"Juan Enriquez's new offering might just be the most important book of the decade. For those of us old enough to remember stars being added to the American flag–and for those who have lived their whole lives under fifty stars–*The Untied States of America* is a warning that a nation's life cycle is a constantly evolving process. Juan enables us to visualize more, or fewer, stars on the most visual icon of nationhood, our flag. Brilliantly researched, Juan's unique writing style enables the reader to easily consume a constant stream of interesting and reinforcing data. Like his first book, *As the Future Catches You,* this is a must-read for all Americans from red and blue states and for policymakers on both sides of the aisle. Interesting, factual, scary, and entertaining–don't miss the opportunity to see our future, read this book."
—RUSS HOWARD, Brigadier General, U.S. Army (retired)

"In his thoroughly researched and documented exploration of the rapid changes in American society in an increasingly competitive and globalized world, Juan Enriquez makes connections and observations that elude other intellectuals of our day. Enriquez deploys a unique prose style filled with multiple fonts, headlines, and graphics that make this provocative essay especially accessible and handy for contemporary hyper-multitasking readers."
—PAULA STERN, U.S. trade representative and member of the Clinton Administration Cabinet

"Juan Enriquez delves into the social gaps caused by ethnic discrimination and inequality of wealth, highlighting the unspoken fissures that sooner or later could threaten the unity of the United States or Mexico. By reminding us that the very existence of these nations cannot be taken for granted, this book invites reflection on why citizens must work to keep them whole."
—OSCAR ARIAS, former president of Costa Rica, winner of the Nobel Prize

"Having had my professional geography dramatically altered by *As the Future Catches You,* I could hardly imagine Juan Enriquez doing it again. He has with *The Untied States of America.* Priority number one for all of us these days, from the White House to Main Street to pillow talk about our lives and careers, is thinking deeply about uncomfortable truths and possibilities. I guarantee that *Untied* will bring on a big case of the intellectual fidgets and provoke deep thought. . . . It is a masterpiece."

—TOM PETERS

"If you think you know North America then you need to read this book. You will learn things that shed a fresh light on who we are and what are the choices for our continent. Freshly written, provocative, and informative."

—SENATOR BILL BRADLEY

"With an outsider's eye and an insider's knowledge, Enriquez is a modern-day de Tocqueville, carefully observing daily customs and mores in a country that is increasingly divided between those who understand and embrace the future and those that seek to maintain yesterday's status quo. This is the best book I have seen on what could happen if we do not immediately address the growing divisions within our society."

**—J. CRAIG VENTER, sequenced the human genome in 2001,
cofounder of Synthetic Genomics, Inc.**

"This is a surprising book, different in format than any you are likely to see. Enriquez has an important message: that nations are always beset with pressures from both outside and within, while history teaches that invariably they do not survive in their original form or size. He convincingly does not exempt the United States. But he presents his arguments with great originality in staccato form, with an astonishingly wide range of data, quotes, and speculation; in sum, persuasive, thought-provoking, and, ultimately, deeply unsettling."

—EUGENE B. SKOLNIKOFF, professor of political science, MIT

"A cold shower of wit and wisdom, revealing the power of nonparadigmatic thinking."

**—GEORGE LODGE, Jaime and Josefina Chua Tiampo professor of
business administration, emeritus, Harvard Business School**

Also by Juan Enriquez

AS THE FUTURE CATCHES YOU

CROWN PUBLISHERS

New York

The **UNTIED**
States of America

...

POLARIZATION, FRACTURING,

and OUR FUTURE

Juan Enriquez

Copyright © 2005 by Juan Enriquez

All rights reserved.
Published in the United States by Crown Publishers,
an imprint of the Crown Publishing Group,
a division of Random House, Inc., New York.
www.crownpublishing.com

CROWN is a trademark and the Crown colophon
is a registered trademark of Random House, Inc.

LIBRARY OF CONGRESS CATALOGING-IN-PUBLICATION DATA
Enriquez, Juan, 1959–
The untied states of America : polarization, fracturing, and our future /
Juan Enriquez.— 1st ed.
p. cm.
Includes bibliographical references.
1. Polarization (Social sciences).   2. Regionalism—United States.
3. Alienation (Social psychology)—United States.   4. Secession—United States.
5. Sovereignty.   6. Nationalism.   I. Title.
HN90.P57E67 2005
306'.0973—dc22
2005013651
ISBN-13: 978-0-307-23752-1
ISBN-10: 0-307-23752-4
Printed in the United States of America

Design by Barbara M. Bachman

10   9   8   7   6   5   4   3   2   1

FIRST EDITION

TO

Mary,

Diana,

and

Nico,

WHO SHARE THE ADVENTURE . . .

C O N T E N T S

INTRODUCTION: UN-TIED (UN TI'ED),—V.T....XII

PART ONE
—
A SOCIAL, POLITICAL,
ECONOMIC PRESSURE COOKER

1. HOW DARE YOU ... 2

There are some things you do not question, like flags, borders, and stars. And precisely because we do not tend to question, we are often surprised when they suddenly alter.

2. UNTIED STATES 30

Given that the U.S.'s flag has rarely been stable for long . . . how many stars do you think it will have in fifty years? Forty-five? Fifty-five? Sixty-five? For most it is easier to see how the number of stars grows, not how they shrink. But even within the prosperous and powerful UNITED States of America there are some who are deeply unhappy. Almost every country in the world faces demands for increased autonomy and even secession.

3. TECHNOLOGY AND RELIGION'S BRUTAL MARCH 59

Some countries, and regions within countries, missed the digital revolution and are now missing the life sciences revolution. Even when fundamentalism does not attempt to slow technology, the challenge is still daunting, even within the most advanced societies.

PART TWO
—
A FEW BILLS PAST DUE

---

4. EXCUSE ME . . . I WAS HERE FIRST   86

*Long-forgotten promises, particularly those involving
signed but trampled treaties, can come back to bite
centuries later. This has happened in Australia, New
Zealand, and Canada. It is also increasingly common
within the U.S. The number and power of self-identified
"Native Americans" is increasing rapidly.*

5. BORDERS BOUNCE: DO YOU *HABLA ESPAÑOL*?   128

For English, press one, para Español presione el
dos. . . . *Parts of the U.S. are rapidly reverting to their
Hispanic roots. Does it become a bicultural society?
Do alienation and income differentials lead to demands
for further integration or further autonomy? And
Hispanics are far from the only alienated minority . . .*

6. DEMOCRACY + OPEN BORDERS =
FOUR MEXICOS?   165

*Mexico is a complex and divided country. The trends are
not all good. The equivalent of one-fifth of Mexico's
population has already voted by leaving the country and
coming to work in the U.S. It is not inconceivable that,
if parts of Mexico continue breeding poverty and violence,
it could someday untie into four separate countries.*

PART THREE

—

A WIDE WORLD OF LESSONS
LEARNED

**7. EUROPE AND ITS DISCONTENTS
(WHAT IS A COUNTRY, ANYWAY?) 208**

*As the European Union expands, and as borders and
constitutions within breed, there is a question of what is a
country really? Within a supranational umbrella, small
countries can oft become very successful. Are the EU
structures a preview of where North America is headed?
Or is Canada, which has held together despite various
pressures to untie, a better model?*

8. LIKE YOUR FLAG? WANT TO KEEP IT? 239

*Three-quarters of today's UN members were not there
fifty-five years ago. Countries and borders continue to
breed promiscuously. Flags, anthems, and borders
are symbols, only as durable as a country's ability
to fulfill its promises to its citizens.*

CONCLUSION: WHAT IS YET TO BE DONE? 267

*January 21, 2008, 8 A.M. The White House.
The Oval Office . . .*

POSTSCRIPT 277

NOTES 279

CREDITS 341

INDEX 343

Often do the spirits

Of great events stride on before the events

And in to-day already walks to-morrow.

—*Samuel Taylor Coleridge* (trans.),
THE DEATH OF WALLENSTEIN
(ACT V, SCENE 1)

INTRODUCTION

UN-TIED (un ti'ed),—v.t. 1. To loosen or unfasten. 2. To free from restraint. 3. A situation resulting from the uncomfortable feeling, beginning in 2000 and intensifying in 2004, that many people from large chunks of the country don't understand their fellow citizens and vice versa. 4. The result when people, regions, companies, and industries on the cutting edge—the sources of innovation, the value adders who pay taxes—look at the laggards and ask themselves: what's in it for me, why am I supporting *those* bums? 5. A process influenced by an accelerated Darwinian system when the small untie from large, clumsy confederations, resulting in new countries that can succeed because of open borders, free trade, universal human rights, democracy, and science. 6. The historical fact of life in much of the world—Europe, Asia, Africa—as gaggles of new nations form and disband. 7. The subject of a book published in 2005 by Juan Enriquez focusing on the untying phenomenon, with a larger purpose of starting a dialogue between citizens about what people who love their country should think about and do to prevent untying. Part I provides the sense of the enormous social, political, and economic pressures facing America and its neighbors and asks if a country can be like a supermarket brand that no longer sells; Part II looks at a few bills past due, the interest on which America has been accumulating for centuries; Part III looks at the lessons to be learned from the wider world, specifically Europe, Canada, and Latin America. It also poses the startling question of "So what?"—the consequence to America—should it care—about countries that collapse as they fail to keep up with the economic driving force of today's world—knowledge.

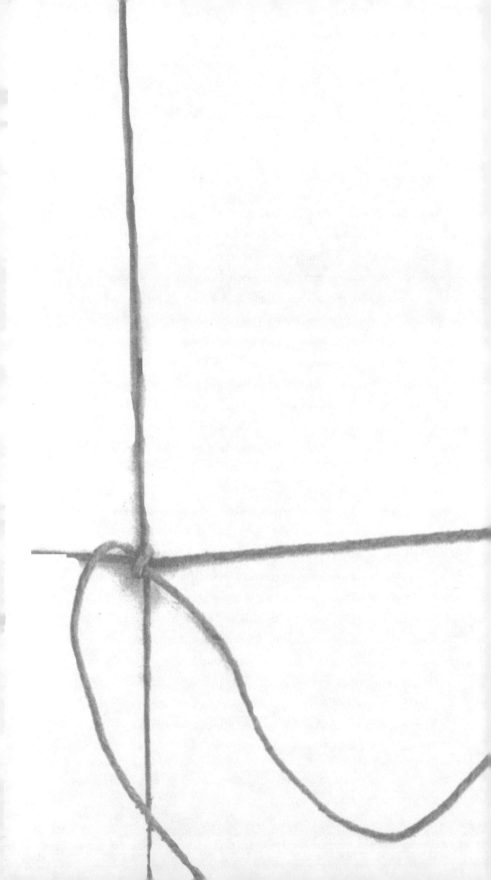

PART ONE

A

Social,

Political,

Economic

Pressure

Cooker

1.

HOW DARE YOU . . .

**"WE WOULD RATHER BE RUINED
THAN CHANGED . . ."**

—*W. H. Auden*

Every week you read about another country falling apart.

Sometimes rich countries, sometimes the most miserable places on earth.

Countries, like marriages, companies, and people, Oft reach a break point, and split up or die.

We watch as it happens to others, but we rarely ask ourselves . . .

Could it ever happen here?

Because most of us truly love the country we live in.

Yet country after country disappears, splits, secedes.

Turns out, regardless of pledges, nations are divisible.

But surely, you might argue, not the U.S.; after all,

it is a hyperpower.

But sometimes instead of just looking at what is today . . .
We might want to look at what could be tomorrow.

And if one were dispassionately to dissect current U.S. trends, one might have a few sleepless nights . . .

Start with the U.S. current account deficit . . .

> In 2004, if you laid enough $1,000 bills end to end to cover the $617 billion deficit, you could circle the earth about 2.4 times.[1]

Pete Peterson, not exactly a radical, was Richard Nixon's secretary of commerce. He has been charging around the country for years, playing Paul Revere.

Peterson's message is consistent:

The U.S. spends a lot more than it earns.

It has done so for years.

This is not sustainable.

Hola? Hello? Anyone paying attention?

According to Peterson . . .

> *"Telltale signs are appearing that suggest America may well be headed for a financial meltdown."* [2]

Peterson is hardly alone . . .

Bob Rubin, ex-secretary of the Treasury, agrees.

("We are confronting a day of serious reckoning.")

As does Gregory Mankiw, Bush's top economic adviser.

(Benefits now scheduled under current laws are not sustainable. They are empty promises.)[3]

As does the comptroller general of the U.S.

("The path we are on is imprudent and unsustainable.")[4]

As does Newt Gingrich.

"Bush's people will get up every morning and worry about the budget."[5]

In fact, so does George Bush II.

("I want you to think about a Social Security system that will be flat bust, bankrupt, unless the United States Congress has got the willingness to act now.")[6]

The list goes on and on.

From time immemorial, the last thing a government does . . .

Is drive the nation to bankruptcy.

Bottom line:

You Cannot Spend 5 to 6% More Than the Country Earns Every Year Without Serious Consequences.

As debt rises, so, too, do interest payments. Other spending is crowded out. Interest rates rise. . . .

Just before Thanksgiving 2004, Fed Chairman Greenspan most cryptically warned:

"Cumulative deficits, which result in a market decline of a country's net international investment position—as is occurring in the United States— raise complex issues . . ."

Indeed, said Wall Street, and the market began to drop. . . .

Greenspan's speech sound obscure? It has consequences; according to ex-secretary of labor Robert Reich:

> *"Greenspan can put the economy into a tailspin simply by tightening his grip. Volcker did it in 1979 and Jimmy Carter was fired. Bill Clinton knows that. Greenspan has the most important grip in this town: Bill's balls in the palm of his hand."*[7]

Fortunately Clinton paid attention; one of his great achievements was generating a budget surplus. But then those promising less government and more fiscal restraint came to power, and deficits exploded.

Government remains a large part of the problem.

Some estimate your household's share of present and future debt is a mere $473,456.[8]

Government spectacularly fudges the numbers every year.

Remember the "Social Security Trust Fund" that you pay into to finance your retirement? It is being used to fund "other government spending.""Special Issue" Treasury bonds, debt if you will, already amount to $1.5 trillion.

Then there is the proposed 2005 budget. The campaign promise was "We'll cut the deficit in half." To accomplish this, the government is using a trick or two. The benchmark is not the actual shortfall ($431 billion) but what was predicted as a shortfall ($521 billion).

(Hurray!!! We already saved $90 billion.)

Tax revenues are assumed to rise (despite further tax cuts) by $517 billion. The small cost of wars in Iraq and Afghanistan are left out altogether ($100 billion).

(This budget, of course, ignores costs beyond 2005 like the $1 trillion for making tax cuts permanent beyond 2009, $500 billion for new Medicare prescriptions . . .)[9]

P.S. The White House announced, before the election, the 2005 deficit would be a mere $331 billion deficit. In January 2005, they changed their minds and projected $427 billion . . . never mind.

This is the kind of accounting that lands CEOs in jail.
It is the reason Sarbanes-Oxley was passed.

But none of this legislation applies to government . . .

Even if you fixed the accounting.

You do not solve the problem because . . .

The underlying trends are ugly.

Despite a weakening dollar, the trade deficit continues to grow, month by month . . . 2003 . . . 2004 . . . to a record-breaking $58.3 billion in January 2005.[10]

The minimum wage in the U.S., in real dollars, is 37% below where it was in 1968.[11]

Even before the baby boomers retire, Social Security obligations are already one-fifth of all federal spending.

In the 1930s there were 41 workers for every retiree . . .

In 1950 there were 16.

1960, about 5.1.

Today there are 3.3.

By 2030, there will be 2.2 . . .[12]

An estimated 48% of the total government's budget will be spent on the elderly by 2015.[13]

Not surprisingly, payroll taxes have increased from 2% to 12.4% of your salary. Care to guess what they will be by the time your kids retire?

Medicare is already 13% of the government budget and likely to become one quarter of all spending by 2030.[14]

Medicare, Medicaid, and Social Security already cost about 7% of everything produced by every American every year.

By 2030? Over 15%.

(In Mississippi, Medicaid spending has doubled in five years, leading the governor to declare it "is a cancer on our state finances.")[15]

Every year medical and retirement spending goes up.
And the U.S. fights wars in Afghanistan, in Iraq.
And fights insurgencies in Colombia, keeps troops in Korea.

> And keeps cutting taxes.
> So you can get more.
> And pay less.
> Yippee!!

Except it does not work out like that.

To finance these growing gaps, government borrows more
and more . . .

> The deficit grows . . .

> So does debt service . . .

> Government borrows more to pay interest . . .

During President Bush's first term, China, Japan, Hong Kong, Korea,
Taiwan, and Singapore increased their holdings of U.S. Treasury debt
by half a billion per day.[16]

> By the end of 2004, the U.S. owed 28% of all it produces in a
> year to foreigners.

As one French analyst so charmingly put it: "[The U.S.] has
become sort of a black hole, absorbing goods and capital but
incapable of providing, in return, equivalent goods."[17]

> Asian banks alone held $1.89 trillion.[18]

One manager in Japan, Masatsugu Asakawa, oversees
$720 billion worth of T-bills.

If he dumped dollars for euros, he could drive up interest rates.[19]

Better pray he does not get up ornery one morning.

The U.S. still has a unique advantage; when it devalues its currency, its debt does not go up, because the loans are dollar denominated, so far.[20]

This stuff matters, if China appreciated its currency 10% it would lose capital equivalent to 3% of what it produces in one year (GDP)

(because the dollars it holds would be worth less in yuan).

Many are even more dependent. . . .
  Korea would lose 3% of GDP,
    Taiwan 8%,
      Singapore 10%.[21]

The world's reserve currency belongs to a debtor nation.

In 1978, the U.S. net foreign asset balance was +9% of GDP.

In 2004, it was -27% GDP.[22]

It would be far harder to control the federal deficit or interest rates if the dollar ceases being the world's reserve currency.

January 24, 2005, will probably be seen as a watershed day. A survey of 65 Central Banks showed they had been buying ever more euros, over the preceding two years.

Central Banks finance 80% of the U.S. current account deficit, the difference between what the U.S. spends abroad and what it earns. If they stop plugging this gap, it could be the end of the dollar's long reign as the currency *primus inter pares*.[23]

Perhaps a good time to remember that when the British Empire overextended, went off the gold standard, and lost its status as a reserve currency, the country also devolved as the dominant global power.[24]

Unfortunately, you can't just blame government . . .

It is not just a Republican vs. Democrat issue.

(It would be easier to fix if it were just one party or just the government acting irresponsibly.)

Turns out companies have also gotten very good at cloning, juggling, accumulating debt.

And companies not only borrow, they speculate with debt. If you ask really smart bankers, "What keeps you up at night?," often they reply, **"Hedge funds."**

There are huge liabilities that no one quite seems to understand . . .

> In 1998, LTCM lost $3.6 billion in five weeks. It took months to unravel what their exposure and liabilities were. One company, unraveling, came very close to hurting the global financial system. The company was run by Nobels in economics.[25]

Even mundane things, like a couple of airlines, are large enough that they can virtually wipe out the entire reserves of the federal government's pension benefit insurance fund.

> After multiple bankruptcies, United and US Air began hinting they might quit paying their pensions. One analyst estimated the top seven airlines underfunded pensions by $20.6 billion.
>
> This could easily break the Pension Benefits Guaranty Corp. (PBGC).[26]
>
> (And by the way, the PBGC likely also insures your pension, along with those of 44 million Americans.)

Meanwhile, Fannie Mae and Freddie Mac, government-chartered purchasers of mortgages, have gotten really good at leveraging assets and hiding liabilities. So much so that Alan Greenspan, chairman of the Fed, warned that they could become a **systemic threat to the economy.**[27]

> Not that these companies really welcomed the oversight. When Congressman Richard Baker began investigating some Fannie Mae practices, the company hired Ken Starr, he of Whitewater fame, to "educate" the staff as to what they had to keep secret.[28]

This is a slightly worrisome problem, given that there is over two trillion dollars outstanding in guaranteed loans.

> Not a lot has to go bad for there to be a really, really major problem.

Individuals also keep piling on debt.

The U.S. has the lowest private savings rate of all major industrialized countries.

(October 2004, average personal savings were 0.2%; if you take home $50,000, you save $100 annually.)[29]

The average household owes over $84,454.[30]

(The average home has $8,000 in credit card debt.)

Most debt is tied up in real estate, an asset . . . as long as prices rise.

For many living in high-tech areas, this has been a great investment.

So, many decided to buy a couple more houses.

Good idea. . . . . so far.

But several folks have pointed out that the place where most of us have chosen to place our nest eggs may be "slightly overvalued."

Shawn Tully, a smart *Fortune* reporter, points out that there is a yawning gap between how much a house costs and how much the average person earns.[31] From 1975 through 2000, houses cost about 2.8 times more than the average person earned in a year.

By 2004, in California, this ratio was 6.4.
Nationwide? 3.4.

Tully points out just how much cheaper it is to rent than to buy.

This makes little economic sense; the price of a house should be about as much as you would be willing to pay to rent the house indefinitely (discounted value of future rents).

The ratio between the cost of owning vs. renting has grown from ten times to sixteen times.

More and more speculators are entering the market.

In the first eleven months of 2004, 8.5% of mortgages went to folks who had no intention of ever occupying their new digs. One-quarter of the 7.7 million homes sold in 2004 were bought as investments.[32]

As more folks made more money, more began to play the same game with ever more properties.

Risky game . . .

By the beginning of 2005, one company estimated the risk of an overall housing-price decline in the top fifty U.S. metropolitan areas was 16%.[33]

In Boston/Cambridge, the risk was 53%.
San José/Sunnyvale/Santa Clara, 53%.
San Francisco/Oakland, 47%.
San Diego/Carlsbad, 43%.
New York/N.J., 36%.

As you observe these trends, you may say to yourself . . . Self, might this imply that a great deal of real estate lives within a bubble?

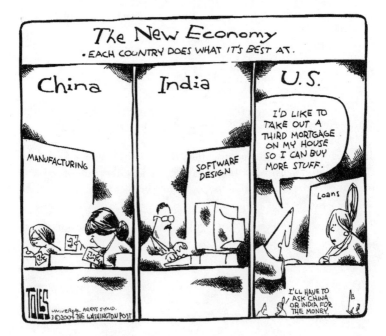

We have gotten very good at taking out second mortgages, at consolidating credit debt.

> Borrowing is not as much of a worry if you are investing in future growth and prosperity. But it is a lousy idea if used to fund immediate consumption, gratification, and pork. Because countries and individuals do, time and again, spend themselves into bankruptcy.

Not that you would find any evidence of this overspending today . . .

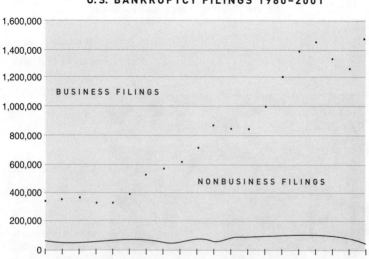

U.S. BANKRUPTCY FILINGS 1980–2001

When you are highly leveraged and have little savings, losing your job or getting sick can quickly lead to bankruptcy.

An average American is already spending 13% of after-tax income to pay interest and/or principal on loans. A 2005 study by Harvard's Dr. Steffie Woolhandler found that half of the country's two million annual bankruptcies are driven by unexpected health care costs.[34] Others are driven by job loss.

Despite this, in March 2005, Congress severely tightened bankruptcy laws.

It will be much easier if you are in the middle class to fall into poverty.

> But, rejoice, the measure will not affect multimillion- or multibillion-dollar corporate bankruptcies.

> (The U.S. is far from alone. . . . British households owe $1.4 trillion, about 130% of annual disposable income.)[35]

The bottom line is . . .

Some generations act like trust fund heiresses . . . and spend all that previous generations accumulated.

And we seem to be living in one such period.

Thank you, Paris Hilton . . .

When this occurs, *if the country is lucky*, it will begin to correct course before it goes irrevocably broke.

Before things get truly ugly . . .

These trends could come together, feed on one another, and generate a perfect financial storm.

(Ever wonder why Warren Buffett now refers to
America as "Squanderville"?)

Let me remind you of the obvious: currency is paper, worth
only what people agree it is worth.

(Particularly since August 15, 1971, when Richard Nixon quit exchanging
U.S. dollars for gold.)

> Every day, a currency's worth is reassessed trillions of
> times, as people decide to buy or sell euros, dollars, yen,
> yuan.[36]

> Technology links systems. A few decision makers can
> have huge leverage. Without setting foot in a country,
> they can help grow or partly destroy an economy.

In 1992, George Soros, a hedge fund manager, assembled enough
financial leverage to force the British pound out of the European
exchange rate mechanism.

This reputedly made him his first billion.

It also created a convenient scapegoat for countries, ranging from
France to Malaysia, to blame for their lousy economic policies.

> Having knocked off a series of currencies, Soros decided the
> consequences of some financial crashes are so severe and
> destabilizing that there should be much more restraint,
> regulation, and supervision.[37] Recently he was incensed enough
> with the government's spending patterns that, instead of
> knocking off currencies, he spent more than $15 million in
> an attempt to oust Bush II.

Soros is far from the only currency cowboy. . . .

In 1994, millions of Mexicans suffered huge losses.

Mostly due to their own government's incompetence.

But also in part due to a secretive speculator living in Lyford Cay,
Bahamas, Joseph C. Lewis. After making a fortune off the collapse of the
British pound, he reportedly bet his wealth against the Mexican peso,
which eventually collapsed spectacularly.[38]

Currency speculators are not a posse motivated by flags and anthems.

They are motivated by money, by the hunt, by the kill.

One currency speculator described himself as a member of a community of "wolves on the ridgeline looking down on a herd of elk . . . by culling the weak and infirm, we help maintain the health of the herd."[39]

And behind this altruistic Darwinism, there is also the small matter of profits and losses. Julian Robertson and Tiger Management made an 80% return for their investors in 1993, 48% in 1996, and 67% in 1997. Citibank made $1.5 billion on currency trades in 1997.

You can also lose spectacularly; in 1998, Harvard faced losses of about $1.3 billion after buying emerging market funds at a discount and then selling these markets short.[40]

The point is, there are huge incentives in the system for volatility and instability.

Any government, any currency, is vulnerable, given severe mismanagement of currency, of budgets, of interest rates.

No one is in charge and everyone is in charge.

Power has unbundled not just from countries to conglomerates and large markets but also to a few individuals.[41] Central banks and governments have ever less control over their own currencies.[42] And it may be impossible for even the most powerful governments to reassert control.[43]

Governments can signal by raising or lowering interest rates, by buying or selling currencies. They can keep managing their finances and keep investors happy, so as to avoid stampedes.

But they cannot assume they alone are sovereign.

Many ignore these lessons and waste billions in futile attempts to prop up their currency. But foreign exchange markets are simply too large.

During 2004, over $461 billion in foreign exchange was traded in the U.S. every day.

Plus $355 billion in derivatives.[44]

If governments and/or traders lose faith in a currency, things can happen very fast. In desperation, after years of mismanagement, some countries have even considered giving up one of the basic attributes of sovereignty, their own currency.

The head of the Mexican Bankers Association argued "we have to analyze openly, in depth and constructively, the benefits of adopting a strong currency."[45]

i.e., Kill the peso, long live the dollar.

A head of a powerful business group was even blunter: "Large businesses are already dollarized. Almost the only thing left in pesos is salary. Having a lot of currencies only enriches speculators."[46]

In one poll, nine out of ten Mexicans agreed with the businessmen and advocated dollars over pesos.[47] Even Mexican government officials wavered and began floating a series of trial balloons.[48]

(Baja California, much of Northern Mexico, and Cancún have, in fact, already dollarized . . . , as have Argentina, Ecuador, and Panama.)

Now, as the dollar weakens, many throughout the world are seeking shelter in euros or elsewhere.

Many have warned about these trends. But few have examined the question . . .

If
    we

        continue

        down

        the

        current

        path,

        so

        what?

It may be time to do so.
For many countries.
Including the U.S.

Monetary problems and inequalities often accentuate, or revive, divisions.[49]

When budget cuts really begin to hurt, there is often a lot of finger-pointing.

The rich try to keep what they have.

(This is one of the reasons suburbs breed: own schools, fire and police departments, beaches and parks.)

The poor try to get more to survive.

You see this separatism pop up in place after place.

A few years ago, as a lark, college professor Frank Bryan wrote up *The Vermont Papers* (with Republican John McClaughry), arguing that an independent Vermont would have significant economic advantages.

> They contrasted local thrift with Washingtonian debt. Many took them seriously. By 1990, seven Vermont communities had voted in favor of secession.[50]

The debate continues. In March 2004, the town of Killington, Vermont, voted to secede and join New Hampshire. Killingtonians were furious that they got back ten cents per dollar paid in state taxes.

> By August 2004, other rich towns—Ludlow, Manchester, and South Dorset—began to sing the same tune.

(The fact that these towns do not border on New Hampshire did not seem to dissuade them.)[51]

These are not the first or last times these debates have been, or will be, heard. They have raged from Boston to the Texas Panhandle, from California through Staten Island and Queens. They are alive in West Kansas.[52] In February 2005, frustrated at liberal Western Washington, Sen. Bob Morton attempted to take twenty of the state counties and generate a 51st state.

> So far he has support from nine other senators.[53]

> Similar debates are going on in Maine, Minnesota, and New York.

Countries can also suffer suburbanization.

They suburbanize and breed new flags and anthems.
> You see this phenomena time and again.

Czechs put up minor resistance when the Slovaks wanted to declare independence.

> Although the new Czech Republic was 40% smaller and had a third fewer people than Czechoslovakia, its income per person was also 20% higher than Slovakia's.[54]

Bottom line, the Czechs felt they were better off joining the EU by themselves.

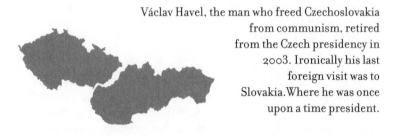

Václav Havel, the man who freed Czechoslovakia from communism, retired from the Czech presidency in 2003. Ironically his last foreign visit was to Slovakia. Where he was once upon a time president.

This is far from a unique case of economic secessionism . . .

Between 1979 and 1988, Yugoslavia's economy collapsed, real wages dropped by one-third. The country fell apart.

The first part to untie was neither the poorest nor the most ethnically conflictive region. It was the region with the highest income per capita in Central and Eastern Europe. Slovenia understood Yugoslavia would not be admitted to the European Economic Community for decades, if ever. . . .

But Slovenia alone was another matter.

Although the new country hosted only 8% of the ex-Yugoslav population, it represented around one-third of the total economy.[55]

Throughout the developing world it is often the regions that think they have the resources to be richer that usually attempt to leave first.

Biafra holds a great deal of Nigeria's oil.

Katanga has much of Congo's copper.

Eritrea had twice the per capita income of Ethiopia.

Chiapas has a great deal of Mexico's gas, timber, and hydropower.

Aceh, in Indonesia, has oil, and three times the average national income.[56]

This is also a trend within developed countries . . .

Politicians in Northern Italy hold rallys hoping to cast off Southern Italy. Part of Belgium's rich North wants to get rid of the French region. As Scotland becomes wealthier and more integrated into the EU, it is also ever more independent. Basques and Catalans, who have some of the highest incomes in Spain, are aggressive secessionists.

Nowadays it is not that hard to dissolve, or split, a country.

Flags, borders, and anthems are delicate.

They are real.

They are also myths. . . .[57]

(One definition of myth:
"the way things are, as people in a particular society believe them to be.")[58]

Yet . . .

*We have paid little attention to how many countries
split and disappear
because our own Hemisphere
has been remarkably stable.*

**We have generated no true new borders
on the American continent since 1910.**

But this stability may be coming to an end.

It is hard to imagine countries falling apart in the Americas. . . .

But bear with me; try the following thought experiment:

Imagine for a moment that you were a member of the British Cabinet. You are sitting in the same room where folks like Blair, Major, Thatcher, Churchill, Balfour, Gladstone, and Disraeli plotted the future of the British Empire.

The year is 1905 . . .

Robert Cecil, marquis of Salisbury, prime minister, presides.

You are looking at a map of your country, of your empire.

In 1909, the British empire governed about 11.5 million square miles and 400 million people, about 20% of the earth's land and 23% of its population.

The map shows increasing power and influence over the course of four centuries.

It looked something like this:[59]

Look at the world as a cabinet minister of the world's most powerful empire. Ask yourself: "What will the map look like in fifty, seventy-five, and one hundred years?" Do you honestly think you, and your fellow ministers, would have gotten it right?

Might you have guessed that your flag would cover more territory?

Or might you have guessed that it would likely be the same?

Few, if any, would have said smaller.

(Likely a terribly lonely position.)

Yet over the next fifty years, the British Empire shrunk by about 11,405,752 sq. mi.[60]

It is now 94,248 sq. mi.

> It does not just happen to the Brits, recall the words of a man who was very smart, and very wrong. David Starr Jordan, president of Stanford University, said: "The Great War of Europe, ever threatening . . . will never come" (1913).

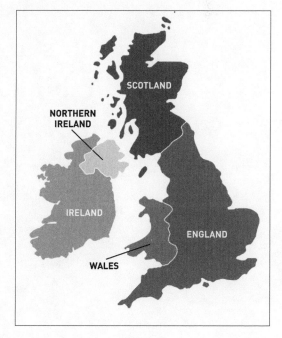

Even if you were part of Margaret Thatcher's first cabinet (1979), you probably would never have guessed that your fractious isle would begin devolving into four parts.[61]

You might have asked yourself the same type of question
and gotten the same answer if you had been part of
Gorbachev's USSR cabinet circa 1987. . . .

With these goggles, with this context . . .

Now transport yourself back to the present.

Sit in the Cabinet Room in the White House circa 2005.

Reread the test the INS administers to those who wish to become
U.S. citizens:[62]

> 1. *What are the colors of our flag?*
> 2. *How many stars are there on our flag?*
> 3. *What color are the stars on our flag?*
> 4. *What do the stars on the flag mean?* . . .

Now ask yourself, How often has this changed?

And how might it change in the future?

In other words . . .

How many stars, Do you think, Will be in the U.S. flag In fifty years?

You probably think you know. . . .

But remember, each of these patterns has officially represented the U.S.

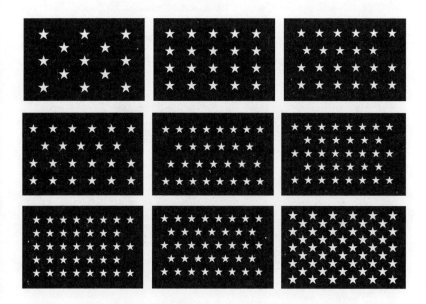

(Before William Howard Taft [1912], only the number of stars was mandated, not their pattern.)

There has yet to be a U.S. president buried under the same flag he was born under.

As generals, astrologers, astronomers, and politicians might say . . .

Stars Happen.

And sometimes unhappen . . .

Likely many will argue that the current flag and border have
been and always will be.

(Just as some believe: "If English was good enough for Jesus . . .")

But there is just a little historic evidence that this argument
does not hold much water. . . .

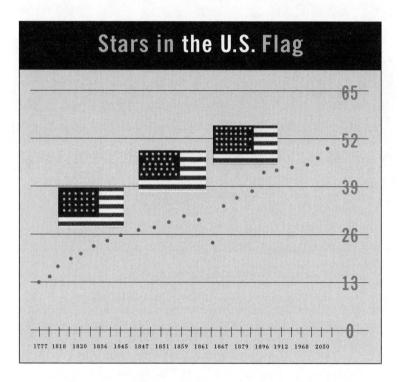

Over the next fifty years there could be anywhere

From seven to thirteen new U.S. presidents. . . .

Think they will all salute exactly the same flag?

Then how many stars will be in the U.S. flag? . . .

What are the paths that lead in one direction or the other?

(Or, if you wish, what could lead to stability?)

Likely this book will anger some and puzzle many.

We tend to take our flags, borders, and stars for granted.

(Like childbirth, we forget just how painful, and common, change is.)

When someone dares question our symbols and their future, we often ignore the question, or we get quite angry; we react viscerally, if you will.

(Or attempt to pass constitutional amendments "to prevent their desecration.")

People often confuse a physical symbol with what it represents.

In 1998, the U.S. House of Representatives voted 310 to 114 to alter the First Amendment to "prohibit the physical desecration of the flag of the United States."

A disabled Special Forces officer, one who served in Beirut, Panama, and Desert Storm, understood the difference between myth and substance far better than most legislators. He testified that soldiers fight not for the flag but for what it represents:

"Flags, no matter how they are honored, do not have rights. People do. "[63]

At this point many protonationalists will likely loudly squawk.

So let's answer up front.

Agreed, the U.S. is not the UK.

Yes, times are different.

Yes, it is a different country.

But humor me; remember: *Courage is the power to let go of the familiar.*[64]

Before you answer questions about the future shape of the U.S. too quickly . . .

Are you aware that three quarters of the sovereign countries jabbering on within the United Nations were not there fifty years ago?

In 1950, there were fifty members.

Today, one hundred and ninety one.

Some of the world's most powerful lost, and continue to lose, a great deal of territory.

From 1900 to 1950, 1.2 new countries were created per year.

From 1950 to 1990, this increased to 2.2 per year.

During the 1990s we saluted 3.1 new sovereignties.

Flags can appear and disappear very quickly.

April 26, 2004, Iraq's Governing Council unveiled a new flag. It was immediately subject to torrents of abuse. The new national symbol lasted just a few hours. . . .[65]

Promiscuously.[66]
Breeding
Are
Countries

Each time a country splits, historians, political scientists, economists, biographers, priests, a myriad of folks, provide hundreds of reasons as to why a particular state contracted, fell apart, reappeared, or disappeared.[67]

Sometimes they are right.

Often, historic cleavages like race, religion, ethnicity, language, culture, and colony help map who will untie from a given country.

And they certainly explain a lot in retrospect . . .

Pulitzer-winning historian Daniel Boorstin said planning for the future, without a sense of the past, is like planting cut flowers.

Some sections of the atlases of the 1700s look similar to maps we see today. The Yugoslav outcome is best understood by looking at these maps. Future maps of Africa may look a lot closer to the precolonial divisions.[68]

But if these fundamental internal cleavages and divisions Have been present for centuries or millennia . . .

Why did the original political unit disappear to begin with?

And why is it reappearing now?

And what other entities will soon reappear?

Perhaps the global proliferation of states and borders will never occur in the Americas. . . .

You may have a hunch, idea, or perhaps a near certainty Of how many stars will be in your flag in fifty years. . . .

Are you willing to bet the ranch on your hunch?

2.

UNTIED STATES

"A HOUSE DIVIDED AGAINST ITSELF CANNOT STAND."

—Abraham Lincoln, from MATTHEW 12:25

Bankruptcy is by no means enough to calve stars . . .

What arguing over money can do is revive old wounds and exacerbate existing tensions.

(Just ask any divorced couple, or group of inheriting siblings, if money, and the lack thereof, or its unequal distribution, ever caused any friction.)

When you can no longer put off hard choices, because you have run out of cash and credit, you tend to have some pretty frank debates as to who is pulling his or her weight in this relationship.

And it turns out, several states, several regions in fact, are a growing burden on all of our taxes.

As favorite programs are cut, more folks may begin to ask themselves: "Why am I footing the bill for these bums?"

Which is why, often, it is the rich regions, not the poor, Nor the ethnically conflictive ones, that untie first.

This debate has raged from Czechoslovakia and Yugoslavia to Spain, England, Italy, and Canada. So one might want to begin by asking, who generates much of the wealth within these fifty U.S. states?

And who spends it?

Start with taxes. Some states get far more money back than they pay out . . .

Who Gets: Who Gives[1]
(Net Tax Benefit 2003)

RECEIVE > THAN THEY PAY	PER $ PAID	PAY > THAN THEY RECEIVE	PER $ PAID
New Mexico	1.99	New Jersey	0.57
Alaska	1.89	New Hampshire	0.64
Mississippi	1.83	Connecticut	0.65
West Virginia	1.82	Nevada	0.70
North Dakota	1.75	Minnesota	0.70
Alabama	1.69	Illinois	0.73
Montana	1.60	Massachusetts	0.76
Hawaii	1.58	California	0.78
Virginia	1.58	Colorado	0.80
Kentucky	1.52	New York	0.80

Curious that the most productive, high-tech states tend to vote Democratic. The most dole-dependent tend to be hard-line, antigovernment, antispending Republicans.

> 75% of Mr. Bush's electoral votes came from Taker states.
>
> 76% of Mr. Kerry's electoral votes came from Giver states.[2]

In the two years leading up to the Bush II reelection, Midwestern politicians tried to outdo each other in generosity to the heartland.

> Farm incomes doubled. Federal subsidies increased 40%, to $15.7 billion in 2005.[3] 70% of these subsidies go to the largest 10% of agribusinesses, not to family farms.

Two Stuttgart, Arkansas, groups, Riceland Foods, Inc., and Producers Rice Mill, Inc., have received $800 million plus.

Knowledge generates much of the U.S.'s new wealth. But not a lot of knowledge grows on farms; in fact, it is highly concentrated, in geographic terms.

Using this lens, take a look at the outcome of the last presidential circus. Republicans and assorted Bushies like this map. . . .

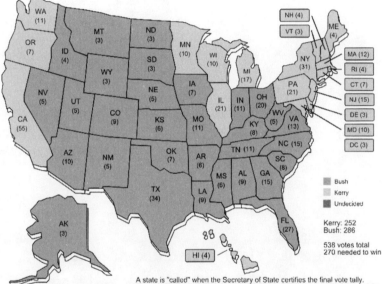

A state is "called" when the Secretary of State certifies the final vote tally. Failing that, the state belongs to the candidate for whom three major networks (ABC, CBS, NBC, FOX, and CNN) declare the state.

But not as much as they like this map . . .

(Just a few small blue patches if you look at it by country.)

While Republicans cover the most land surface, they do not generate most of the knowledge.

NUMBER OF UTILITY PATENTS GRANTED PER 100,000 POPULATION, BY METROPOLITAN AREA, 1998

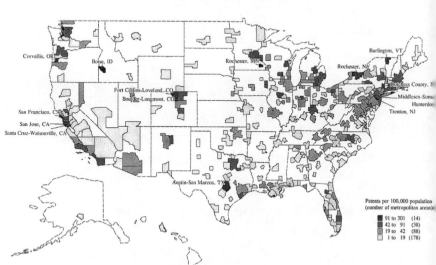

There is a significant difference between where technology, knowledge, and money is generated and where it is spent.

On average, it takes about 3,000 Americans to generate one U.S. patent. The states where it takes fewer people tended to vote Democratic. The opposite was true in Republican states.

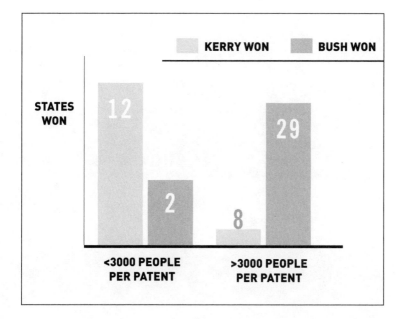

If money was the only thing to fight about, the only major cleavage, one would not dare contemplate the idea of an UNTIED States of America.

But there are other fundamental differences. . . .

It is sometimes hard to understand just how divided the U.S. is by just looking at red states and blue states.

> When accused of being a "Liberal," the publisher of the *New York Times* responded: "What we saw play out in this election was urban vs. suburban-rural, not red state vs. blue state". . . "We are from an urban environment; it comes with the territory."[4]

Many of the cities on the East and West Coasts have a lot more in common with Canadians than they do with those living in red states.

They are, in general, wealthier, more liberal, more secular, pay more taxes, believe in some government. . . .

Some creative folk understood these trends and posted this map on the Internet just after the 2004 election. . . .

It spread like wildfire because it reinforced existing prejudices, on both sides.

Especially after February 2005, when Canada's Parliament began debating gay marriage and the prime minister gave a strong speech in favor of the measure.

After the 2004 election, Immigration Canada reported daily inquiries from the U.S. increased from 20,000 per day to 115,000.[5]

The divisions that lie within the UNTIED States are more complicated than this map indicates, of course. When you break out elections county by county, there is a lot of blue within the red, and vice versa.

Mississippi is among the Reddest of the Red States.
But Winstonville, Mississippi, voted 228 to 14 for Kerry.
Mound Bayou voted 1,073 to 92 for Kerry.

That is not the problem. The problem is that many of these divisions have been gerrymandered, ossified.

(Often by mutual consent of reelection-seeking congress folk.)

There are very, very few really competitive seats.

In 1976, Carter vs. Ford, 26.8% of voters lived in landslide districts (60% + for one candidate). In 2000, Bush vs. Gore, 45.3% lived in landslide counties.[6] In 2004, less than one in fifty congressional races was for real . . .

As districts gerrymander with ever more precision, people tend to hear the same opinion over and over, from their representatives, from their neighbors.

Prejudices, half truths, and accusations against the "others" are reinforced daily, weekly, yearly. Of the 3,140 counties contested during the Bush-Kerry election, only 65 were won or lost by less than 1%. Some claim turnover in congress is now lower than it was in the Soviet Politburo.[7]

In the 2004 general election, only four House incumbents were defeated.

It is not just the political process that divides. Media is becoming ever more of a business, targeted toward its specific audience's most treasured beliefs.

Politics and media reflect, and reinforce, deep-rooted divisions. Many folks are simply not on the same page, literally.

After putting aside Harry Potter . . .

During 2003 and 2004, two books dominated best-seller lists. Both use adventure-novel formats and various derring-dos by unlikely heroes to get across their point.

They both had to do with religion . . .

The *Da Vinci Code* portrays a profoundly corrupt church.[8]

The *Left Behind* series portrays a profoundly corrupt society because not enough pay attention to the church.[9]

Most of the folks who live near me, in the People's Republic of Massachusetts, have read *Da Vinci*.

But they had never heard of the second series.

Because I travel a lot, speak to various audiences, and cannot pass by a bookstore without stopping . . .

I began to see large displays of the *Left Behind* series in places like Northern Kentucky, Kansas, rural Illinois, South Carolina, parts of Florida. After reading a couple of the books, I got more interested in this phenomenon and began asking questions.[10]

During each talk I gave, I would put up the two book covers and ask people if they had read these books. Usually a large percentage of the audience had read one, but almost never the other.

And usually people were shocked when told how many copies the other book had sold.

By May 2004, *The Da Vinci Code* had sold more than 7.3 million copies.

By February 2005, the twelve volumes of *Left Behind* had sold more than 70 million. . . .

**We are, according to many, in the midst of the
final battle between good and evil.**

The Rapture folk take the daily news and place it in the context of the imminent end of the world. Here are some of the headlines they had during the last week of February 2005:

Rapture-Ready News

*If therefore thou shalt not watch I will come on thee as a thief,
and thou shalt not know what hour I will come upon thee.
(Rev. 3:3)*

- **A Third Intifada?**
- **Iran Nukes Would Trigger Regional Proliferation.**
- **Russian Nuke Theft "Has Occurred."**
- **Fury as Pope Links Abortion to Holocaust.**
- **World Must Act on Bird Flu or Face Pandemic.**
- **California Braces for More Wicked Weather.**
- **U.S. Prepares for Germ Attack.**
- **Pope Declares Democracy "Godless."**
- **Pope Calls Gay Marriage Part of the "Ideology of Evil."**

(Want to see today's news? Surf over to http://www.raptureready.com/.)

P.S. After you read the day's rapture news, scroll down to the "Bible Based Truth Section." Here you see:

"Your Final, Final Warning: This Time We're Serious."

(So, for God's sake, send in your donation NOW!)

One can understand how the crowd that comes home to watch *Sex and the City* may not overlap a lot with the *700 Club* crowd. . . .

(Although *Desperate Housewives* seems to be a
common theme in Red and Blue states.)

A computer programmer called Valdis Krebs looked at the books Amazon recommends to anyone who buys one of their books.

(People who bought this book also purchased . . .)

Krebs found there is virtually no overlap in reading material between the left and right.[11]

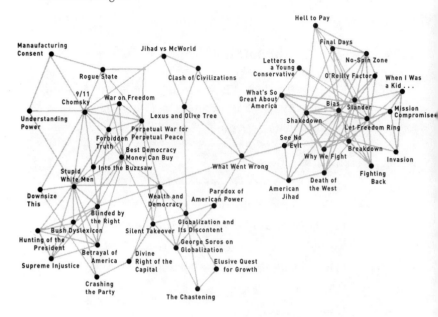

The only point of overlap? Books on Arabs, e. g., Bernard Lewis's *What Went Wrong?*

American households still watch eight hours of TV per day, but usually different channels in different rooms. No more togetherness on the family couch to watch Uncle Walter (Cronkite).[12]

Candidates and pundits often reinforce these divisions to increase ratings and motivate their base.

Forget about whether these authors are on the right or left; just reflect on the divisive nature of these titles.[13]

Weapons of Mass Distortion
The Death of Right and Wrong
Stupid White Men
Slander
Rogue Nation
Deliver Us from Evil
Tales From the Left Coast
Fanatics and Fools

Regardless of which side you are on, you have to recognize that these are fundamental differences in how many folks see the world. . . .

And they are growing ever more polarized.

These are not divisions that have to do with who the specific presidential candidates are in any given year.

Presidential campaigns mirror underlying cleavages.

Right now there is enough space and money to keep everyone more or less happy and somewhat apart. But it could be a very different story going forward . . .

Despite these divisive trends, many will surely take an absolutist position.

How dare you question the very integrity of my country!!!

Expectorating arguments veiled in the most compelling nationalist rhetoric and righteous indignation . . .

Some of which echoed in the halls of the old Soviet Union, Czechoslovakia, Yugoslavia, East Germany, and Franco's Spain . . . or old boys clubs in Imperial France, Germany, and Britain for that matter.

So let me be clear.

It is not my wish or desire . . .

That the U.S. have fewer stars in its flag.

But it is not my choice.
It is a choice of citizens.

Globally, autonomy and untying are increasingly common options.

Hiding divisions,

wishing them away,

pretending they do not exist,

does not eliminate the underlying rot.

(And rot eventually leads to the dissolution of even the proudest and strongest of states.)

Country splits often become irreversible long before they are recognized de facto and de jure.

So if you love your flag, your country, you have to be honest enough to recognize a country is a temporary myth, sustained, supported, and strengthened by people like yourself.[14]

And you should continuously remind yourself just how often citizens end up supporting alternate myths.

(Edmund Burke: "Commonwealths are . . . artificial creations . . . arbitrary productions of the human mind.")[15]

It has been shown time and again that it is easy to make many out of one.

Just ask the Romans about their old Empire . . .

Citizenship is buying into a national brand.

Brands and countries both strive to "create loyalty beyond reason."[16]

Country: A brand, an idea, sometimes so powerful that one may be willing to sacrifice one's life, and even the lives of one's children, for that brand.

But when brands promise one thing and deliver another,
When they disappoint or hurt their consumers,
They erode, they lose support.

Old brands are removed from the supermarket shelf. . . .
Old countries are removed from maps. . . .

Marketing professors, like NYU's Scott Galloway, argue:

You have to evaluate a country brand
With no malice, with no mercy

If leaders promise a lot and deliver ever less . . .
Or even worse if they lie . . .
The brand is in trouble.

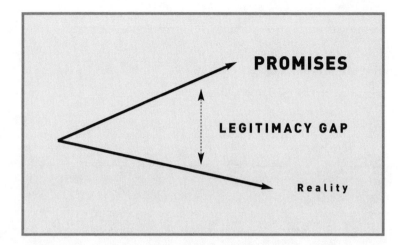

As the Brits like to say: "Mind the Gap."

Sometimes the gap between what is promised and what is real grows so broad, the whole country myth becomes unsustainable.

Then you can watch a country disappear, live, on CNN.

Remember this flag?

Everything it stood for disappeared
in eleven months.

East Germany disappeared into another sovereignty,
into an old rival,
after forty years of relentless indoctrination.

**Not even the toughest opponents of the German
communist regime wished to eliminate the country.**[17]

**But all it took was a chink in the Berlin Wall; the process
became unstoppable.**[18]

The day after the Berlin Wall was breached,
Bulgaria, too, ousted its "supreme leader."

Turns out, in many countries, few wanted to be there;

**There was little to support the country's
symbols and myths.**

You have to be careful to keep your promises, especially when it
is a matter of life and death . . .

Many Americans are more than willing to defend their country. Thousands volunteer for the Navy, Army, Air Force, Special Forces. They put themselves in harm's way, volunteer to fight, perhaps to give up their lives. Despite this, when they are abroad, one of the first things many do is begin checking off dates. They know exactly how many days they have left in the country. Often they reenlist . . .

But what is important is that it is their choice.

So it is really delicate when a country, when a government, breaks its pact, breaks its promise. When government unilaterally extends tours of duty in war zones for tens of thousands . . .

As has now happened, time and again, in Iraq. Given that 40% of soldier's in Iraq are "weekend warriors" with families and careers, many feel cheated, lied to.

Not surprisingly, National Guard recruitment is down 30%.[19]

The danger is that eventually, if promise and reality diverge too much . . .

Grandchildren may decide it is not worth the effort
To defend the same symbols, beliefs, flags,
And borders of their grandparents.

**("A nation is the desire of many individuals
to do great things together.")**[20]

After all, even the United States, once upon a time, lost seven stars. Then the rebel flag grew again until thirteen had joined.[21]

Some countries, despite ongoing massive challenges, have successfully rebranded. The U.S. has been masterful at changing, restructuring, rebuilding. Even India, often a pit of poverty, caste prejudice, and ethnic-religious strife, is now successfully selling "smart, English-speaking people, at a great price."

India now sells engineering consulting in Germany. . . .

China, not exactly a democracy, nor a rich country, has convinced itself and the world it is well on its way to resurrecting its historic role as the world's Middle Kingdom.

The United Kingdom brand, once upon a time the most storied and powerful in the world, is now but a shadow of its former self.

Turns out the sun did set on the empire . . .

It has taken decades of restructuring and pain to get the country moving again.

(Meaning former downtrodden, pitiful Ireland has a higher GDP per capita than the UK.)[22]

Meanwhile, the U.S. brand, despite its overwhelming military power, economic dominance, educational and cultural hegemony, is in trouble globally.

It seems a brand which garners ever less respect, sometimes even within.

In 1991, George Bush I had a 75% approval rating among Germans and 72% among Russians.

In 2004, George Bush II had a 14% approval rating among Germans and 28% among Russians.[23]

In this context it is interesting to see how different U.S. regions brand themselves. . . .

One has to remember that the U.S. is a really young country.

But a lot of territory has already changed hands.

Many flags have flown over large parts of the present-day U.S.

"Six flags over Texas" is not just an amusement park. It is a political reality. . . .

Spain (1519–1685), France (1685–1690), Spain (1690–1821), Mexico (1821–1836), Republic of Texas (1836–1845), Confederate states (1861–1865), and USA (1865–).

Autonomy, even untying, is not a completely alien and abstract concept in the U.S.

It was not that long ago that: *"We the delegates of Texas, in convention assembled, have passed an ordinance dissolving all political connection with the Government of the United States of America . . ."*[24]

Perhaps no flag other than the stars and stripes will ever fly over Texas . . .

Or perhaps not.

As of 2004, should you move to Texas, you could get a new license plate. Its motto:

"Texas: It's Like a Whole Other Country"

(Indeed . . .)

There is more emphasis on state history in Texas than in any other state.

Fourth graders and seventh graders spend a full year on the state's history. As of 2003, Senate Bill 83 required all public school students to also recite the Texas Pledge of Allegiance:

> *"Honor the Texas flag. I pledge allegiance to thee, Texas, one and indivisible."*[25]

Being a "Texian" is a continuous state of mind.[26] It is ingrained from childhood. It is nontrivial.

The feeling of "better off alone" is reinforced daily through a variety of "Lone Star" symbols and myths.

The State Flag . . .

Gov. Rick Perry explained the new Lone Star quarter: "This quarter will remind all of the proud and rich history of the state that was once its own sovereign nation."

And do not forget Lone Star Beer: *"The National Beer of Texas."*

(Sadly, not everyone loves Texas. Gen. Phil Sheridan once said: *"If I owned Texas and Hell, I'd rent out Texas and live in Hell."*)

Polls taken during Gov. George Bush's campaign showed that 42% of Texans would be in favor of untying, if they could maintain a confederated status with the United States.

> Sovereignty is not an abstract notion for fringe groups, like the "Republic of Texas"; they claim a sovereign country that includes pieces of the "old Texas," parts of Oklahoma, Kansas, New Mexico, Colorado, and Wyoming.[27]

I am not predicting, or promoting, untying Texas.

But I do want you to reflect on the fact that even compact and tight historical units like the British Isles and Spain can suffer surprising challenges from rich regions.

And so, too, someday, might the U.S.

Like Texas, Alaska has sat on the fringes and reinforced its better-off-alone attitude. . . .

> Alaska's history, as a part of the U.S., is not very long. Through 1741, maps of the North Pacific tended to peter out around northern California. Then a Russian empress sent an expedition to "discover" the Aleut's "great land."[28]

(Al-a-aska is larger than the next three largest U.S. states combined, stretching a distance the equivalent of from Atlanta to San Diego.)

Until October 18, 1867, the official maps of Alaska were Russian:[29]

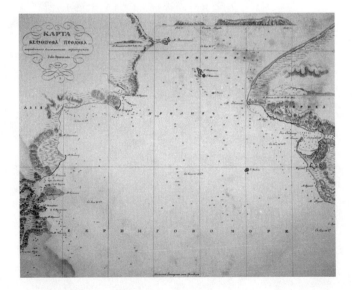

Baron Eduard de Stoeckel, Russian ambassador to the U.S.,
negotiated the sale of the territory, for $7.2 million.

Many thought Secretary of State William Seward paid way too much.

(Seward was a busy little imperialist who dreamt of a vastly expanded
U.S. "He also wished to acquire Alaska, Canada, Greenland, Iceland,
Mexico, Darien Island, Hawaii, the Danish West Indies, Santo Domingo,
Haiti, Culebra, French Guiana, Tiger Island, Cuba, Puerto Rico, and
St. Bartholomew. . . . He even devoted serious consideration to the new
location for the capital of this far-flung empire, deciding on Mexico City
as the most strategically placed site.")[30]

Cynics had several nicknames for the Alaska purchase:

*"Hyperborean Solitudes, Seward's Folly,
Seward's Iceberg, Walrussia."*[31]

It was so hard to get real news from so far away that
one could report the totally false.

Agapius Honcharenko began printing the *Alaska Herald*
without ever setting foot in Alaska.[32]

Had a single senator changed his vote, Alaska might not have become a star in the flag.[33]

Most of Alaska's population was indigenous. They were not
exactly respected . . .

In 1885, the aptly named Governor Swineford reported that his
district had 49,900 inhabitants: whites, 6,500; practically white
creoles, 1,900; civilized natives, 3,500; wholly uncivilized natives,
35,000.[34]

The Organic Act of 1884 provided that: "(Indians) shall not be disturbed
in the possession of any lands actually in their use or occupation or now
claimed by them."

Guess how long that was respected . . .

A lot have come, taken, left bitter feelings behind. *Discovery*
became a free for all in which species after species was
slaughtered.

The sea cow and the speckled cormorant soon became extinct.[35]

However, in a small serving of just deserts, the 1884 act failed to specify
how anyone could acquire land. This was "reserved for future legislation
by congress."

Nobody bothered to fix Alaska's real estate folly for almost three-quarters of a century, which led to many outright land grabs and massive discrimination.

In 1942, Nathan Margold, solicitor of the Department of the Interior, argued:

"Original occupancy establishes possessory rights in Alaskan waters and submerged lands, and that such rights have not been extinguished by any treaty, statute or administrative action."

But it is hard to claim land if you are not a citizen. And until 1924 natives could become citizens only "if they severed all tribal relationships and adopted the habits of a civilized life."[36]

Finally, Minook, born of Russian father and Eskimo mother, sued for citizenship. Judge James Wickersham granted the request; not the end of the story, of course . . .

In 1945, when an antidiscrimination bill was being debated in the Alaska Senate, one opponent argued:

"The races should be kept further apart. Who are these people, barely out of savagery, who want to associate with us whites with 5,000 years of recorded civilization behind us?"[37]

But legal ambiguity and past wrongs can come back to bite, decades or centuries later.

Through 1954, congress had yet to find the time to legislate under what conditions Alaskan Indian lands could be sold.[38]

This implies most land titles were invalid. . . .

Soon native populations began claiming one-third of Alaska for their exclusive use.[39]

Of course claiming and getting are not the same. One suit was thrown out because the native's attorneys were "not approved by the Secretary of the Interior."[40]

The natives did not go away.

Suits mounted; soon natives were claiming 380 million acres, more than the total land mass of the state.

While the claims were outstanding, it was hard to drill for oil.

The energy-hungry federal government initially settled for a payout of $1 billion and 44 million acres.[41]

We might expect to see increasing demands for autonomy and self-governance, and not just among native Alaskans. Many Alaskans have felt exploited by a faraway capital.

"Alaska has been cursed . . . (by) absentee landlordism where the people who control the resources of the country do not reside in the country and have no interest in it."[42]

It took eighty-nine years of stewing, petitioning, and begging for Alaska to become a state.

There were heated debates over whether the territory should become one, three, or four new stars.[43]

On November 6, 1923, those living in southeastern Alaska voted to secede from the territory and become a separate state within the United States.

The vote was 1,344 in favor and 89 opposed.

Feds did not care what Alaskans or Hawaiians wanted. Democrats and Republicans kept blocking each other's attempts to make one territory a state but not another.

Finally President Eisenhower signed the bill admitting Alaska.

He signed the bill in private, wary of the reaction of his fellow Republicans.

And it was not just Republicans who were deeply unhappy.

So were some Alaskans, some of whom can make the Lone Star Texas seem downright neighborly.

"(Using) the term 'Outside' to designate any place except Alaska has been common for a long time."[44]

Even today local government is far away;
You cannot drive to Juneau, the state capital.
You have to either fly or take a boat.

A new star was not a great celebration . . .

In the 1980s, Joe Vogler founded the Alaskan Independence
Party (AIP).

In 1990, AIP candidates won the governorship and lt. governorship.

AIP became one of the few successful third parties in the U.S.

Joe Vogler was murdered in 1993.

The debate faded, for a while . . .[45]

It is easy to forget that U.S. history is littered with threats and attempts to untie.[46]

New Englanders threatened untying at least four times.
Southerners also threatened to secede over the following
issues:

Jackson's tariffs (1828).

American Indian's rights (1820s and '30s).

And over slavery, leading to the Civil War . . .

And, in fact, the U.S. has lost several potential stars already.

Notice any particular pattern in these flags?

**Care to guess why each of these flags is red, white,
and blue and contains a star or two?**

The U.S. tried very hard to keep the Philippines.

1901 sedition laws in the Philippines led to prison and/or death for
those advocating independence.

"Pacification" may have killed up to one million natives.

But, unlike Puerto Rico, there was no offer of citizenship for these
"savages."[47] Nevertheless, the U.S. kept large military bases, Clark
and Subic Bay, and actively intervened in Philippine politics until it
was kicked out in 1992.

Panama was never formally annexed. Its inhabitants never
became U.S. citizens.

But the U.S. did carve the country out of Colombia in 1903, to
protect the canal.[48] The U.S. remained the key employer and de
facto kingmaker in a country governed by the U.S. military and
the canal for eighty-five years.

(And when all else failed, the U.S. simply threatened or intervened:
1903, 1918, 1921, 1925, 1941. . . .)

On January 9, 1964, when students dared attempt to raise
their country's own flag, inside a high school within the
canal zone, U.S. troops killed twenty-three people.

In 1989, just before the U.S. invaded to oust General Noriega, the
country's new president was sworn in, not on sovereign Panamanian
territory, but on a U.S. military base.

Through 2000, the country was literally cut in two, by a ten-mile-
wide canal zone. The currency was, and remains, the U.S. dollar.
Many in congress are still furious Carter dared "give up U.S.
territory."

Then there is Puerto Rico; it became a territory in 1902, elected its first governor in 1950, became a commonwealth in 1952. . . .

Yet those born on the island are merely statutory citizens of the U.S.

In legal terms, this means the U.S. Congress can unilaterally declare Puerto Rico, and its inhabitants, independent and no longer part of the United States.[49]

(Bye, bye. Nice knowing you for a hundred years . . .)

Think about this for a minute, much as various neocons might wish to do so, they cannot yet legally revoke the citizenship of the inhabitants of the Commonwealth of Massachusetts.

But they can cast off the Commonwealth of Puerto Rico with a simple majority vote.

This is a curious form of democracy, indeed—kind of reminds you of the bumper sticker *"Liberty and Justice for All. Offer not available in some areas. (Prices subject to change.)"*

The mayor of San Juan, Puerto Rico, claims: *"Puerto Rico is a Hispanic country with ties of citizenship to the American nation."*[50]

(U.S. citizenship was granted through the Jones-Shafroth Act, in 1917, so Puerto Ricans could be drafted into WWI.)

Yet the relationship between island and mainland remains schizophrenic at best.

(The Supreme Court ruled that Puerto Rico is "foreign in a domestic sense.")

In one poll among Puerto Ricans, 62% considered Puerto Rico, rather than the U.S., their nation. But if forced to choose a citizenship, 54% would become Americans.[51]

A vote on Puerto Rican vs. U.S. citizenship is not an abstract concept. In 1998, after a very contentious debate, the U.S. Congress passed HR 856 . . . by one vote. This bill allowed Puerto Ricans to choose statehood, independence, or the status quo.

Given the option of statehood, Puerto Ricans said, thanks, but no thanks.

(Just as they did in 1967 and 1993.)

So the U.S. continues to compete against its own citizens in a broad range of events.

In 2001, a bitterly disappointed Miss USA, one of five finalists for the modestly titled "Miss Universe" contest, lost to Puerto Rico's Denise Quiñones. During the 2004 Greek Olympics, the NBA dream team got slaughtered, 92–73 in its first game, by Puerto Rico.

(Stunning given that NBA/Olympic teams had a 24 W–1 L record.)

One none-to-subtle sportscaster reacted by asking: *What do you make of the Americans getting knocked around by a fake country?*[52]

It is not that the U.S. did not try, very hard, to annex P.R.

(Before 1952, those flying a Puerto Rican flag were arrested.)

Yet Puerto Rico remains a complicated, multiracial, Spanish-speaking isle.

It is full of *blancos, blanquitos, rubios, trigenos, morenos, mulatas, indios, negritos, prietos, jabaos. . . .*[53]

But almost half of all Puerto Ricans live on the U.S. mainland.[54] Many of these English-speaking nuyoricans, who are returning to the island to retire, favor the U.S.[55]

It is not clear whether Puerto Rico will someday be a star gained or a star lost.

Statehood would be neither easy nor smooth. Some Republicans worry that this would likely add two (D) senators and several (D) congressmen. So one might expect a series of hurdles such as meeting minimum economic growth targets, more English in schools, federal taxation, and cuts in local government.[56]

Guam remains in a similar limbo. It could, someday, claim statehood.

One-third of their land lies behind U.S. military checkpoints. Its quasi-U.S. citizens are allowed to send representatives to the U.S. Congress. And sometimes, in committee, not in the general session, these representatives are even allowed to vote. But if and only if their combined votes are not enough to overturn the committee's vote. In other words, the vote counts if, and only if, it makes no difference.

American Samoa ("an unorganized, unincorporated U.S. territory") is another odd place.[57] Great football. In 2002, every PAC-10 team recruited at least one Samoan, not to mention the more than twenty-eight NFL players . . . which makes a Samoan forty times more likely to get to the NFL than the average American.[58]

In 1986, another U.S. territory was cut loose, Micronesia.

> And some cynics even dared accuse the U.S. of a divide-and-conquer strategy, just because it took an inhabited land area smaller than Rhode Island and carved it up into four different political entities. . . .

The U.S. Commonwealth of the Northern Marianas, the U.S. Free Associated Republic of the Marshall Islands, the U.S. Free Associated Federated States of Micronesia, the U.S. Free Associated Republic of Palau.

> These "countries" are now independent and free. Hurray!
> Yet they maintain a Compact of Free Association with the U.S.

> > (And, until recently, they received the highest level of per capita U.S. aid.)[59]

The U.S. controls their defense and foreign relations. And any citizen of Palau, Micronesia, or the Marshall Islands is free to work in the U.S.[60]

Noncitizens with quasicitizen rights?

The Northern Mariana license plates still read "USA."

Those who live on these islands have "undetermined" citizenship.[61]

Perhaps one way to figure out whether this region might add a star to the flag someday, is to ask your friendly CIA. . . .

"Under U.S. administration as part of the UN Trust Territory of the Pacific, the people of the Northern Mariana Islands decided in the 1970s not to seek independence but instead to forge closer links with the U.S. Negotiations for territorial status began in 1972. A covenant to establish a commonwealth in political union with the U.S. was approved in 1975. A new government and constitution went into effect in 1978."[62]

Confused? So am I. . . .[63]

> These are citizens . . . except they cannot vote for any U.S. presidential candidate. They retain local control over immigration, customs, labor, and taxes. But U.S. district courts have jurisdiction. Meanwhile, the Chinese are building up trade and tourism, and could soon become more important to these folks than the U.S. is.[64]

Closer to home? The U.S. Virgin Islands . . . perhaps another star someday?

The bottom line is that minor legislative changes

(Just defining the legal status of nations that are already within the U.S. border)

Could someday add five or more stars, or turn them loose. . . .[65]

By now I hope you agree with me that "U.S. citizenship" is a little more layered and complicated than it may seem at first.[66]

There is a zoo of citizenships within the U.S.

How well the U.S. is able to sell its model, its values, its myth on the periphery today may be a harbinger of what could occur within the core tomorrow.

But even though you can see the fraying edges of empire on the periphery, it is still really hard to see what could soon lead to significant untying in the core of the U.S.

> But it is not impossible.
> Think Britain, Spain, Italy, Canada.

There remain deep historical fault lines within the greater and within the core of today's United States of America. They are by-products of an occasionally brutal history of conquest and modernization.

Given that there are still many wounds.

> It is key not to assume continuity.

> Today is the time to mediate conflict.

> Before it is someday too late.

Decisions and policies put in place today will determine what the flag and border look like fifty years out.

In an era of ever fewer heroes, decreasing institutional legitimacy, and ever greater political polarization, might you at least want to ask . . .

What might strengthen or even expand the borders of a country?

And what could weaken them and cause them to contract?

So even though flags, borders, and anthems are delicate subjects . . .

Please try not to get too defensive or angry.

Let's you and I have a conversation. . . .

There is plenty of space on the pages that follow for you to comment, add, cross out, agree, disagree, and question.

Let's have an honest debate over what makes a country stronger.

And what can make it weaker.

Not just a discussion about trends . . . but also about consequences.

(And let's try to find some answers, before a flag or border suddenly gets altered, here or next door.)

3.
TECHNOLOGY AND RELIGION'S BRUTAL MARCH

"OUR DEEPEST FEAR IS NOT THAT WE ARE INADEQUATE.
IN REALITY WE ARE POWERFUL BEYOND MEASURE.
IT IS OUR LIGHT, NOT OUR DARKNESS, THAT MOST FRIGHTENS US."

—*Marianne Williamson*, A RETURN TO LOVE

If you do not educate your own . . .

If you do not attract some of the smartest

Or if you wrong the most educated and entrepreneurial . . .

They leave and . . .

You will not grow,

You will not be competitive, and

Long term, you may not be a viable country.

And if you are not a viable country,

If most of the smart ones have left,

Or were not educated to begin with,

Then, in real-politick terms,

Why would anyone bother with you?

You know that. I know that.

Hell, even politicians know that.

There is not a politician on Earth who does not say things like:

The future of our country lies in our children.

Nothing is more important than education.

Teachers are the building blocks of society.

Yada, yada, yada . . .

If it is so obvious, if it is such a cliché, then why is it so
hard to implement?

Why do so few countries and governments
really act in consequence?

It is not as if the trends aren't clear. As if there is no evidence
of what succeeds and what fails.

Want to ensure **no** economic growth in your community?

Do a lousy job educating your kids.

Ignore women, marginalize them.

Do not innovate.

Get rid of all those who have political, cultural, and business ideas
that differ from "the way we do things around here."

Become dependent on government pork.

(And soon you, too, can become another one of the 117 U.S. cities,
or a myriad of countries, with below-average rates of patent
production, investment, and growth.)[1]

Think about what happened in Brazil. Decades ago it decided to
become the best in the world. Scouts scoured each and every village
to find the most talented kids.

It did not matter if they were rich or poor, were black, brown, or white,
lived in a village or a big city, had powerful parents or were orphans.

If they were good, they were supported, mentored, tracked, and trained.

And eventually, the country won. Time and again . . .

Until there was no doubt they were the best.

Brazil beat the world five times.

The tragedy is that Brazil chose to do this in soccer.

In 2003, 92% of Brazil's schools had no access to the Internet and 52% did not even have a phone line.[2]

> If you live in North East Brazil, your life span is likely seventeen years shorter than that of a southern Brazilian.[3]

Meanwhile, South Korea chose to do exactly the same thing . . . **in math and science.**

Very different outcomes . . .

In 2004, Samsung's net income was higher than that of Intel or Microsoft. By 2005, Samsung had the highest value of any non-U.S. tech company ($77 billion).

It is not just Brazil that is in competitive trouble; so, too, is the U.S.

China used to generate one-sixth as many engineers as did the U.S. Now it graduates four times more.

Korea, with one-sixth the U.S.'s population, graduates the same number of engineers.

The high school dropout rate in the U.S. has been growing since 1983.

The dropout rate is now 32%.[4]

Recall Descartes:

Cogito, ergo sum.

"I think, therefore I am."

Descartes got here after deconstructing every aspect of knowledge.

He could not prove he was not dreaming, that what he saw was not distorted.

But he knew he thought. . . .

And that confirmed he existed. . . .

A modern corollary is . . .

Countries that don't think, cease to exist.

Of course technology can also be used to veto existence.

Today's H bombs weigh 4% of what the bomb dropped on Hiroshima weighed and are 7,000 times more powerful.[5]

A knowledge economy generates an accelerated Darwinian system.

Countries succeed and fail, appear and disappear, very quickly.

This is not a new story.

Latin American states started "Europeanizing" and building strong central governments more than a century before the U.S. and Canada.

Mexico, Peru, Brazil, and Colombia had universities, courts, printing presses, centralized tax systems, and hospitals up and running decades before the *Mayflower* was built. Mexico's National Autonomous University was up and running in 1553. Harvard? 1636.

In 1700, the British, Spanish, and Portuguese colonies of the Americas were about equally productive. Cuba was producing 67% more wealth per person than the U.S. Through 1800, Cuba's GDP per capita exceeded that of the U.S.[6]

There was a basic difference in outlook between the pilgrims and most Spaniards and Portuguese.

These were not particularly nice people. All three were exceedingly noxious to natives. But the former came with dreams of building a new life and exercising religious freedom.

They had no plans to go home.

The Spanish disembarked and unloaded an ossified version of religion and brought plenty of bureaucrats with them.

Their dream was to plunder and go back home.

Because they were just here "for a little while," few Spaniards took the time to invest in people, develop broad science literacy, or to build lasting, autonomous institutions.

(Until very recently, it was common for Spaniards to leave "to make their Americas"—that is, to go work somewhere and then return home and retire.)

In one society, pride and class was an expected virtue.

In the other, it was a sin.

One can see the contrast in permanence by comparing Anglo and Latin constitutions.

In Latin America, as in the U.S., presidents swear to uphold and defend the constitution. But the U.S. has had the same constitution for more than two centuries.

Only seventeen amendments have passed since 1791.

Meanwhile, throughout Latin America, constitutions are continuously redrafted or simply scrapped.

Just three examples of new constitutions or major redrafts: Argentina (1813, 1819, 1826, 1853, 1860, 1866, 1898, 1949, 1957); Brazil (1820, 1824, 1832, 1888, 1889, 1891, 1925, 1926, 1934, 1937, 1946, 1965); and Mexico (1813, 1814, 1819, 1821, 1836, 1843, 1857, 1877, 1917).

It is not unusual for the constitution to suffer significant amendments every presidential period.[7]

As long as the basic rules keep changing, not many will invest for the long term.

Instead, many will simply snatch what is available now and run.

Between the late 1700s and the 1800s, the income gap between Anglo America and Latin America grew and grew.[8] Political stability, technological know-how, and broad investment in human capital made a huge difference.

> During the postindependence chaos, most Latin American countries simply missed much of the industrial revolution. By the 1820, the U.S.'s GDP per person was about twice that of Mexico; by 1900, it was just under four times as much.[9]

What was critical in the 1800s and 1900s is ever truer today.

As political squabbles rage, science and technology do not stand still.

The knowledge economy is accelerating change almost beyond comprehension.

Over the next five years we will double the data generated by all human beings throughout history.[10]

At the beginning of this century, scientific databases doubled every fifty years. In 1998, the U.S. granted one-third more patents than in 1997.

> If you tried to store the data from your computer hard drive on a 1950s' hard drive, it would cover 2½ square miles.

(Today's hard drives can store 100 billion bits per square inch.)[11]

Some countries "get it," and the results are spectacular. In 1981, a diminutive Deng Xiaoping launched a "responsibility system" for Chinese farmers. Deng based his heresy on a simple phrase used by Mao Tse-tung in 1957: *"Let a thousand flowers bloom, a hundred schools of thought contend."*

Within the dance of veils that shrouds Chinese politics, all in the know understood. China would, once again, tolerate entrepreneurship.

Soon Deng, leader of the largest communist nation on Earth, was saying: *"To get rich is glorious."*

One small phrase which may turn out to be a key break point in history, placing a dirt-poor country on a path toward becoming a major economic power.

No other world leader, ever, has gotten so many people out of poverty as quickly. The Chinese economy has been doubling every five to eight years.

> There are already around 300,000 Chinese millionaires. Not evenly distributed, of course, by the early 1990s, those living in Shenzhen, China, were making more than $5,700 per year in a country where most incomes averaged $317.[12]

The income differential between those living in the East and those in the agricultural West is tenfold.[13]

> Many Chinese want to reclaim their four-millennial status as a political, technological, and economic superpower. Meanwhile, many of the folks they compete against in the West are comfortable. They earn a decent living. Some have held the same job for decades. Often, they are really good at what they do, and they have a vested interest in the system.

> Tweaking it is OK; blowing it up is very uncomfortable.

The Chinese understand the way to take on the West is
not to imitate.

It is to outwork and to out-think.

One of my nutty friends, Jonathan West, is a wonderful
Tasmanian who taught at the Harvard Business School before
founding his own competitiveness institute. We enjoy traveling
together to various odd places, studying, learning, writing.

His 2004 trip to China truly scared him.

Jonathan went into factory after factory and found that the
Chinese were manufacturing ever more products, cheaper,
faster, with higher quality.

But that was neither new, nor particularly scary.

When Jonathan began to deconstruct what made the Chinese
so successful, he found that over one-third of Chinese college
grads had science, math, or engineering degrees.

What powers China is regions like Haidian. Likely you have never
heard of it. . . .

It is home to 40 universities, 138 science research
institutes, and 810,000 engineers.[14]

As they build new industries, Chinese entrepreneurs are able
to take apart products and reverse-engineer them. But unlike
the Japanese, they do not just retool and export.

What the Chinese are doing is breaking up products so
that people, not machines, do the assembly. Those doing
the assembly, by hand, are, more often than not,
engineers.

This provides a lot of work.

But gradually it dawned on Jonathan that there was a
second, far more important, implication. Those on the
line have the knowledge to continuously improve the
product, piece by piece, day by day.

They can redesign on the fly. They can fix. They can cut cents off.

The Chinese have adopted a strategy similar to that which made the U.S. the most powerful nation on earth. . . .

The U.S. made science its dominant religion.[15]

Science promises ultimate truths, answers to ever more fundamental questions . . .

> PhDs are the modern priests, teaching "absolute" truths. Labs, hospitals, and universities are the new cathedrals, promising cures, accumulating wealth, dazzling with miracles.

Anyone who does not believe in science is oft accused of heresy.

So far, science works better than any other system we know of.

> (Try keeping a plane in the air using faith alone. . . .)

Countries in which technology is a part of daily myth and ritual have a tremendous advantage. Countries that ignore science, or that stop learning, tend to fall behind very fast.

> In 1975, only Japan generated more graduates as a percentage of population than did the U.S. By 2003, the U.S. had fallen to 14th place.[16]

Science will dominate as long as we do not come up with an even more powerful system of myths-beliefs-truths.

Education and technology fuel a knowledge-based economy.

> Street markets in Taiwan are very different from those of Latin America; next to piles of vegetables and plastic goods, one also sees stall after stall of computers and computer parts.[17] A South Korean is half as likely as a Brazilian to have a TV, and ten times as likely to own a computer.[18]

One quick way to weaken or even lose your flag and country is to become ever more intolerant and ever more ignorant.

Quit bringing in new people, new ideas.

In 2003–2005, throughout the southern United States, several science museums refused to air various films.[19]

Apparently they were insulting some audiences.

Here are some of the horrid notions many U.S. kids will be protected from:

The Cosmos (what do you mean the universe is billions of years old!)

Galápagos (nasty subject, evolution and the heretic Darwin)

Volcanoes of the Deep Sea (life originated in the deep sea?)

These subjects create a ticker tape of emotions:

"It's blasphemous." "I hate it when the theory of evolution is presented as a fact."

Never mind the films are scientifically accurate.
After all, why teach geology, astronomy, biology? . . .

(Ironically Darwin set out to be a pastor.)

A key driver of economic growth is generating a belief system where nothing is sacred if disproved by contradictory data.

(*"When theory collides with reliable data, theory must go."*)[20]

When societies forget science and depend more and more on faith alone, they get into real trouble and eventually fall further and further behind. There are good and logical reasons why, in developed countries:

"Nations replaced universal religions as sovereign arbiters of life and death."[21]

> And people began to get just as passionate about
> their flags as they did about their gods.

This does not imply religion cannot be a very positive force. It can help guide a society, build institutions, preserve and promote a moral conduct. But one has to be very clear on what religion can and cannot accomplish in the context of a knowledge economy.

William J. Bernstein, neurologist, author, investor, argues there are four key questions:

Who? Why? What? How?

Religion must focus on the first two . . .

(and allow scientists to focus on what and how).

Religions that attempt to explain and control all

Leave no room for growth and discovery.

> And they stifle the state, ideas, and growth.
> Eventually gaps between dogma and reality
> Weaken even the religion itself.

This is just one of the reasons why a rise in fundamentalism is so damaging.

Arab-speaking states, once upon a time, had some of the highest incomes in the world. Around AD 1000, the best mathematicians, astronomers, hydrologists, botanists, engineers, architects, doctors, and pharmacists congregated in the great universities in Damascus, Shiraz, Esfahán, and Córdoba.

But when Arabs quit learning, researching,

Incomes began to erode, for centuries.

And they continued to fall . . .

11% of rich country's (OECD) incomes in 1980 . . .

5% in 1990.
4% in 2000.
Despite oil.[22]

When a lot of people in a country are absolutely certain that something is true . . .

And when those who do not share these beliefs are heathens,
And no one is allowed to learn or practice something different,
The country is in deep, deep trouble.

During the Dark Ages, the Catholic Church banished learning, research, technology.

But not corruption, or lust for land and gold. In 1342–1343, Pope John XXII granted 624 dispensations of legitimacy; 484 went to children of the clergy.[23] Then came the Inquisition and Savonarola; write a book like the one you are reading and be tortured.

If history teaches anything, it is that mixing religion and governance can be catastrophic.

> One can trace the fall of Spain to getting the balance between church and state wrong. In 1492, Isabella and Ferdinand consolidated the country. Then they celebrated by expelling some of the best and brightest scholars, scientists, researchers, because they were Jews and Moors.

Excerpts from The Alhambra Decree, March 31, 1492:

". . . by diabolical astuteness and suggestion that continually wages war against us may easily occur unless the principal cause of it be removed, which is to banish the said Jews from our kingdoms."

"We order all Jews and Jewesses of whatever age they may be, who live, reside, and exist in our said kingdoms . . . that by the end of the month of July next of the present year, they depart from all of these our said realms and lordships, along with their sons and daughters, menservants and maidservants, Jewish familiars . . . under pain . . . they incur the penalty of death and the confiscation of all their possessions."[24]

The Inquisition let loose against scholars, students, and foreigners, preventing any new idea or technique from entering the country.[25]

Disaster was temporarily offset by gold and silver from the New World, but for centuries, Spain remained a relatively insular and closed society.

Spain learned little, adopted little, from those it conquered.

If you go to London, you can eat great Indian and Chinese food. Then you can visit marvelous archeological museums, celebrating the wealth and achievements of many former colonies.

If you go to France, the Vietnamese and African foods are wonderful. The whole of Paris circles the great Egyptian obelisk. The Louvre contains uncountable treasures.

But then go to Madrid, and try finding decent Mexican, Peruvian, Argentine food, . . . Attempt to find the nonexistent Aztec, Maya, or Inca archeology museums. There was not enough respect for these cultures to bother to preserve them, much less showcase them. Many of the greatest Nahua-Aztec sculptures were destroyed to build the Mexico City Cathedral.

And if you go to Córdoba,visit the great mosque.
But don't bother looking for any Arab food.
Centuries of life and custom left little mark.
Just archeological ruins.

If Spain is to become a great power again, it is going to have to recall just how much learning it ignored and squandered, and it is going to have to overcome past prejudice.

Throughout the world, religious fanatics continue to repress and destroy. . . .

(Post-9/11 graffiti in D.C.: "Dear God, save us from the people who believe in you.")[26]

Religion has probably started more wars, altered more borders, and destroyed more countries than any other force on the planet.

But religion, along with nationalism, has also built more countries than any other force on the planet.

In almost every country, nationalism and religion still partly underlie theory and legitimacy of governance.

Getting the balance right between science, morals, and faith is essential if a country is to survive long term.

It is not that current U.S. religious practices, per se, are dangerous.

It is that religious beliefs are being manipulated to win elections.

The law is very clear. How and when we die is the most personal choice we can make. You have a right to avoid extraordinary measures if terminally ill or brain dead.
If you cannot decide, then your spouse, your children, and your parents can decide, in that specific order. In the Terry Schiavo case, the Supreme Court declined to intervene, or overturn lower courts, six times.

None of this seemed to matter to President Bush II and many in congress. They used a family feud as a theocratic political platform. They passed legislation allowing the federal courts to take up a local case. They then accused judges and lawyers of being "the personification of evil" and murderers. Bush II interrupted his Crawford vacation and flew back to sign the bill.

Their argument? All life is sacred and must be preserved at all costs. (A curious argument coming from the pro–death penalty ex-governor of Texas, after executing 134 people.)
(And curious given that Tom DeLay allowed his father to die in 1988 after a similar tragedy.)

Bill Frist and Tom DeLay flew down for a gruesome "photo op," propping up the victim between them.[27]
Finally, DeLay attempted to subpoena a woman who had not said a word for fifteen years. . . .

Tell us about your condition?

Even after she died, Schiavo was featured on Corpse TV. The coroner's truck, with her body inside, was followed, à la O.J., by gaggles of TV helicopters.

Jesse Jackson arrived in a white stretch limo to go on CNN. . . .[28]

These are extraordinarily divisive and polarizing issues, with relatively small groups of fanatics and fundamentalists yanking political chains.

Never mind that 82% of the U.S. population opposed congress on this issue. Never mind 74% thought it was all about politics.

A very brave ex-senator (R-Mo.), ex—UN ambassador John Danforth argued:[29]

"Republicans have transformed our party into the political arm of conservative Christians.

"In my state, Missouri, Republicans in the General Assembly have advanced legislation to criminalize even stem cell research. . . . They argue that such cells are human life that must be protected, by threat of criminal prosecution, from promising research on diseases like Alzheimer's, Parkinson's, and juvenile diabetes.

"I am and have always been pro-life. But the only explanation for legislators comparing cells in a petri dish to babies in the womb is the extension of religious doctrine into statutory law.

"When government becomes the means of carrying out a religious program, it raises obvious questions under the First Amendment. But even in the absence of constitutional issues, a political party should resist identification with a religious movement. While religions are free to advocate for their own sectarian causes, the work of government and those who engage in it is to hold together as one people a very diverse country. At its best, religion can be a uniting influence, but in practice, nothing is more divisive.

"As a senator, I worried every day about the size of the federal deficit. I did not spend a single minute worrying about the effect of gays on the institution of marriage. Today it seems to be the other way around."

Remember, even the most fundamental beliefs change over time.

Many regarded other races as inferior; women were supposedly weak and incompetent, royalty had different blood. . . .

For millennia, and even today, few things get people more riled, faster, than discussing . . .

My God(s) vs. Your God(s) . . .

(Pablo Neruda: *"There are words that have blood in their syllables."*)[30]

Particular gods used to rule when to plant, what to eat, learn, and sacrifice.

Specific deities seemed all powerful and absolute.

Until they weren't. Until the rules changed.

Until there were more practical, more powerful, beliefs to live by.

When the gap between what was preached and what was observed daily got too wide, societies rewrote, reinterpreted, edited, altered, changed, and rejected basic beliefs.

When St. Paul was preaching a single God in the great Greek amphitheater in Ephesus, Turkey, his message was reasonably well received. Until those in the audience who sold statues and amulets related to various Gods realized their market was about to drastically shrink.

So they attempted to lynch the future saint, who was forced to escape through the narrow crawl space at the back of the stage.

(Perhaps one of the first victims of protests against free trade?)[31]

If you can change, alter, reinterpret, and redefine God . . .

You can certainly redefine, rethink, restructure, or bury . . .

A flag, a border, a country . . .

*No matter how powerful and dominant
it seems at any given time.*

Within the U.S., religion-moralism, always a powerful force, seems to rise once again.

> You can see this in the violent reaction against the Janet Jackson bare-breast incident during the Super Bowl, or in Baptist compounds spreading north, or in the massive Baptist-vote turnout for Bush II.

Historically, this is not unusual. . . .

When a very successful civilization is yet again challenged by waves of change, often the reaction is to slow down, to try to reroot oneself in fundamental beliefs.

> I am happy with things as they are. We are losing what we have.
>
> Stop this new nonsense. . . .

Those overwhelmed or marginalized by change sometimes react very aggressively.

> Eleven U.S. states now limit the teaching of evolution. Cathy Cox, Georgia's superintendent of schools, typified the breed. She tried to eliminate references to evolution and the earth's age from biology textbooks "because it reminded people of that monkeys to man sort of thing."[32]

> Kansas conservatives now dominate the school board, which had already voted once, in 1999, to eliminate all mention of evolution. A bill in Missouri would require at least one chapter with alternatives to evolution.[33]

(As Madison Ave. might say, 10% more Americans prefer creationism over Darwin.)[34]

It is hard to overstate how fast our world is changing now.

(Although many Wall Street analysts certainly overstated how fast monetary rewards will flow.)

The largest databases in the world are now biology databases. About half of this data is free.[35] Most of it did not exist five years ago.

> (Free public biodatabases increased from 171 at the beginning of 2004 to 719 by January 2005.)[36]

This data changes what we can research and how we deal with food, feed, fiber. It will change energy, computing, insurance. Likely life code will substitute the digital world as the greatest single driver of economic wealth on the planet.[37]

> Some thrive in this environment. They start new industries, launch new academic disciplines, develop company after company.

But very few countries are bothering to read these free biodatabases. The first map of how genomics data flows globally shows that the U.S. is overwhelmingly dominant in terms of generating and consuming bio information.[38]

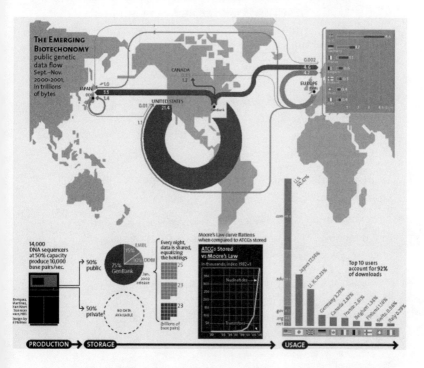

Most knowledge flows within the U.S, and to Japan, and to Europe.

In a knowledge-driven economy, development is concentrated within a few cities and regions rather than across whole countries.

> Almost all life science research and business development occurs inside a few zip codes; in northern California, for instance, in 94080. In Southern California, most of the action is within Salk-Scripps-UCSD.

> > (92121 happens to be above a nude beach, but I do not think that is the dependent variable.)

As knowledge concentrates, you see significant increases in the wealth of the community.

> Look at real estate prices for instance: 41% of the U.S.'s million dollar–plus houses are in California. 11.6% of the single-family homes in Cambridge, Mass., cost more than a million.[39]

Technology will likely continue to generate large disparities in wealth and knowledge within borders as well as across them.

As incomes diverge, the stakes of adopting one model or another increase.

Often both sides dig in, certain they are right and the others are fools.

Many of the smartest migrate to where they respect research and new ventures. There is ever less incentive for technologically sophisticated people to remain within relatively backward states or countries.

Among the most talented and mobile, single citizenship is rapidly eroding.

> Eighty-nine countries now allow dual citizenship. Governments grant these rights because they want to attract capital, skilled workers, the young and talented.[40]

Regions that do adapt and advance often begin to argue they have little to gain from subsidizing the rest of the state. As rich areas grumble about having to support the "backward," those who are increasingly poor are also likely to become increasingly resentful and militant.

Broadening technology gaps could lead to further fragmentation of states.

Even quite homogenous states like China might cleave a few states because the technological value added by nations like Tibet and the Uighur are quite low.

If countries do not restructure, their strength can fade quickly. Those with advanced science degrees have no trouble crossing borders and finding jobs.

And as the smart leave, countries go into an economic death spiral.

One of the determinants of U.S. technological leadership was attracting smart foreigners. This would have been hard to accomplish had the 1882 Chinese Exclusion Act remained in place. It was an attempt to block Chinese from entering the country and denying those already here citizenship. In which case 40% of the CEOs in Silicon Valley, who are Indian or Chinese, would likely be working elsewhere.

We like to think we are past these xenophobic eras and live in a more enlightened time. But post–September 11, many foreign students are treated as suspects.

They increasingly choose to go elsewhere. There has been a 50% drop in foreign students taking graduate tests (GREs) to study in the U.S. Foreign student applications declined 28% in 2004 in the U.S. and increased 15% in Britain and 10% in Germany.[41]

Not so good given that about one-third of U.S. Nobel winners were born abroad.

The loss of foreign talent would not be as serious if U.S. students were filling the gap.

Unfortunately this is not the case. The U.S. ranks 15th out of 40 in mathematical literacy (TIMMS). Not bad . . . if your main competition is Latvia. . . . But more than a slight problem when you import more and more from Singapore, Korea, Hong Kong, Taiwan, and Japan . . . #1 through #5 in math.[42]

The good news is that the problem was recognized by President Bush.

He proposed educational reforms that would place the U.S. at the top within a decade.

The bad news is, it was Bush the First who proposed this . . . in 1990.[43]

In 2001, the U.S. graduated 59,536 engineers. China? 219,563.[44]

The first key to long-term success and survival is:

K I P

(Knowledge Is Power)

This, of course, has been true for ages.

But it has a very different meaning, and far broader consequences, when the global economy is based on knowledge, rather than manufacturing or agriculture.

Google is putting whole libraries, including Harvard's, into its search engine.

This is a global system within which you can build or destroy countries very fast.

Even successful countries will face huge obstacles if they allow great disparities in education and knowledge creation to grow between ethnic groups, between regions, between religions.

You can easily divide large countries and generate a series of successful, and not so successful, smaller states.

Gaps in educational attainment and income can Eventually become national security issues.

Only 3% of the scientists in the U.S. are Hispanic.
Only 10% of Hispanics graduate from college.[45]

If two or more populations consistently diverge, if they become increasingly isolated, there is ever more opportunity for recrimination and blame.

Some of the best studies of what discriminatory policies can lead to were done by Russian scholars after the Soviet Union collapsed. One conclusion: "The task of politicians is to avoid the strict channeling of ethnicity along social lines, to prevent the emergence of obvious disproportions in social conditions . . . and guarantee the equal availability of social mobility."[46]

(Now ask yourself, are all Democratic and Republican representatives being good boys and girls under this criteria . . . or are they constantly pushing and prodding to get one group to blame the other?)

"If demography is destiny, the United States is entering a perilous era . . . much of our population growth includes millions of people with very little education and few skills to prepare them for the bitterly competitive global economy."[47]

This could someday even end up costing the country stars . . .

PART TWO

A

Few

Bills

Past

Due

EXCUSE ME . . . I WAS HERE FIRST

4.

One Native American Web page opens with
a couple of pertinent quotes:[1]

"AMERICAN HISTORY IS LONGER, LARGER, MORE VARIOUS,
MORE BEAUTIFUL, AND MORE TERRIBLE THAN ANYONE
HAS EVER SAID ABOUT IT."

—*James Baldwin*

"MEMORY SAYS, 'I DID THAT.'
PRIDE REPLIES, 'I COULD NOT HAVE DONE THAT.'
EVENTUALLY, MEMORY YIELDS."

—*Friedrich Nietzsche*

No one would argue that Native Americans have
been treated fairly.

But most people say let bygones be bygones.

Judge George Folta made this clear back in 1952:

> *"It is a matter of common knowledge that today the Indians of south-*
> *eastern Alaska prefer the white man's life despite all its evils and*
> *shortcomings . . . racial discrimination is virtually nonexistent."*[2]

Never mind that Arizona did not allow Native Americans to vote until
1948; New Mexico, till 1962. Or that in 2000 the Washington State
Republican Convention voted to eliminate all tribal governments.

Delegate John Fleming: "We think it can be done peacefully . . . but if
the tribes were to resist . . . then the U.S. Army, Air Force, and the
Marines, and the National Guard are going to have to battle back."[3]

In Boston, in 2004, ninety-two Native American
delegates and alternates attended the Democratic
National Convention . . .

Which technically made them felons.

The Indian Imprisonment Act of 1675 prohibits Native
Americans from entering Boston if not accompanied by two
musketeers. The law was still valid in 2005.[4]

What you and I may regard as an historical oddity makes
other folks' blood boil.

Turns out the Muhheconnews had been trying to get the Boston
law repealed since 1996.

After millions of deaths, and being exiled to "the rez," discrimination continues. Just try to rent a house as a Native American.

A 2003 survey on rental discrimination found . . .
21% of Asians were rejected . . .
22% of African-Americans . . .
26% of Hispanics . . .
29% of Native Americans.[5]

Peoples murdered and oppressed for centuries still face enormous obstacles.

Even Native American jewelry is under attack.

About 40% of the "authentic handicrafts" sold in Gallup, New Mexico, are made in China and India.

Often the sellers are Arab merchants.[6]

But country after country is finally beginning to realize that, if even a few folks survive, things can get very sticky . . .

Many an old treaty is finally coming home to roost.

This has occurred in places like Australia, Canada, Ecuador, New Zealand, and South Africa.[7]

And sometimes it can have serious territorial consequences.

In Australia, for instance, the Government of Australian Colonies (and thereafter the Governments of the Commonwealth, States and Territories of Australia) long based their sovereignty and land claims on a concept of *terra nullius*.

(A quaint notion that the "discovered" land was "empty.")

Ironic given the initial explorers' detailed descriptions of settled natives, tilling the land and handing down properties from father to son.

This fictional veil of just ownership lasted through 1992. Then the Australian High Court ruled that the land title of Indigenous Peoples, Aborigines, and the Torres Strait Islanders was to be recognized as common law.

The court rejected *terra nullius* as anachronistic and unreasonable.

This implies that native title rights predate European colonization.

And if the crown did not explicitly "extinguish" a land title, it could pass via inheritance.[8] (In practical terms, if the crown held on to aboriginal land, it would have to give it back.) If title had been transferred to settlers, it had effectively "extinguished" the native title.

New Zealand is living through an even more complicated process.

Originally, the English crown claimed land on the principle of "discovery."[9]

But then, when the French began meddling in the area, the Brits decided to strengthen their claim through a treaty with hundreds of Maori chiefs.

Of course you remember . . . The 1840 Treaty of Waitangi.[10] But so what, you may ask . . .

For over a century and a half the Maori remained mostly powerless, and the treaty was ignored and mostly forgotten.

Until there was a Maori political resurgence . . .

In the 1970s and 1980s, New Zealand began to respect the Treaty of Waitangi.

> (Once again promising to really, really do what it had promised it was going to do in 1840.)

Maori judges began investigating legislative or executive actions that violated the treaty.

> And, yes, this does have consequences.

> Courts began to order the government acquire lost Maori lands, at market price, and return them to tribes that claimed them.[11]

In 1992, the government gave the Maori $150 million to buy an interest in New Zealand's largest fishing company and 26% of the country's fishing quota in return for limiting Maori personal fishing rights to certain reserve areas.

> It was just the beginning . . .

> New Zealand continues to be embroiled in complex and expensive disputes. But most claims are now adjudicated through arbitration and compromise instead of suits.

(This may be a good model for future U.S. and Canadian claims.)[12]

Complex rulings are crossing the Pacific and coming ever closer to home . . .

In 1997, the Delgamuukw case recognized aboriginal titles in Canada.

> In 2003, the Dogrib gained control over natural resources and industrial development in an area slightly smaller than Holland. The Deh Cho slowed a $6 billion gas pipeline. In November 2004, British Columbia's Supreme Court ruled that the Haida should be consulted over land use in their traditional lands.[13]

("The government's duty to consult with Aboriginal peoples and accommodate their interests is grounded in the principle of the honour of the Crown, which must be understood generously.")

Native claims can now slow, if not stop, mining, drilling, forestry, off-shore drilling.

So ask yourself . . .

If *terra nullius* does not stand up to scrutiny in Australia,

Nor does "discovery" in New Zealand . . .

If land titles are getting somewhat fuzzy throughout Canada . . .

Just how long will the Doctrine of Discovery,

the basis for settling the Americas, stand judicial scrutiny?

In other words . . .

If you can have these debates in former British colonies, like Canada, New Zealand, and Australia, and have tough rulings, based on former British law . . .

Just what makes you think that the U.S. will remain an immune outlier . . . forever?

But, of course, if one is to make such a claim, one would have to seek evidence that what is occurring in other Anglo countries might also be occurring within the U.S. . . . .

Which is why I urge you to take a little drive through Connecticut . . .

As you drive through the state, you can sometimes spot spectacular specimens of citizens dressed in fuchsia, lime green, and sunflower yellow, carrying their golf clubs . . .

You can detachedly observe a world of order, rank, privilege, and law. Every blade of grass is placed *comme il faut.* Houses are ordered just so. Woods are protected just so . . .

And only those that are just so are allowed into the clubs . . .

Nothing as tacky as a casino would ever be allowed to muddy this orderly and rarified existence.

No resident of Connecticut is allowed to open a casino.

So how come the largest casino in the U.S. lies within the borders of this state?

Ironically, this wildly successful enterprise belongs to the Pequots, a tribe that so typified doom and extinction that Melville used it as the name of the boat in *Moby-Dick.*

Strange karma.

Turns out the casino is not in Connecticut, after all;
it is in a separate nation.[14] And separate nations within Connecticut
could someday claim up to one-third of the state's lands.

Connecticut is no exception.

Victorious in a series of court battles, 175 tribes have built
232 casinos, mostly within states that prohibit casinos.[15]

There are several hundred sovereign nations within the U.S.

American Indian status and residency, treaties and
obligations, are yet another part of the quilt that
makes up the zoo of exceptional citizenships
that coexist within the U.S.'s borders.

Each sovereign nation makes up its own rules, has its own police forces, is mostly exempt from taxes, chooses its own citizens, and has its own governing council.

That is what it means to be sovereign . . .

Casinos and other sovereign perks are not just a matter of
charity or goodwill toward oppressed indigenous tribes.
It is a matter of obeying national and international law and
precedent.

And, thanks to the Constitution's 14th amendment,
Indians are not subject to taxes.

(Although many tribes do pay "voluntary" contributions to states.)

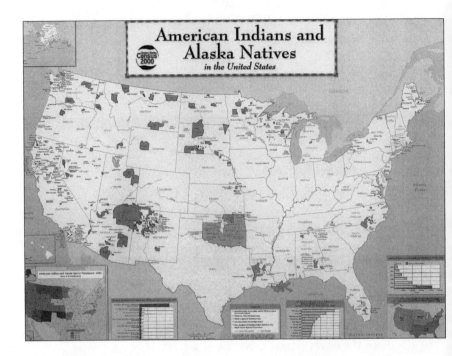

What is the source of this odd quilt of laws, nationhoods, and sovereignties?

Papal bulls gave Europeans "the right" to conquer non-Christian lands.

After Reformation, the English maintained "their rights" to conquer.

However, military campaigns were expensive.

It was better to negotiate.

So colonial governments established a *first crucial precedent*:

Land was purchased from tribes that had the status of sovereign nations.

Then King George III, in an effort to control further colonial expansion and prevent alienating tribes that might ally with France, attempted to regain control of all land transactions with native tribes.[16]

(Everything beyond the Appalachians was supposedly off limits to white settlers.)

This established a *second crucial precedent*:

Only a sovereign could obtain lawful land title from native tribes.

These precedents survived independence. . . .

On September 19, 1778, the newly sovereign U.S. signed its first treaty of alliance with a Native American Nation.[17]

The treaty was signed between the Lewis brothers and three Delaware Indians: White Eyes, John Kill Buck, and Pipe:[18]

"Whereas the United States are engaged in a just and necessary war, in defence and support of life, liberty and independence, against the King of England and his adherents, and as said King is yet possessed of several posts and forts on the lakes and other places . . .

"The Delaware nation . . . do hereby stipulate and agree to give a free passage through their country . . . Whereas the enemies of the United States have endeavored, by every artifice in their power, to possess the Indians in general with an opinion, that it is the design of the States to extirpate the Indians and take possession of their country to obviate such false suggestion, the United States do engage to guarantee to the aforesaid nation of Delawares, and their heirs, all their territorial rights."[19]

This treaty established a *third precedent*, which is now coming back to haunt various states and property owners:

Indian nations signed treaties with the U.S. as sovereign entities.[20]

Through 1871, the U.S. signed 371 treaties, which recognize Indian tribes as sovereign entities.[21]

In 2004, there were 562 federally recognized tribes in the U.S. and close to three hundred more groups seeking recognition.[22]

For a long time tribes were so downtrodden and marginal that these treaties seemed to have no consequence. . . .

There were ample warnings that the actions that followed may not have been entirely kosher in legal terms:

Chief Justice John Marshall ruled against President Andrew Jackson.

He favored the Cherokees.

The president's response?

"Marshall has made his decision; let him now enforce it if he can."

A lot was promised, codified, made legally binding.

Little was actually respected, delivered, fulfilled. . . .

U.S. treatment of the Sioux provides a particularly egregious example of law ignored.[23]

In 1851, the federal government and the Sioux signed a treaty. Sioux would allow pioneers to cross their land. The U.S. would not invade their land.

(Gee, just like the Delawares.)

Surprise . . . the government built several forts in Sioux territory.

After two years of fighting, the new Fort Laramie Treaty (1868) prohibited settlers from crossing the Great Sioux Reservation. Then, under pressure from miners, President Ulysses S. Grant sent troops in, which led to the Battle of Little Bighorn.

Following the U.S. defeat, the government invalidated the Fort Laramie Treaty and took much of the Sioux property. In 1889, the U.S. government dispersed the Great Sioux Reservation over seven smaller reservations and gave the remaining land to the new states of North and South Dakota.[24]

The status of the remaining sovereign nations is ambiguous.

One circuit court held that:

"Indian tribes are not states. They have a status higher than states. They are subordinate and dependent nations possessed of all powers as such only to the extent that they have expressly been required to surrender them by the superior sovereign, The United States."[25]

This ambiguity was reinforced in the final report of the Sen. James Abourezk's (D-S.D.) Commission.

"The relationship of the American Indian tribes to the United States is founded on the principles of international law. . . . It is a political relation: a relation of a weak people to a strong people; a relationship of weak governments to a strong government."[26]

(And you wonder why Native Americans are sometimes so angry?)

As anyone who has read much about ongoing disputes having to do with borders, ethnicities, and international law knows . . .

Treaties between sovereign nations can have significant legal consequences decades, or even centuries, after being signed.

This is not just a battle over casinos.

You have to remember, for the U.S., for Canada, for Latin America . . .

"Indigenous groups are the only ethnic groups whose claims challenge the territoriality of states."[27]

Native Americans claim 28 state names originate from their languages. A few examples:

Alaska	"Object towards which the action of the sea is oriented" in Aleut
Arizona	"Silver bearing" in Aztec
Arkansas	"Downstream place" in Sioux
Connecticut	"Place beside a long river" in Mohican/Algonquin
Hawaii	"Homeland" in Hawaiian
Illinois	"Warriors" in Algonquin
Kansas	"South Winds People" in Sioux
Kentucky	"Land of Tomorrow" in Iroquois
Massachusetts	"A large hill place" in Algonquin
Michigan	"Great waters" in Chippewa
Minnesota	"Sky-tinted water" in Dakota Sioux
Mississippi	"Great Waters" in Chippewa
Missouri	"Town of the large canoes" in Missouri
Nebraska	"Flat water" in Otto
North Dakota	"Friend" in Sioux
Utah	"People of the mountains" in Ute

It goes on and on across states, counties, cities; you get the idea.[28]

Not that everyone recognizes and respects this ancestry . . .

After World War II, the U.S. government attempted to implement a policy of "termination."

Finally a little truth in advertising?

It was a ham-handed attempt to no longer recognize distinct tribes, with their own territories, laws, and rights.

This is far from the first time "termination" was attempted. December 29, 1890, about 300 Lakota were massacred at Wounded Knee. For these "heroic acts," 23 soldiers won the Congressional Medal of Honor.

Merry Christmas . . .

Five days after the massacre, the *Aberdeen Saturday Pioneer* ran an editorial that argued:

"Safety depends on the total extermination of the Indians. Having wronged them for centuries, we had better, in order to protect our civilization, follow it up by one more wrong and wipe these untamed and untamable creatures from the face of the earth."

You know the guy who wrote this editorial . . .

L. Frank Baum went on to write *The Wizard of Oz* a decade later.[29]

Attempting to ignore and bury Indian claims and territories led to protest and upheaval.

It got ugly.

Soon the government began reversing itself and granting ever more petitions. The Indian Self-Determination and Education Assistance Act (1975) began allowing control over school boards and history lessons. The Tribal Government Tax Status Act (1982) amended the IRS code so tribes could be treated as states.

And so on and so forth . . . Many rights have accumulated.

Each society, each group within a society, makes up stories, historical myths, to pass on to the next generations. Sometimes these stories are based on fact, sometimes they are embellished, sometimes they are made up.

The first Thanksgiving apparently took place in Texas. They did not eat turkey in Plymouth for Thanksgiving. Plymouth was neither the first, nor the first permanent, settlement in North America. George Washington apparently never cut down a cherry tree.

Pointy-headed historians point out these things time and again. But like Dracula, these common myths are so powerful they revive time and again.[30]

But not all myths are shared by all citizens. It is not entirely surprising, after a couple of hundred years of unpeaceful coexistence, that Narragansett leader Tall Oak said:

Your Heroes are not our Heroes.[31]

Native Americans are not particularly fond of Teddy Roosevelt. He apparently said: *"I don't go so far as to think that the only good Indians are dead Indians, but I believe nine out of every ten are, and I shouldn't like to inquire too closely into the case of the tenth."*[32]

Many Native Americans do not share, and often reject, many of America's common myths.

The battles over who is a true hero, large and small, continue today.

In 1823, Congressman Francis Baylies argued: "Our natural boundary is the Pacific Ocean . . . it is no invasion of the rights of man to occupy a territory over which the savage roams, but which he never cultivates. . . ."

Some consider Abe Lincoln a mass murderer for ordering the largest mass hanging in U.S. history; thirty-eight Sioux were killed the day after Christmas 1862.[33]

> More recently, Longmont, Colorado, named a street after Civil War hero Col. John Chivington. But in the late 1970s, mid-1980s, and 1991, various Native Americans protested. Turns out Chivington also led the 1864 Sand Creek Massacre, killing Arapaho and Cheyenne.
>
> Residents refused time and again to change the name. Positions radicalized. Tony Belthem of the Four Winds Council then suggested naming the street "Ted Bundy or Hitler Av."

After twenty-seven years and multiple protests, the town council voted 6–1 to change the name of the street. But not everyone is pleased, as one resident put it: "The residents of Chivington can hardly talk to each other civilly about this matter."[34]

Many of the symbols, myths, and heroes that created a common nationhood have very different implications for Native Americans.[35]

There is the small matter of changing the name of Custer State Park to Chief Crazy Horse Park . . . The South Dakota legislature has been postponing this debate.

> (According to United Native America's Mike Graham, they were too busy trying to vote the official state dinosaur and bread.)

Some colonists not only raped, pillaged, stole, and murdered; they also brought smallpox, bubonic plague, typhoid, influenza, mumps, measles, cholera, malaria, and scarlet fever.

> Contagion began way before the *Mayflower* showed up; Spanish expeditions brought pigs into contact with natives who had no immunity.

Historians like Henry Dobyns argue these scourges killed up to 96% of the total population of the Americas.[36]

> So many had died by the time the British colonizers arrived that they described finding thousands of abandoned pyramid-like earth mounds all over the U.S. Whole towns abandoned.

> Some argue that a few of the societies that got wiped out may have been larger, richer, more populous, than some of those in Europe.

> To get a sense of what it might have meant for world history if the plague had wiped out 99% of Europe's population, instead of just a third, read Kim Stanley Robinson's *The Years of Rice and Salt.*

(China, India, Arabia become the dominant powers. Europe is a mostly abandoned wasteland. The Americas have time to develop peacefully. . . .)

This issue of historic rights and wrongs keeps coming up again and again. Conservative columnist Ann Coulter recently dismissed all claims that soldiers had deliberately spread smallpox among Indians:

"The settlers didn't understand the mechanism of how disease was transmitted. Until Louis Pasteur's experiments in the second half of the 19th century, the idea that disease could be caused by living organisms was as scientifically accepted as crystal reading is today. Even after Pasteur, many scientists continued to believe disease was spontaneously generated from within."[37]

Native Americans were quite displeased by this analysis:

"Perhaps she should read the letters between Colonel Henry Bouquet and General Amherst dated 13, July, 1763 to 16, July 1763 in which Bouquet and Amherst discuss their intentions to give the Indians blankets and handkerchiefs infected with small pox.

"They knew the disease was spread through the seeping wounds and sweat left on the blankets. That is why the blankets and other materials were routinely burnt. They intentionally kept these blankets and sent them to the Indians to infect them, not caring whether they were killing children or adults. It is stated in their own words in these letters. This is germ warfare and a form of TERRORISM."[38]

After fighting head on, being ignored and marginalized, left behind . . .

Tribes are increasingly using courtrooms to reestablish their rights and increase their economic wherewithal.

The number of Indian lawyers increased tenfold in two decades.[39]

Recent petitions include:

Restitution of constitutional treaty-making authority . . .

Freedom to publicly address the U.S. Congress . . .

A review of treaty commitments and violations . . .

Resubmission of nonratified treaties to the senate.[40]

Two sample clauses from Senate Resolution 37 (2004):[41]

(3) acknowledges years of official depredations, ill-conceived policies, and the breaking of covenants by the United States Government regarding Indian tribes;

(4) apologizes on behalf of the people of the United States to all Native Peoples for the many instances of violence, maltreatment, and neglect inflicted on Native Peoples by citizens of the United States;

Skirmishes over small, seemingly trivial, rights establish, or resurrect, precedent after precedent.

In 1997, there were about 1,200 living on the Muckleshoot reservation. It was described as "the most dilapidated of any Washington tribe."[42] But they built a casino and used their newfound wealth and political clout to reestablish their ancestral rights to hunt.

To the dismay of many a homeowner, they began harvesting shellfish at will on "private" property that lies within their reservation.

But as Newton stated, in his third law of motion;

For every action there is an equal and opposite reaction.

A group of angry Washington State folk put together United
Property Owners, an antisovereignty lobby. Soon big businesses,
some of which have enjoyed virtually free "leases" on
Indian lands, joined in.

("One Nation of Oklahoma" is supported by the Southern Oklahoma
Water Alliance, Oklahoma Farm Bureau, Oklahoma Petroleum
Marketers Association, and Oklahoma Independent Petroleum
Association. Oklahoma, you recall, was supposed to be Indian lands.)

Now they have merged and claim to be "One Nation United," ready
to do battle against the Indians once again.

Here is what they seek:

Tax Indians.
   No "treatment similar to states."
      Limited campaign contributions.
         Stop sovereign tribal immunity.
            No more recognition of tribes.
               No more lands outside reservations.[43]

No one paid much attention to Indian claims until they began
winning court battles, and rights, and building up their own
economy. But now that a few are successful, many want to
retake what little the Indians have achieved.

There is a lot of pressure building up inside Native America versus non-native America.[44]

And vice versa . . .

You can see case after case where sovereignty clashes. . . .

Despite the U.S.'s support of the International Whaling Commission's ban on all commercial whaling, the Makah can hunt and kill
whales in U.S. waters because of an 1855 treaty.

Consider the following statement issued by the Environmental Protection Agency:[45]

> *Under Section 301(d) of the federal Clean Air Act, the EPA is authorized to treat Indian tribes as States. As such, Indian tribes do not fall under the permitting authority of State or local agencies. Instead, EPA retains permitting authority for all sources of air pollution that are located on tribal lands. However, EPA is currently in the process of developing regulations which will enable EPA to transfer permitting authority over to tribal governments on a case by case basis.*

Sovereignty can have unintended consequences; some reservations are being used as toxic dumps. Utah's Goshute Indian reservation is surrounded by army nerve-gas storage facilities and coal-fired power plants. So they decided to store highly radioactive nuclear waste.[46]

In 2005, you could easily manufacture and sell methamphetamines within the Navajo reservation. Use was up 100%.[47]

These debates and legal battles are not confined to western states, and sometimes the overall impact of these skirmishes can be very significant.

In 1972, the Penobscots and the Passamaquoddies set about recovering 12 million acres.

(About two-thirds of Maine.)

They settled in 1980 for just over $80 million.

Like Martha's Vineyard, MA? Careful where you buy land. . . .

At least three hundred Native Americans live on the Vineyard.

They, and five hundred fellow Wampanoags, have challenged the incorporation and ownership of the town of Gay Head.[48]

Gay Head is now officially called Aquinnah. . . .

Turns out, under the federal Trade and Intercourse Act of 1790, states cannot acquire land from Indians without federal approval.

So Massachusetts may have seized this illegally.[49]

The Wampanoags could very well win.[50]

And speaking of respecting the founding father's wills and desires . . .

It was George Washington who signed this law.

New Yorkers are not safe from history's long reach and bite, either. Over the course of two centuries, the Oneidas lost more than 99% of the land they were granted by treaty. Eventually, they were left with a measly thirty-two acres. And they were mad.

Tough, said Albany and NYC; time for lawyers, said the Oneida nation . . .

They based their claims on the Treaty of Six Nations 1784:

"The Oneida and Tuscarora nations shall be secured in the possession of the lands on which they are settled. . . . A line shall be drawn, be-ginning at the mouth of a creek about four miles east of Niagara, called Oyonwavea, or Johnston's Landing-Place, upon the lake named by the Indians Oswego, and by us Ontario; from thence southerly in a direc-tion always four miles east of the carrying-path, between Lake Erie and Ontario, to the mouth of Tehoseroron or Buffaloe Creek on Lake Erie; thence south to the north boundary of the state of Pennsylvania; thence west to the end of the said north boundary; thence south along the west boundary of the said state, to the river Ohio; the said line from the mouth of the Oyonwayea to the Ohio, . . ."

In the 1970s, three groups of Oneidas, from New York, Wisconsin, and Ontario, Canada, joined together in an attempt to regain control over 270,000 acres.

By 1985, the Supreme Court had upheld a test case over 900 acres.

Many got nervous, negotiations began . . . and stalled for over a decade.

Meanwhile, the Oneidas opened a successful casino and hotel, as well as a series of tax-free shops and gas stations.

> They invested part of the profits in lawyers and lobbyists and part in furthering their own knowledge, skills, and education. They, again, became formidable opponents and warriors.

By 1998, the Oneidas had forced the U.S. Justice Department to support their suit. Twenty thousand current property owners suddenly found their property rights at risk.

And now the other side was furious. . . .

Governor Pataki's spokesman was blunt: *"The Federal Government has turned its back on the people of central New York."*

One New Yorker argued: "It's amazing that they basically sided with a foreign nation against us. . . . You ask where do my tax dollars go, against me?"

> But, despite anger and frustration, the Oneidas are pressing ahead. As are the Mohawks (along the St. Lawrence River), the Senecas (near Buffalo), the Stockbridge-Munsee (Wisconsin), and the Cayugas (in the Finger Lakes).[51]

On February 3, 2005, Governor Pataki authorized five new casinos in the Catskills in an attempt to mediate some of these claims.

In March 2005, the Onondaga Nation filed suit claiming 3,100 square miles, from the St. Lawrence Seaway to Pennsylvania.

> Quite ambitious considering their current land holdings are 11 square miles. They even claimed Syracuse.

They claim their suit was not an attempt to build casinos or get money; it was an attempt to force a cleanup of one of the dirtiest lakes in the U.S., Onondaga Lake.

> Turns out their sacred site now hosts 165,000 pounds of mercury and other pollutants.[52]

Ask the U.S. Census Bureau where you might find one or two Native American communities, they will provide you with the following list:[53]

Acoma Pueblo and Off-Reservation Trust Land, Agua Caliente Reservation, Alabama-Coushatta Reservation, Allegany Reservation, Alturas Rancheria, Annette Island Reserve, Augustine Reservation, Bad River Reservation, Barona Reservation, Battle Mountain Reservation, Bay Mills Reservation and Off-Reservation Trust Land, Benton Paiute Reservation, Berry Creek Rancheria and Off-Reservation Trust Land, Big Bend Rancheria, Big Cypress Reservation, Big Lagoon Rancheria, Big Pine Reservation, Big Sandy Rancheria, Big Valley Rancheria, Bishop Reservation, Blackfeet Reservation and Off-Reservation Trust Land, Blue Lake Rancheria, Bois Forte Reservation, Bridgeport Reservation, Brighton Reservation, Burns Paiute Colony and Off-Reservation Trust Land, Cabazon Reservation, Cahuilla Reservation, Campbell Ranch, Campo Reservation, Capitan Grande Reservation, Carson Colony, Catawba Reservation, Cattaraugus Reservation, Cedarville Rancheria, Celilo Village, Chehalis Reservation, Chemehuevi Reservation, Cheyenne River Reservation and Off-Reservation Trust Land, Chicken Ranch Rancheria, Chitimacha Reservation, Cochiti Pueblo, Coconut Creek Reservation, Cocopah Reservation, Coeur d'Alene Reservation, Cold Springs Rancheria, Colorado River Reservation, Colusa Rancheria, Colville Reservation and Off-Reservation Trust Land, Coos, Lower Umpqua, and Siuslaw Reservation and Off-Reservation Trust Land, Coquille Reservation and Off-Reservation Trust Land, Cortina Rancheria, Coushatta Reservation, Cow Creek Reservation, Coyote Valley Reservation, Crow Reservation and Off-Reservation Trust Land, Crow Creek Reservation, Cuyapaipe Reservation, Dresslerville Colony, Dry Creek Rancheria, Duck Valley Reservation, Duckwater Reservation, Eastern Cherokee Reservation, Elko Colony, Elk Valley Rancheria, Ely Reservation, Enterprise Rancheria, Fallon Paiute-Shoshone Colony, Fallon Paiute-Shoshone Reservation and Off-Reservation Trust Land, Flandreau Reservation, Flathead Reservation, Fond du Lac Reservation and Off-Reservation Trust Land, Forest County Potawatomi Community and Off-Reservation Trust Land, Fort Apache Reservation, Fort Belknap Reservation and Off-Reservation Trust Land, Fort Berthold Reservation, Fort Bidwell Reservation, Fort Hall Reservation and Off-Reservation Trust Land, Fort Independence Reservation, Fort McDermitt Reservation, Fort McDowell Reservation, Fort Mojave Reservation and Off-Reservation Trust Land, Fort Peck Reservation and Off-Reservation Trust Land, Fort Pierce Reservation, Fort Yuma Reservation, Gila River Reservation, Goshute Reservation, Grand Portage Reservation and Off-Reservation Trust Land, Grand Ronde Community and Off-Reservation Trust Land, Grand Traverse Reservation and Off-Reservation Trust Land, Greenville Rancheria, Grindstone Rancheria, Guidiville Rancheria and Off-Reservation Trust Land, Hannahville Community and Off-Reservation Trust Land, Havasupai Reservation, Ho-Chunk Reservation and Off-Reservation Trust Land, Hoh Reservation, Hollywood Reservation, Hoopa Valley Reservation, Hopi Reservation and Off-Reservation Trust Land, Hopland Rancheria and Off-Reservation Trust Land, Houlton Maliseet Trust Land, Hualapai Reservation and Off-Reservation Trust Land, Huron Potawatomi Reservation, Immokalee Reservation, Inaja and Cosmit Reservation, Indian Township Reservation, Iowa Reservation and Off-Reservation Trust Land, Isabella Reservation and Off-Reservation Trust Land, Isleta Pueblo, Jackson Rancheria, Jamestown S'Klallam Reservation and Off-Reservation Trust Land, Jamul Indian Village, Jemez Pueblo, Jicarilla Apache Reservation, Kaibab Reservation, Kalispel Reservation, Karuk Reservation and Off-Reservation Trust Land, Kickapoo (KS) Reservation, Klamath Reservation, Kootenai Reservation, Lac Courte Oreilles Reservation and Off-Reservation Trust Land, Lac du Flambeau Reservation, Lac Vieux Desert Reservation, Laguna Pueblo and Off-Reservation Trust Land, La Jolla Reservation, Lake Traverse Reservation, L'Anse Reservation and Off-Reservation Trust Land, La Posta Reservation, Las Vegas Colony, Laytonville Rancheria, Leech Lake Reservation and Off-Reservation Trust Land, Likely Rancheria, Little River Reservation, Little Traverse Bay Reservation, Lone Pine Reservation, Lookout Rancheria, Los Coyotes Reservation, Lovelock Colony, Lower Brule Reservation and Off-Reservation Trust Land, Lower Elwha Reservation and Off-Reservation Trust Land, Lower Sioux Reservation, Lummi Reservation, Makah Reservation, Manchester-Point Arena Rancheria, Manzanita Reservation, Maricopa (Ak Chin) Reservation, Mashantucket Pequot Reservation and Off-Reservation Trust Land, Menominee Reservation and Off-Reservation Trust Land, Mesa Grande Reservation, Mescalero Reservation, Miccosukee Reservation, Middletown Rancheria, Mille Lacs Reservation and Off-Reservation Trust Land, Minnesota Chippewa Trust Land, Mississippi Choctaw Reservation and Off-Reservation Trust Land, Moapa River Reservation, Mohegan Reservation, Montgomery Creek Rancheria, Mooretown Rancheria, Morongo Reservation, Muckleshoot Reservation and Off-Reservation Trust Land, Nambe Pueblo and Off-Reservation Trust Land, Narragansett Reservation, Navajo Nation Reservation and Off-Reservation Trust Land, Nez Perce Reservation, Nisqually Reservation, Nooksack Reservation and Off-Reservation Trust Land, Northern Cheyenne Reservation and Off-Reservation Trust Land, North Fork Rancheria, Northwestern Shoshoni Reservation, Oil Springs Reservation, Omaha Reservation, Oneida (N.Y.) Reservation, Oneida (Wisc.) Reservation and Off-Reservation Trust Land, Onondaga Reservation, Ontonagon Reservation, Osage Reservation, Paiute (Utah) Reservation, Pala Reservation, Pascua Yaqui Reservation, Passamaquoddy Trust Land, Pauma and Yuima Reservation, Pechanga Reservation, Penobscot Reservation and Off-Reservation Trust Land, Picayune Rancheria, Picuris Pueblo, Pine Ridge Reservation and Off-Reservation Trust Land, Pinoleville Rancheria, Pit River Trust Land, Pleasant Point Reservation, Poarch Creek Reservation and Off-Reservation Trust Land, Pojoaque Pueblo, Port Gamble Reservation, Port Madison Reservation, Prairie Band Potawatomi Reservation, Prairie Island Indian Community and Off-Reservation Trust Land, Puyallup Reservation and Off-Reservation Trust Land, Pyramid Lake Reservation, Quartz Valley Reservation, Quileute Reservation, Quinault Reservation, Ramona Village, Red Cliff Reservation and Off-Reservation Trust Land, Redding Rancheria, Red Lake Reservation, Redwood Valley Rancheria Reservation, Reno-Sparks Colony, Resighini Rancheria, Rincon Reservation, Roaring Creek Rancheria, Robinson Rancheria and Off-Reservation Trust Land, Rocky Boy's Reservation and Off-Reservation Trust Land, Rohnerville Rancheria, Rosebud Reservation and Off-Reservation Trust Land, Round Valley Reservation and Off-Reservation Trust Land, Rumsey Rancheria, Sac and Fox/Meskwaki Reservation and Off-Reservation Trust Land, Sac and Fox Reservation and Off-Reservation Trust Land, St. Croix Reservation and Off-Reservation Trust Land . . .

Plus another 386 locations.

Throughout the U.S., a number of Indian nations are arguing that local and state laws are not applicable or valid over their towns/territories.

And they are winning.

Not all of these claims respect modern borders . . .

For centuries, there was an informal understanding that Tohono O'odham, Yaqui, and Kickapoo Indians were free to cross the U.S.–Mexico border without documents. In 1996, increased fear of drug trafficking and aliens broke down this arrangement.

Angry tribe members found it ever harder to travel back and forth for medical, religious, or family reasons. As a result the O'odham are trying to incorporate a nation recognized by both the U.S. and Mexico.[54]

Many oppose, do not like, do not favor Native American sovereignty. But things are different today.

Those who still do not get it are increasingly held in contempt.

(Literally.)

After various treaties were signed in the 1880s, the U.S. government began holding billions of dollars in "trust" for millions of Indians.

Each Indian was supposed to own 80 to 160 acres.

Over the last century, various tribes tried to get the government to provide an account of these trusts.

(The government leased lands to oil, timber, and gas businesses.)

Government officials paid little heed.

Then they discovered that long-lost rights can resurrect in a most unpleasant manner. . . .

In 1999, for the first time in American history, two cabinet officers were simultaneously held in contempt of court. The government's long-standing position had been that it was impossible to keep track of who owned what and who was owed what. . . .

A Federal District Court disagreed. It ruled that the government had deliberately delayed and lied.

(Imagine that . . .)

Judge Royce C. Lamberth did not exactly mince words:

"[The government has] engaged in a shocking pattern of deception. . . . I have never seen more egregious misconduct by the Federal Government."[55]

This had consequences . . .

Secretary of the Interior Bruce Babbitt, and Secretary of Treasury Robert E. Rubin were held in civil contempt for failing to provide records.[56]

And the saga continued . . .

In 2002, Interior Secretary Gale Norton and an aide were found guilty of four counts of civil contempt.[57]

The Native American Rights Fund (NARF) suit alleges extreme mismanagement of 500,000 peoples' trust accounts and seeks damages of $132.7 billion. . . .[58]

(For 120 years, through October 2004, the government could sell oil, timber, grazing leases, property in general, without even notifying the Indian landowners.)

In an attempt to hide what they have done (or not done), government lawyers have resorted to extraordinary tactics.

The U.S. government has already spent $50 million of your tax dollars battling this Indian suit. Meanwhile, at the end of the 20th century, per capita income on reservations averaged $4,478 per year, 53% of homes had no phone . . .[59]

To defend the indefensible, some government attorneys alleged they could not provide documents because: "they were located on high shelves and could not be safely retrieved." Or they "were covered with rat droppings and would put workers at risk of contracting hanta virus."[60]

**Not surprisingly, Judge Lamberth refers to the Interior
Department's handling of Indian affairs as: "The gold standard
for mismanagement by the federal government for more
than a century."**[61]

Recognition and redress are sometimes a little slow. In September
2004, the Smithsonian opened its National Museum of the American
Indian . . .

Meanwhile, newly minted Indian lawyers like Echohawk have
reached one conclusion:

*"Successful tribes are those that have made use of
litigation and exercised sovereignty"*[62]

And this is a lesson they are unlikely to forget.

(Syracuse University's Institute for Advanced Sovereignty teaches
"lawyering skills that will allow them to pursue new legal and
nonlegal strategies to promote tribal sovereignty and Indigenous
freedom.")

There is a growing pride and awareness of indigenous rights.

After all . . .

**"Treaties were agreements between sovereign
nations that granted special peace, alliance,
trade, and land rights to the newcomers."**[63]

Native American challenges and demands for increasing
sovereignty are not going to simply fade away. In February
2005, Judge Lamberth ruled a full accounting for all Indian
trust assets must be finished by January 6, 2008.

This potentially means 500,000 land claims
have to be settled within three years.[64]

There is ever more incentive to reclaim one's
native roots and fight back . . .

The new motto and T-shirts for United Native America?

American Indian Homeland Security

Fighting Terrorism Since 1492

There is enough bitterness on all sides that even battles on the
radical fringe can escalate very quickly.

As long-lost legal and property rights resurrect, American Indian communities grow larger and more powerful.

The number of citizens that self-identify as American Indians more
than tripled between 1960 and 1990. (523,591 to 1,878,285).[65] And
then it increased an additional 119% from 1990 to 2000.[66]

40% of those living in the South now claim an Indian ancestor.

Tribes long considered extinct are resurfacing.

Through the 1700s one of the largest and most powerful tribes was
the Apalachee. Their territory was so extensive, colonists named the
distant mountains after them (the Appalachians). Most were killed
by colonists. Then they were hunted by slaves working on behalf of
cotton owners.

In the 1900s, KKK members chased them with dogs and clubbed
them to death.

In 1997, an archeologist named Bonnie McEwan began rediscovering
an extinct tribe. Three hundred survived, hiding out in the southern
U.S.—a proud people, driven into hiding for centuries, now seeking
recognition.[67]

Some folks are going on the war path. . . .

If you were near Shasta Lake, California, in September 2004, you might have witnessed a ritual that had not taken place since 1887, a Winnemem Wintu war dance.

> The 125-member tribe was outraged by the proposal to raise the dam, thus drowning a further twenty sacred sites, including burial grounds.[68]

It was bad enough that the government took all their lands in 1851 and promised a reservation that never materialized.

> The individual tribe members then had to make due with individual land allotments, which in turn vanished under dam waters.

> (In 1941, the Central Valley Project–Indian Lands Acquisition Act (55 Stat 612) granted to the United States, "(a) all the right, title, and interest of the Indians in and to the tribal and allotted lands.")

Californians living in the Central Valley have a lot at stake in this battle. Farms and cities cannot continue to grow without more water. But they will face a lot more folks who do not want to lose ancestral lands.

The Winnemem Wintu's are just one of fifty-seven groups seeking recognition within California.

These battles are just starting in the U.S. and everywhere.

More income and more education are likely to make some Native American movements more demanding rather than less.

> Canada's problems with the Quebecois, Spain's problems with the Basques and the Catalans, and England's problems with the Scots did not go away when income and education levels increased.

> > > Often, just the opposite occurred as people realized they had rights and that those rights had been trampled.

Many indigenous movements are coming together globally, learning from one another, imitating one another, pushing one another to demand more.[69]

(A convention at Lake Chargoggagoggmanchauggagchaubunagungamaugg?)[70]

> Some Indian activists remain more focused on protecting their traditional national rights than on integrating into the United States.[71]

The language of Indian petitions is increasingly framed in terms of violations of international law.

Consider an excerpt of a speech given in Europe, by Arvol Looking Horse:

"There were more 'casualties' in the so called Indian wars than in WW I and WW II combined. . . . Apartheid and genocide exist in America and will continue to exist unless the world pressures the U.S. to deal justly and honorably with the First Americans."[72]

One center of an increasingly global debate is an obscure United Nations Sub-Commission on the Promotion and Protection of Human Rights, established in 1982.

> The debate then led to the UN Permanent Forum on Indigenous Issues, established in July 2000.[73] Various indigenous people are communicating with one another and are making claims for autonomy based on their rights as peoples, as nations.[74]

Some tribes have sought independent recognition from the UN and other countries.

(More political-scientism: indigenous citizenship is the right of a people to an autonomous territory within the state.)[75]

But if Native Americans were to go before an international court to take on the United States Government, what possible evidence could they offer?

Well, they might start by bringing in a star witness, says the head of the government organization in charge of protecting their rights and welfare, the Bureau of Indian Affairs (BIA).

On September 8, 2000, a bunch of folks got together in D.C. to "celebrate" the 175th anniversary of the BIA. Kevin Gover, assistant secretary of Indian Affairs, gave a speech. Here are a few verbatim excerpts:

"We must first reconcile ourselves to the fact that the works of this agency have at various times profoundly harmed the communities it was meant to serve. . . . The first mission of this institution was to execute the removal of the southeastern tribal nations. By threat, deceit, and force . . ."

"This agency participated in the ethnic cleansing that befell the western tribes . . . it must be acknowledged that the deliberate spread of disease, the decimation of the mighty bison herds, the use of the poison alcohol to destroy mind and body, and the cowardly killing of women and children made for tragedy on a scale so ghastly that it cannot be dismissed as merely the inevitable consequence of the clash of competing ways of life."

"This agency set out to destroy all things Indian. . . . This agency forbade the speaking of Indian languages, prohibited the conduct of traditional religious activities, outlawed traditional government, and made Indian people ashamed of who they were. Worst of all, the Bureau of Indian Affairs committed these acts against the children entrusted to its boarding schools, brutalizing them emotionally, psychologically, physically, and spiritually."

These are the words of the government, not the accusations by the aggrieved.

Native Americans may have a case after all.[76]

And these cases could get very, very expensive.

Once upon a time, House Speaker Newt Gingrich visited with Albert Hale, the president of the Navajo Nation, whose reservation is about the size of West Virginia.

> In Arizona, Navajo land claims exceed the total land area of Connecticut, Delaware, New Jersey, and New Hampshire combined.

Gingrich asked the chief to explain the growing sense of sovereignty and nationhood. Hale responded:

"When I come to Washington, you don't send me to the Bureau of Indian Affairs . . . you have a state dinner for me."[77]

But instead of state dinners, many Native Americans continue getting fleeced in D.C.

> In 2004, two lobbyists, close to very prominent Republicans, were accused of taking more than $80 million in fees from Native Americans. Meanwhile, they were sending e-mails to each other mocking tribal chiefs as "morons," "troglodytes," and "monkeys."[78]

Not that this is a completely isolated attitude.

If you scratch the surface a little, you will still find a lot of racial hatred toward Native Americans.

> In March 2005, a very disturbed teenager killed ten in the U.S.'s second-worst school massacre ever.

It occurred on the Red Lake Indian reservation.

This type of Colombine High School horror normally brings out the best in people—flowers, prayers, donations, condolences flow toward the bereaved.

Not in this case.

Here are some of the verbatim responses to the tragedy posted on Yahoo Internet message boards:[79]

> Did he have his war paint on? Where was the medicine man? 10 Dead Prairie Niggers?!? Woo Hoo!!! Red savages! They shouldn't have any weapons but a bow and arrow. Heap big pile of injuns killed! How embarrassing for their "tribe." I guess they lost a few potential blackjack dealers.

Perchance you think I exaggerate, that over the next fifty years, past wrongs, old treaties, this mothballed native and indigenous stuff will have no impact . . .

If that is the case, I would urge you to take a vacation in Hawaii; it is, after all, a lovely place to surf, sunbathe, and drink mai-tais.

> But if you take a minute out from your vacation, and focus on the world around you,

There are a few dissonant notes. . . .

After you land in Honolulu, you can buy a book called *A Call for Hawaiian Sovereignty* at the airport newsstands.

> As you drive to your hotel, you might notice some cardboard License plates. They reproduce the originally assigned numbers and letters, but under the words:

"Kingdom of Hawaii."

This is not an abstract notion, a lot of native folk still believe this is the only legal government.

The story begins in a fashion similar to that of
Native Americans . . .

By the late 1800s, much of the native population of the Pacific had
been wiped out by diseases, poverty, and slaughters. Hawaiians had
declined from around 300,000 in 1778 to fewer than 50,000 in
1890.[80]

> Most major Pacific real estate had been annexed, by one power or
> another.[81] In Hawaii's case, the U.S. got into the business of
> imperialism because of a bitter battle over sugar. U.S. planters
> wanted to annex the island and its rich fields.[82]

In 1893, troops invaded and gave Queen Lili'uokalani a choice:

Abdicate or be shot.

> And so ended Hawaii's monarchy and its independence.[83]

> President Grover Cleveland agreed the takeover was illegal.

> So very sorry . . .

Foreign workers soon flowed in to work on plantations and
overwhelmed the native population.

> Although not all "guest workers" were happy campers. Filipino
> sugar cutters were not allowed to bring in brides because of anti-
> Asian immigration laws, and they could not marry non-Filipinas
> because of the laws against miscegenation . . . racial mixing.[84]

(And, in 2004, Massachusetts' governor Romney resurrected
these charming legal precedents in an attempt to prevent same-sex
marriage.)

Even before annexation, a matriarchal society had already
started to be overwhelmed by European laws.

The 1860 Act to Regulate Names forced Hawaiian women to take their
husband's name, give the child the father's surname, and separate
names by sex.

> This helped undermine the enormous power
> Hawaiian women had wielded for centuries.[85]

But despite death, exile, and change, not everyone forgot their roots as an independent country. The state motto:

Ua mau ke ea o ka aina i ka pono.

Which, translated for mainlanders, sometimes means:

"The life of the land is perpetuated in [by] sovereignty."[86]

You could see a few signs of unrest brewing.

> In 1941, the U.S. Navy seized a small Hawaiian island, Kaho'olawe. They used it for target practice, pounding it into dust. This drove native Hawaiians nuts and generated a rallying point for nationalist sentiments, particularly after some were convicted of criminal trespass in 1977.[87]

Pressure from the Protect Kaho'olawe 'Ohana (PKO) finally became so intense that the military abandoned the island in 1994.

By the way, this is far from the first time the Navy has lit the fuse for autonomy.

> A very similar policy become a rallying point for Puerto Rican autonomy.
>
> For sixty years, the Navy used a little island near Puerto Rico, Vieques, for target practice.
>
> Protests simmered.
>
> Assorted political fauna like Al Sharpton made it a sport to fly down and get arrested.

All great fun until 1999, when an errant bomb killed a Puerto Rican guard; then tensions exploded. And those well-known softies Rumsfeld and Wolfowitz ordered a halt to all bombing.[88]

About one-fifth of Hawaii's population considers itself native.

Several hundred have attempted to renounce their U.S. citizenship and seek to create a Hawaiian nation, Ka Lahui Hawai'i. They are demanding the UN include Hawaii in the list of non-self-governing territories.[89]

Faced with growing pressures and demands, somewhat surprisingly, the U.S. government issued an official apology. Congress and President Clinton acknowledged the:

"100th anniversary of the illegal overthrow . . . which resulted in the suppression of the inherent right to sovereignty of the native Hawaiian people."[90]

Then things began to cascade; for the next five days, the Stars and Stripes was banished.

And only the Hawaiian flag flew over state buildings.

Hawaiians began singing "Hawai'i Pono'i," an anthem written by the deposed queen in 1893. A lawsuit claimed redress of 1.8 million acres,

(Approximately 45% of the state's land, including Pearl Harbor, the University of Hawaii, and a part of the airport.)

In 1995, a group called the Nation of Hawaii asserted independence and adopted a "constitution."[91] In 1996, native Hawaiians held a referendum; 73% of voters were in favor of sovereign nation status.[92] Thousands marched on August 12, 1998, the hundredth anniversary of the takeover.

Protests continue today.

A series of court rulings further embittered the debate by clawing back meager gains.

In 2000, the U.S. Supreme Court "rejected the idea that only native Hawaiians or those who traced their ancestry back to the state's original residents could vote for trustees of the Office of Hawaiian Affairs (OHA) . . . such distinctions amount to an illegal racial distinction."[93]

In 2001, the Hawaiian Supreme Court invalidated the segregation of 20% of income from ceded lands to the OHA for the benefit of Native Hawaiians.

In 2002, the same court upheld the state's right to sell ceded land despite unresolved native claims to it, and the private Kamehameha School admitted a non-Native Hawaiian, causing widespread outrage and protests.[94]

Some have had enough.

Hawaii's Congressman Akaka and Senator Inouye submitted a bill *"to provide a process for the recognition by the United States of a Native Hawaiian governing entity for purposes of continuing a government-to-government relationship."* [95]

This would give native Hawaiians "dependent nation" status, establish a U.S. office for native Hawaiian relations, and provide a process for recognizing a native Hawaiian governing entity. [96]

Someday, one star gone?

Protests are coming to the mainland.

October 19, 2003, San Franciscans watched an "Aloha March" rally for Hawaii's independence. [97]

And in September 2004, thousands of native Hawaiians marched in Honolulu demanding independence.

Hawaii, one symptom?

Or one of many? [98]

If you want to get a sense of where things could eventually be heading . . .

You might want to look north.

Canadians started finding seeds of untying in many places.

As Quebec demanded special privileges and calling for secession . . .

Other Canadian provinces also began reexamining their own status.

Some began calling for greater autonomy.[99]

The Assembly of First Nations, for one, began disputing the idea that Canada was founded by English and French.

(They argued a number of nations were sovereign throughout the territory centuries before the current state was founded.)

It is *not* a theoretical debate. . . .

Indigenous issues can lie buried for centuries.

And then they can revive in most unpleasant ways.

Canada's Constitution Acts of 1774, 1791, and 1840 do not mention any status or rights for natives. Parliament was given authority over Indian lands in 1867.

For a long time it was as if natives simply did not exist. But even today there are more than a thousand aboriginal communities.

And Canada finally recognizes them as "first peoples."

One way to postpone unpleasant debates over the past is to keep Indians from voting . . .

(As Canada did until the 1950s and 1960s.)

The other way is to keep Indians from ever getting near a court. According to the 1927 Indian Act (Section 141):

Every person who, without the consent of the Superintendent General expressed in writing, receives, obtains, solicits or requests from any Indian any payment or contribution for the purpose of raising a fund or providing money for the prosecution of any claim which the tribe or band, shall be guilty of an offense and liable upon summary conviction for each offense. . . .[100]

For all intents and purposes, for most of its history, Canada ignored most native claims.

But as countries develop and begin promoting human rights and democracy abroad, they are often forced to begin by tidying up their own house.

In the 1970s Canadian natives began winning a series of court cases . . .

In the 1970s and early '80s, aboriginal inhabitants won an average of 36% of their suits.

In the late 1980s and early '90s, they won 37.5%

Now they are close to 50%.

And claims are snowballing.[101]

Canadian courts have become very liberal in granting ancestral land, hunting, fishing, and governance rights to six-hundred-plus Canadian native communities.[102]

The Delgamuukw decision is probably the single-most important precedent. It establishes that:[103]

Aboriginals have rights and title.

Titles lead to exclusive ownership.

Resource development can require consent.

Some are entitled to compensation.

Canada is in a particularly delicate position; unlike the U.S., it has been a strong supporter of international laws and international tribunals.

When Canada and other countries are sued in international courts by natives claiming land, they can no longer claim just territorial rights without informed consent . . .

Nor can they defend themselves using doctrines like . . .

Discovery . . .
Terra Nullius . . .
Conquest . . .
Or Adverse Possession.[104]

The basis for the Crown's claims to Canada have Steadily eroded in case after case . . .

Land is not the only issue First Peoples are suing over.

Turns out they are also angry about . . .

Suppression of Government . . .

Forced Taking of Children . . .

Criminalization of Economic Pursuits . . .

Negated Religious Freedoms . . .

Loss of Due Process and Equality.[105]

Now, within the context of Canada's autonomy and self-governance debate,

The Inuit carved out part of the Northwest Territories, forming the Territory of Nunavut in 1999.

(Nunavut? "Our Land" in Inuit.)

Its 25,000 inhabitants now govern an area twice the size of France.[106]

Ironically, Inuit may someday wish to reclaim parts of Northern Quebec from the pro-secession Francophiles.

Because part of their land was absorbed into the Quebec Province in 1912 . . .

Because these lands are still inhabited primarily by English-speaking Inuit peoples.

After all, if Canada must respect and appease its French-speaking minority . . .

Then the Quebecois must also respect the minorities within their own borders . . .

N'est ce pas?[107]

In 2003, in a virtual replay of Bill Clinton's apology to Hawaiians, British Columbia's premier recognized that governments "failed aboriginal people across our province."[108]

Cash and casinos buy a little time, but the future of Native Americans depends to a large extent on how well they understand and integrate into a knowledge economy.

Education provides alternatives and a context with which one can maintain one's identity.

But this has not been a national priority.

Harvard's 1650 charter created an Indian College.
Wampanoag Caleb Cheeshahteaumuck was the first graduate.
And the only Native graduate for the next three hundred years.
(Ironically, this staved off Harvard's bankruptcy since many donated to educate "the heathens.")[109]

Native Canadians, like Native Americans, may just be getting started in their demands. . . .

5.

BORDERS BOUNCE:
DO YOU *HABLA ESPAÑOL?*

"I HOPE VERY MUCH I AM THE LAST U.S. PRESIDENT IN
AMERICAN HISTORY WHO CANNOT SPEAK SPANISH."

—*Bill Clinton, June 2000*

For centuries, equestrian statues have commemorated heroes and great deeds. Perhaps the largest equestrian statue in the U.S. will not sit in an august Yankee city or in a genteel southern town. Perhaps it will rise in El Paso, Texas.

It does not honor an "American."

It honors Juan de Oñate, whose 1598 expedition established the first European settlements in the western U.S.[1]

(He arrived twenty-two years before the *Mayflower* landed, before the birth of those perennially obnoxious cocktail conversations in the rarified Hamptons air . . . "Oh, yes, great-great-grandmother Dorothy was the seamstress on the *Mayflower*, Daahling. . . .")

But why pay attention to dusty old statues or buildings or past deeds?

Because . . .

**Borders have a funny way of bouncing back,
Even after centuries or millennia.**

In 1945, the U.S. population was 87% white and 2.5% Hispanic. Now it is 75% white and 12.5% Hispanic.

By 2050? 53% white and 25% Hispanic?[2]

In some regions, the change is overwhelming.

In 1975, about one-quarter of those born in California were Hispanic. Ironically, on July 4, 2001, for the first time since 1850, the majority of those born in California were Hispanic.[3]

In Los Angeles, over 72% of the kids in public schools are Hispanic.[4]

The most common baby name in California hospitals? Jose.

When the U.S. took land from Spain and Mexico, there was a strong culture with deep roots.

And if you look really hard, perhaps you can spot some traces of it. Say . . .

Alameda	(Park)
Amarillo	(Yellow)
Boca Raton	(Mouse Mouth)
Chico	(Small)
Colorado	(Red One)
El Paso	(The Pass)
Florida	(Flowery)
Fresno	(Ash Tree)
Las Cruces	(The Crosses)
Lima	(Lime)
Los Alamos	(The Poplars)
Los Angeles	(The Angels)
Los Gatos	(The Cats)
Montana	(Mountain)
Nevada	(Snowed)
Pueblo	(Town)
Punta Gorda	(Fat Point)
Sacramento	(Sacrament)
Salinas	(Salt Ponds)
Santa Fe	(Holly Faith)
Tejas	(Tiles)

Never mind Durango, Laredo, Las Vegas, Nuevo Mexico, Orlando, San Antonio, Santa Ana, San Bernardino, Santa Clara, Santa Cruz, San Diego, San Francisco, San Jose, San Juan, San Luis Obispo, San Marcos, Santa Barbara . . .

In 2003, whites were 49% of the Texas population, a minority for the first time since the early 1800s.

This brings out the worst fears in folks like Harvard professor Sam Huntington. Never one to fear controversy, Huntington has turned from predicting a clash of civilizations, primarily between the West and Islam, to focusing on the brown menace to white-Anglo-Protestant America.

(Many follow Huntington; Lou Dobbs, CNN, anguishes daily . . .)

Huntington argues Mexican immigration is unlike any other in U.S. history because:

> *It comes from a contiguous, poor country.*
> *The scale of migration is massive.*
> *Many continue to enter illegally.*
> *The population is regionally concentrated.*
> *Family reunification makes migration persistent.*

Ironically some of those on the left reinforce these fears through movies like *A Day Without a Mexican*, which show just how vital this population has become to California.

At least half of all the folks who pick U.S. crops are undocumented. Agriculture, lodging, and construction would likely collapse without the 10 million illegal workers.[5]

The bottom line, according to Huntington, is:

"No other immigrant group in U.S. history has asserted or could assert a historical claim to U.S. territory."[6]

Actually, historically, Canada could; perhaps they're too kind?
Puerto Rico could. The Philippines did. Polynesians did. Hawaiians might.

But the basic statement is right.

58% of Mexicans believe the U.S. Southwest should belong to Mexico.[7]

Much of the U.S. was assembled out of the pieces from five other countries.

A lot of this was Spanish-speaking territory.

This is what Mexico's border looked like (pre-1845).[8]

This is the census map showing where Hispanics live in the U.S.

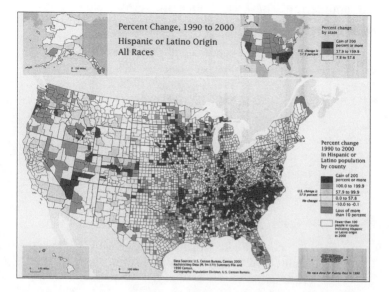

Curious coincidence?

Spanish speakers are rapidly repopulating the old Spanish-Mexican borders.

In 1970, there were 9.6 million Hispanics in the U.S.
 2000, around 35.3 million . . .
  By 2020, an estimated 60.4.

This was definitely not the founding fathers "plan A."

**From 1542 through the 1960s, around 80%
of the immigrants to the colonies and
the U.S. were white Europeans.**

Asians and Hispanics were deliberately excluded.

The National Origins Act (1924) sought to freeze the mix of the U.S. population as reflected in the 1920 census.

Between 1924 and 1965, 82% of immigrant visas
were given to northwestern Europeans.

In 1960, those of Mexican origin were about 1% of total U.S. population. There was even a little ethnic cleansing going on . . .

> During the Depression, over a million people of Mexican descent were forcibly deported from the U.S.

Many were citizens, others were legal residents.

> Never mind, good-bye . . .[9]

(Not the first time this had happened, in 1855 an antivagrancy law, specifically targeted at Mexicans, was charmingly nicknamed the "greaser act.")

But time and again, past wrongs can come back to bite you.

> Born in L.A. in 1926, Emilia Castañeda was summarily expelled, with her family, in 1931. They had one day to pack what they could and get on a train. She went to a country she did not know, to a life of poverty and discrimination.

Emilia was one of a half million Mexicans and Mexican-Americans deported during the Depression to open up jobs for "real Americans."

> In 2003, she and the Mexican American Legal Defense Fund launched a class action lawsuit.[10] Joe Dunn, chairman of California's Senate Select Committee on citizen participation, estimates 1.2 million U.S. citizens were summarily deported. Between 300,000 and 400,000 are still alive. This could turn out to be a very expensive lawsuit. . . .[11]

World War II led, again, to a labor shortage. Suddenly a lot of Mexican and Latin *braceros* (day laborers) were allowed to take low-paying jobs on a non-immigrant basis. This gradually began de facto reversing the trends in population, if not in citizenship.

As the civil rights movement exploded, immigration laws and quotas were torn down and the ratios of immigrants changed radically.[12]

Immigration to the U.S.[13]

	WHITE	HISPANIC
1940	94.8%	3.7%
1970	73.4%	18.7%
1990	31.2%	39.7%
2000	22.0%	45.5%

We are long past the period described by Israel Zanguill: "America is God's Crucible: A great Melting-Pot where all the races of Europe are melting and reforming."[14]

After 1990, there have been more legal Mexican immigrants than European immigrants.[15]

So guess what . . .

Hispanics are now the largest minority in the U.S.[16]

There are now more U.S. Hispanics than there are people in Canada. One among many benefits: it is finally worth watching U.S. soccer. N.Y. alone hosts nine Mexican leagues with 262 teams.[17]

The ratio of Hispanics to African-Americans and whites will continue rising.

One Hispanic wag argues that the motto for African-Americans was "We shall overcome," while that of Hispanics is "We shall overwhelm."

Enough Hispanics have already migrated into the U.S. that second-generation Hispanics will be the key driver of growth . . .

Not new immigrants.[18]

Between the 1970 and the 1990 censuses, whites decreased from 87.5% of the population to 80.3%. Hispanics increased from 4.5% to 9.0%.

Now Hispanics exceed 13.3%.[19]

**This implies that even if you just shut the
border with Mexico tomorrow,
the Hispanic population would continue growing.**

Furthermore, current immigration laws continue to strongly
favor family unification.

Those who already have family members who are U.S. citizens, or
who live in the U.S., are getting two-thirds of all visas.[20]

In the measure that many Hispanic immigrants do not
improve their overall education, this could be damaging
to U.S. competitiveness.

In 2005, H1-B visas, those given to the smartest and most qualified,
were exhausted in one day. . . . Sorry, come back next year. . . .[21]

The political impact of Hispanic immigration, so far, has been
relatively low-key.

Many of those who crossed over from Mexico dreamt of going
home; they delayed becoming citizens.[22]

Among major immigrant groups, Latin Americans are the least
likely to become citizens.

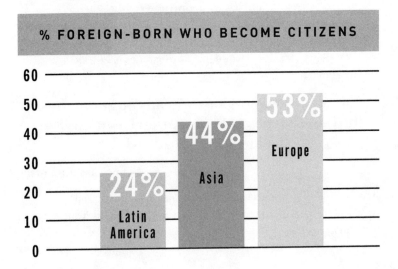

% FOREIGN-BORN WHO BECOME CITIZENS

Latin America 24% Asia 44% Europe 53%

But this is changing.

The Immigration and Reform Control Act of 1986 provided a carrot and a stick.

Amnesty for those already within the U.S. borders.

(For those who entered prior to January 1, 1982,
and resided continuously in the U.S.)

Much tougher restrictions on illegal immigrants . . .

And even on legal immigrants.

If you are convicted of a felony and have not naturalized, you are in deep doo-doo. No matter how long you have lived here, become a criminal alien and lose most of your rights. You will likely end up on a plane deported to a country you do not know, a vacation spot like Syria, Salvador, or Cambodia.[23]

As border controls tightened,
the ebb and flow of folks waned.

Mexicans who used to cross into the U.S., work, and go home, found it harder and harder to cross.

(They were joined by refugees from various Latin American wars and U.S. interventions, folks from places like Haiti, Nicaragua, Salvador, Cuba, and Guatemala who could not go home.)

In 1983, half of those arriving in San Diego expected to remain in the U.S.

By 1996, over two-thirds did.[24]

Folks not only stayed; they brought their families.

They sought citizenship.[25]

(By 1996, around 83% of legal immigrants as well as 75% of the undocumented wanted to become U.S. citizens.)[26]

Many Hispanic citizens do not vote yet—only 5.4% of total votes in 2000.

But Hispanic voter turnout increased 19% from 1990 to 2000.

In some states the number of Hispanics is getting to be so large that even with minimum participation, they could begin to tip crucial elections. This is especially true in states where presidential elections are traditionally contested.

STATE	HISPANIC POPULATION % (2001)	GROWTH OF HISPANIC % (1990–2000)[27]
New Mexico	42	32
California	33	43
Texas	33	54
Arizona	26	88
Colorado	17	73
Florida	17	70
New York	15	30

Between 1978 and 1998, votes cast by Hispanics in governors' races throughout the country tripled.

This is one of the reasons that Bush II has been so careful to court Hispanic voters. He certainly did better as governor of Texas than his Republican counterparts did in California.

In 2004, "family values" and moral issues pushed by the Bush campaign resonated with many Hispanics.

Some claim Bush II got up to 44% of Hispanic vote in 2004.[28]

Hispanics will continue changing U.S. politics.

Throughout the 20th century, California was a bastion of Republicanism. Only four of its governors were Democrats.

In the 1980s, Pete Wilson ran for governor on an antiimmigrant platform. . . .

The Wilson bunch advocated, and passed, Prop 187,
a measure intended to cut all services to illegal immigrants.

No schools, no medical help, no nothing . . . *nada!*
Wilson got a lot of support . . . at first.

But as many Hispanics got poorer, angrier, and desperate,
voters gradually realized these folks were not simply going
to pack up and go away.

And Hispanics understood that some Republicans could hurt
their chances for education, welfare, and family reunification.

Everyone had a family member or
friend who was scared, hurt, hunted.

Many Hispanics began voting
against Wilson and other "Anglo
Only" Republicans.

Even the most conservative
regions, those which fueled
Richard Nixon and Ronald
Reagan's bids for the presidency,
transformed radically.

In 1996, a nine-term congressman from Orange County,
Robert Dornan, was challenged by a woman who had recently
moved into the district.

He laughed. Loretta Brixey, from the elegant Palos Verdes area,
did not seem like much of a challenger. Her previous political
experience was coming in eighth, out of sixteen, for city council.

But then she began using her maiden
name again, Loretta Sanchez. . . .

Suddenly it was Hispanic vs. white power. Dornan lost
by 984 votes . . .

Over the next two years he cried fraud and used every legal artifact
to try to regain his job.

Then came the rematch.
Sanchez beat Dornan by 12,235 votes.
In 2002, Loretta's sister Linda was also elected.
The first sisters ever to serve together in congress.

There was one Hispanic elected official in California in 1965;
by 1992, there were 682; by 2003, they had reached 987.[29]

By 2000, the Republicans had all but given up on California.

Even George Bush acknowledged the difficulty he faced in
getting the all-important California Latino vote:

"It's going to be tough, just because I've got 'Republican' by my name."[30]

Because half of all U.S. Hispanics live in California and Texas,
you have yet to see the full impact of the Hispanic vote.

In 2000 and 2004, California was a write-off for Republicans,
just as Texas was for Democrats. However, please never
underestimate the extraordinary ability Democrats have to lose
what they once conquered; think southern politics . . .

Democrats took California for granted and fed every type
of special interest until . . .

A group of folk long buried and left for dead, revived and attacked.

(Just as keeps happening in *Terminator* movies.)

One key to "Ahnold's" victory was Gov. Pete Wilson
and his old advisers.

> (As well as running against a thoroughly lackluster governor,
> the aptly named Gray Davis, and an equally incompetent
> lieutenant governor, Cruz Bustamante.)

These are the same folks who polarized California with
Proposition 187 in 1994.

And they may yet again be making a fundamental mistake.

> Hispanic immigrants are not looking for welfare. They are looking
> for jobs, for low taxes, for the ability to send money back home.
> Mostly Catholic, they tend to be conservative, respectful of the
> military and of authority.

Too many people speaking Spanish terrifies many folks.

This debate and divide could get increasingly bitter. Twenty-seven
states have made English their official language.[31]

> It is easy for some politicians to rail against Hispanics . . .

In 1988, just over half of Arizona's voters approved an initiative to
make English the only language used by "all government officials and
employees during the performance of government business."[32]

> (An initiative voted on seven times and vetoed time and again.)

Short term, this can be politically useful.

Long term, not a good strategy.

It can lead to what the CIA calls "blowback."

French-Canadians often recall the multiple forms of economic, cultural, and language discrimination they suffered from English-Canadians.

Politicians used this resentment to fuel the secessionist movement.

Every license plate in Quebec recalls past insults and transgressions:

Je me Souviens

(I Remember)

**Slash-and-burn tactics used against
Spanish speakers today—**

**Mass deportations, no bilingual education,
blocking basic health and education—**

Are likely to be remembered well into the future.

How the debate is framed really matters. One can argue bilingual education is not as effective as full immersion, and many Hispanics would agree. But if the argument is that Mexican-Americans have no right to preserve their mother tongue, those become fighting words.

You see occasional flash points. . . . In August 1999, the town council of El Cenizo, Texas, voted to make Spanish its official language and become a safe haven for illegal immigrants.

All discussions by and documents from elected representatives had to be in Spanish.

There is ever more political activism and organization on both sides. Millions are spent on campaigns for and against bilingual teachers.

Debates and battles seesaw back and forth across an increasingly bitter divide.

If disparities in health care and educational attainment continue to widen, a white society will likely get richer and large swaths of a brown one relatively poorer.

If one were to search for the seeds of dissent today that might eventually grow into demands for autonomy-secession, here are a couple of things one might look for:

A concentrated population that self-identifies.

Alienation from the group that governs the society.

Low levels of participation in the political system.[33]

More political scientism: "awareness of their economic displacement and political alienation in Mexico has also intensified a deep ambivalence—if not complete cynicism—among working-class ethnic Mexicans towards the state-centered nation systems."[34]

A better way to explain this is with a popular Mexican song: "I am not from here, nor from there. I have no age or future."[35]

For many Anglos the temptation is to slam the door shut now.

(Before "America the Beautiful" morphs into "Cielito Lindo.")

The U.S. has been militarizing its southern border.[36]

Border patrol agents doubled between 1992 and 1998: "The Attorney General in each of fiscal years 1997, 1998, 1999, 2000, and 2001 shall increase by not less than 1,000 the number of positions for full-time, active-duty border patrol agents within the INS above the number of such positions for which funds were allotted for the preceding fiscal year."[37]

(By 1996, there were more INS agents trying to plug borders than there were DEA agents fighting drugs or FBI agents chasing terrorists.)[38]

But despite tougher laws, more deportations, and higher budgets, there is little evidence of significant change in the patterns of legal or illegal migration.

This is not just a U.S. problem.

Almost one-tenth of the population in the Netherlands comes from Muslim countries. Many consider the country overrun and over-crowded; the political slogan is "Full Up." Immigrants account for about half of the prison population.

Increasingly fed up, many Dutch are emigrating to places like Australia, New Zealand, Canada. In 1999, about 30,000 left. In 2004, almost 40,000.[39]

September 11 showed, once again, just how hard it is to plug a border in today's world.

After the attacks, there was one, single, overriding objective:

We have to take control of our border.

The tough folk got to work, passed draconian laws, took extraordinary measures.

Did you know that the USA Patriot Act is actually an acronym? The official "short title" is the "Uniting and Strengthening America by Providing Appropriate Tools Required to Intercept and Obstruct Terrorism (USA PATRIOT) Act of 2001."[40]

But even after giving the military and intelligence agencies far more leeway, policymakers began to realize just how hard it is to enforce a border.

Take drug prices, for instance . . . Every service and agency, including Army, Navy, Air Force, Coast Guard, Secret Service, FBI, CIA, NSA, and other three-letter species, were hell-bent on battening down the U.S. border. Now ask yourself . . .

Why were the prices of street drugs about the same in 2004 as they were in 2000?[41]

(And why had 51% of twelfth graders tried an illicit drug?)[42]

By the way, the same trends are true in Britain . . .

You can try to clamp down on your own border and take over someone else's borders **and still** strike out.

Afghanistan and Myanmar produce much of the world's raw material for heroin.[43] After the U.S. takeover of Afghanistan, opium poppy cultivation increased to 80,000 hectares.

In 2004, U.S. occupation continued and poppy cultivation went up 64% in one year.

And the number of provinces involved in this illicit trade?

18 in 1999

24 in 2002

32 in 2003

And given that, the average Afghani makes $194

While the drug-producing farmer makes $594 . . .[44]

In some places the poppy fields go on forever. Afghanistan provides about 90% of the heroin sold in Europe.

Perhaps the EU should intervene in the U.S. for enabling drug trafficking?

(After all, this is the logic behind sending U.S. troops to Panama, Colombia, Peru. . . .)

It is hard to get a reliable estimate of illegal migration, but it, too, does not seem to be dropping post-September 11.

In the mid-1990s, a bi-national study on migration found that Mexico was sending about 105,000 people to the U.S. per year.

The Pew Hispanic Center estimated 600,000 people have arrived in the U.S. every year, since 2000, in search of jobs.

As more vigilantes and INS agents patrol the Mexican border, more and more folks are ending up dead.[45]

By 2004, more than 3,000 had died.[46]

Most of these deaths result from an enforcement strategy focused on forcing crossings deep into the desert. Arizona is talking about fencing off three-quarters of its border with Mexico.[47] Many now cross through inhospitable terrain, and face drowning, dehydration, hypothermia, bandits, and poisonous animals.

But . . .

The U.S.-Mexico border runs 1,933 miles.

38% of Mexicans make under \$2 per day. . . .[48]
Wal-Mart pays \$8.50 per hour. . . .
50% of Mexicans are unemployed or underemployed. . . .

As long as extreme income differentials persist between Latin America and the U.S., large-scale migration is likely To continue no matter what types of walls are built.

2003	U.S. Average	U.S. Hispanics	Mexico
Household Income (\$)	47,800	33,000	8,000
Live in Poverty	12.5%	22.5%	35–66% [49]

In a last-ditch attempt to "protect Florida against a future migration outflow," Governor Chiles earmarked \$533,000 of his 1998 budget to support the development of beekeeping, blacksmithing, pig farming, organic farming, and youth camps.[50]

But not in Florida. . . .

The dollars were spent in Haiti, Dominica, Saint Lucia, Grenada, Antigua, and various Latin American nations.

Despite barbed-wire walls, foreign loans or grants, and discriminatory propositions on ballots, it is going to be very hard to stop a partially Hispanic States of America.

By 1993, Los Angeles' most popular radio station aired in *Español*.

By 1999, the top three radio stations were all *Español*.

It's not just California. In Miami, three-quarters of all residents speak a language other than English at home.

67% do not consider themselves fluent in English.[51]

More and more students are coping with these changes by studying Spanish. . . .

Trends in College Language Studies[52]

Language	Students Registered in 1995	Trend 1990–1995 (%)	Students Registered in 2002	Trend 1995–2002 (%)
Spanish	606,286	+14	746,267	+23
French	205,351	-28	202,065	-2
German	96,263	-28	91,100	-5
Japanese	44,723	-2	52,238	+17
Italian	43,760	-12	63,899	+46
Chinese	26,471	+36	34,153	+29
Russian	24,729	-45	23,921	-3

February 2, 2005, Mel Martinez broke a 216-year-long senate tradition. He spoke Spanish in his maiden floor speech.
The senate stenographer had no idea of what to do. The transcript appeared as "speaking Spanish."[53]

Major cities are changing very quickly.

Houston's Racial Distribution[54]

	1980 (%)	1990 (%)	2000 (%)
Anglos	52	41	29
Black	27	28	25
Hispanic	18	28	39

By 2025, Hispanics will be the majority population within Texas.

You can see the initial battle lines being drawn around celebrations like the Victory at San Jacinto.

Traditionally a nativist Texan holiday, it marks . . .

Triumph over the Mexicans . . .

The loss of half their territory,

The beginning of Texan independence.

School districts are redrafting their history textbooks to include "Texas' 300-year history as part of Spanish Mexico."[55]

> One Houston educator observed, "As the Mexican and Mexican-American population moves toward forming a majority in this state, Texans can no longer look back on the historic victory over Mexico as a win for us over them. . . ."

There is even a raging battle in Texas over what to call itself, with ever more advocating:

"TE-jas."[56]

California is changing even faster than Texas . . .

Since 1970, it has hosted a disproportionate percentage of newcomers.

In 1990, California attracted one-third of all immigrants.[57]

Anglos were a comfortable 57% majority in 1990; they are now 47%.[58]

> "In 10 counties, including Los Angeles, Fresno and Monterey, Hispanics make up more than 40 percent of residents, rising to more than three-quarters in Imperial County."[59]

Soon California will have no majority race.

During Mexican president Zedillo's visit, California Governor Davis waxed eloquent:

> *"In the near future, people will look at California and Mexico as one magnificent region."*

> (Try Googling this quote to get a sense of the passionate hatred this particular statement generated.)

Governor Davis's sentiments are shared by Mexico's president:

"The Mexican nation extends beyond the territory contained within its borders."[60]

No Kidding!

It is not likely that Mexico, Latin America, and the Caribbean will soon stop sending their "tired, poor huddled masses, yearning to breathe free. . . ."

So how do you cope with, and adjust to, an increasingly

Hispanic Estados Unidos de America?

Some cope with humor:

> 'Twas the night before Christmas and all through the casa,
> Not a creature was stirring—Carambas! Que pasa?
> Los niños were tucked away in their camas,
> Some in long underwear, some in pijamas,
> While mama worked in her little cocina,
> mi Viejo was down at the corner cantina.

> Their stockings were hanging with mucho cuidado,
> In hopes that saint Nicolas would feel obligado
> To bring all children, both buenos and malos,
> A nice batch of dulces and other regalos.

> Outside in the yard there arose such a grito
> That I jumped to my feet like a frightened cabrito.
> I ran to the window and looked out afuera,
> And who in the world do you think quien era?

> Saint Nick in a sleigh and a big red sombrero
> Came dashing along like a crazy bombero.
> And pulling his sleigh instead of venados
> Were eight little burros approaching volados.

> I watched as they came and this quaint little hombre
> Was shouting and whistling and calling by nombre:
> "Ay Pancho, ay Pepe, ay Chucho, ay Beto,
> Ay Chato, ay Chopo, Macuco, y Nieto!" . . .[61]

Others have a little less sense of humor:[62]

Perhaps these folks never read Isaac Asimov? *Violence is the first refuge of the incompetent.*

Some folks, with sunburned necks, frustrated by more and more Spanish wine, women, and song, still wander around north of Miami with bumper stickers and signs that read:

"Will the last American to leave please turn the lights off"

But consider the following.

First, this is not an unprecedented debate.

As wars and famines raged, 60 million Europeans dispersed throughout the world to find better lives.

In the beginning of the 1800s about 5,000 people per year emigrated to the U.S.

By the 1830s . . . 600,000.

1840s . . . 1,700,000.

1850s . . . 2,600,000.[63]

In the 1850s, blacks were beating up the Irish in Poughkeepsie.

By 1910, 14.7% of the U.S. population was foreign born, versus 11.5% in 2002.[64]

The U.S. grew into a great and powerful nation fueled by immigration.

And whether you do end up getting a Social Security check might depend on legal immigration; if it increased by a third over the next seventy-five years, the Social Security deficit could drop by 10%.[65]

As folks start to have a stake in the system, a reason to play by the rules, an American Dream to strive for, they build up the economy.

Second, **expatriates leave their home country to make a better life.**

In poll after poll, Latinos are most interested in the same issues as Anglos—education, economic opportunity, and safety.[66]

When there is a conflict between U.S. interests and the interests of Latinos' countries of origin or ancestry, many support the U.S. positions.

Even on the issue of further immigration, U.S. Hispanics are split: 43% support, 44% oppose, 57% think politicians have the right to call for tougher immigration policies.[67]

So it is not numbers of immigrants or their politics that should scare you.

Long term, the trend that should worry you,

The one that does lead to separate and unequal,

Is education, integration, or lack thereof.

Poor education quickly translates into poverty.

Hispanics in the U.S. earn 57% of the national average. They are more likely to drop out of high school than Anglos or blacks. (27% of Hispanics have less than a ninth-grade education.)[68]

Half of all Latino, black, and Native American kids do not graduate from high school in four years.[69]

Completed High School (%)[70]

POPULATION 25 YEARS AND OLDER

	1970	1980	1990	1995	2000
Hispanic	—	44.5	50.8	53.4	57.0
Black	36.1	51.4	66.2	73.8	78.9
White	57.4	71.9	81.4	85.9	88.4

Little education, lower wages, little hope: not a recipe for stability.

(Ever wonder why the U.S. jails more of its citizens than any other developed country on the planet?)

Little education makes it far harder for Hispanic single mothers to get off welfare.

During New York City's boom years (1995–1998), 57% of whites left welfare, 30% of blacks, 7% of Hispanics.

By 1998, 5% of welfare recipients were white, 33% black and 59% Hispanic.[71]

Not because Hispanic women are not talented, smart, and hard-working, but because we are not training them to follow careers in science, math, engineering, biology . . .[72]

(There is a rumor around Harvard that the highest-achieving undergraduates are not Asians but Hispanic women, though of course, in this litigious era the administration would never admit to measuring things this way . . .)

Even if a Hispanic States of America seems very distant today, you have to recall that demands for autonomy-secession can crop up, time and again, even within small, well-established, rich countries.

Belgium, a tiny country, headquarters of the European Union. The North speaks Dutch/Flemish and generates most of the wealth through technology and commerce. The South speaks French and lost coal, steel, and textile dominance. These splits are mirrored in political parties: Christian Democrats, Liberals, and Socialists split to reflect region, not to unite country.[73]

**Is it inconceivable that as the southwestern
and the southern corners of Texas become mostly Hispanic,
they could, if mistreated today, lobby for statehood
or even autonomy in a few decades?**

(Under its Constitution of 1845, Texas claims the right to split into
four states plus the original Texas.)

**Is it inconceivable that increasingly diverging Northern and
Southern California could choose to part ways?**

Fifty years is a long time. . . .

**It is not that Mexico is going to reconquer New Mexico. More
likely, Hispanic regions could give rise to an in-between state.**

One which could demand ever more autonomy . . .

of language,

of governance,

of culture.

**The growing Hispanic population could be integrated
successfully and support the status quo.**

**Or it could begin demanding its own statehood governance,
thereby adding stars to the flag.**

**Or it could begin demanding what so many minorities across
Europe are demanding . . .**

(Ever greater autonomy, and perhaps even untying,
within an umbrella of free association.)

Thereby removing stars from the flag.

As you think about the future of the U.S. and its borders, it is
important to remember . . .

Current citizenship does not always imply . . .

Permanent and unconditional allegiance and support.

The English have found that even core borders can bounce back.

> King Edward I's 1282 conquest of Wales was made official with the Statute of Rhuddlan in 1284. Scotland was conquered in 1286, then freed and reconquered several times.

> Speaking Gaelic or Welsh in schools was verboten for centuries. Many ethnic English settled in Scotland and Wales. By the 1950s, the United Kingdom seemed integrated and united.

> In the 1980s, Welsh and Gaelic language instruction resumed. Between 1981 and 1991, the percentage of children aged five to nine who spoke Welsh rose from 17.8 to 24.7%. In the ten- to fourteen-year-old group, the percentage rose from 18.5 to 26.9%[74]

In 1997, a majority of Scottish voters chose to establish a new Scottish Parliament in Edinburgh. The peaceful transfer of power from Westminster occurred in 1999.

And soon thereafter Scots began asking why half of all private land was in the hands of 343, mostly absentee, landowners . . .[75]

Meanwhile, back in Wales, an old tongue spread among shopkeepers and government officials.

(Remember the Armenian saying: "For every language you know, you become a different person.")

Allegiance over time depends how you are treated by your own country.

It is worth recalling that Hispanics in the U.S. are not the only alienated population.

Race remains a major issue and fault line in many parts of the world,

Including the U.S.

Some wounds of past wrongs are still healing, some remain open.

We all know the 2000 and the 2004 presidential elections were quite bitter and divisive.

Here is one electoral analysis, posted on the Web:

"On November 4, 2003, Mississippi voters set descendants of African slaves back a 'long way' to the plantation, crushing a vaunted attempt by the Black Caucus to seize state-government. The main casualties of the drive to integrate the Magnolia State had been Negrophile Governor Ronnie Musgrove, who had appointed Negroes to office, Gary Anderson, a Negro vying for State Treasurer, who had been a Musgrove appointee, and Negress Barbara Blackmon."[76]

Alabama's ex-chief justice Roy S. Moore was kicked out after refusing to remove a massive Ten Commandments sculpture from the lobby of his office. He became a source of inspiration for the Alabama League of the South . . .

The league's objectives, in their own words, "is the cultural, social, economic, and political independence and well-being of the Southern People. We affirm the proud legacy of our predominantly Anglo-Celtic civilization with no apology. We lay proper claim to the political vision of America's Founders, to the heroic struggle of our Confederate ancestors against 'consolidated' government, and to our underlying Christian heritage."[77]

Many state constitutions banned marriages between whites and "other" until quite recently.

California banned miscegenation in 1948. Nevada? 1959. The U.S. Supreme Court did not strike down these discriminatory laws until 1967. South Carolina's state constitution prohibited the "marriage of a white person with a Negro or mulatto or a person who shall have one-eighth or more Negro blood" until November 3, 1998.[78]

Alabamans had an opportunity to eliminate the following passage from their state constitution in 2004:

"Separate schools shall be provided for white and colored children, and no child of either race shall be permitted to attend a school of the other race."

They chose to keep the law as is.[79]

The Alabama State Motto? "We dare defend our rights."

These are the kinds of laws that were written to prohibit folks like "Cablinasians," which would be a tragic loss.

(Tiger Woods coined the term; he is Caucasian, black, Indian, and Asian.)

While one side is suing to eliminate, or at least defang, affirmative action, the other side is pondering what stake it has in the current system.

Just as occurred with Native Americans and casinos/land claims, when minorities begin succeeding economically, politically, or in admissions to elite universities, there is usually a backlash.

Sometimes it is racially motivated, sometimes a parent who thinks their kids should have gotten that benefit, that job, that admissions letter.

The Harvard Business School was threatened with several suits because it dared run a one-week summer program for promising minorities. Some claimed this discriminated against whites . . .

I was proud to teach in that program.

One would hope that the political system, or the "free market," could be used to redress and resolve these disputes and disparities, but it does not always work that way.

Paul Davis, philosopher-in-residence at Biotechonomy, our little venture capital firm, serves as a sports computer, tech adviser, and political oracle. He is usually way ahead of the rest of us in understanding trends, and then he puts this data in his own twisted perspective.

He argues "one man, one vote" is one of the great American myths.

It was partly true till 1921. . . . (After that, women got the right to vote.)

Constitutionally blacks had no constitutional guarantees they could vote until the fifteenth amendment (1870).

Even then various Jim Crow measures such as literacy, means, and residence tests (as well as outright violence) prevented many from exercising their rights for more than a century. The Civil Rights Act (1957) and the Voting Rights Act (1965) began to redress these wrongs.

But it turns out, even today,
not all votes are equal. . . .

During the 2000 election a U.S. Civil Rights Commission investigation concluded: "An African-American was 900 percent more likely to have his or her vote invalidated than a white voter." "In New Mexico, a Hispanic voter is 500 percent more likely than a white voter to have her or his ballot lost to spoilage."[80]

There are almost 40 million African-Americans.

There is one African-American senator.

There are eight white senators in Wyoming, North Dakota, South Dakota, and Montana. They represent 2.7 million people.

(Georgia alone has about 2.3 million blacks.)

STATE	TOTAL POPULATION	STATE	BLACK POPULATION
Wyoming	494	Georgia	2,374
North Dakota	642	South Carolina	1,204
South Dakota	755	Alabama	1,201
Montana	902	Mississippi	939

Then there is Washington, D.C. . . .

It has more people than Wyoming.

60% of D.C.'s inhabitants are African-American.

Not a single senator or congressman . . .

Just a single "delegate," Eleanor Holmes Norton.

Motto on every D.C. license plate?

"Taxation Without Representation"

Or look at it another way: 40 million people

Are represented by 46 U.S. senators.

40 million African-Americans are represented by one senator.

This does not imply that only blacks can represent blacks or only Hispanics represent Hispanics . . .

But there sure are few role models given the number of folks in these constituencies.

(As a % of the population, one might expect to see ten black senators.)

The situation is especially egregious in the southern U.S.

55.3% of African-Americans live in the South.

Ever seen a black southern senator?

(Not since reconstruction . . .)

You might assume you would occasionally see one given that the highest percentages of blacks as a percentage of state population are in Mississippi (33%), South Carolina (30%), Georgia and Maryland (29% each), and Alabama (27%).[81]

> As you look at presidential elections today throughout the U.S. South, on a state level, you see solid red.[82] But if you break down results by district, there are several long waves of blue. The region includes ten districts, each housing about 650,000 citizens, represented by African-Americans in Congress.

From Robert "Bobby" Scott in Virginia to Eva Clayton and Melvin Watt in North Carolina to James Clyburn in South Carolina. From Sanford Bishop, Cynthia McKinney, and John Lewis in Georgia to Harold Ford, Jr., in Tennessee to Earl Hilliard in Alabama and Bennie Thompson in Mississippi.

Some of the counties, from the District of Columbia through Virginia, North Carolina, South Carolina, and Georgia are among the "bluest" in the country.

But, as Paul Davis sees it, in the United States Senate, more than seven million citizens, mostly Democratic, and mostly African-American, are represented by fourteen Caucasians.

All Republicans.

Thirteen men and Libby Dole.

It would not take a lot of imagination to gerrymander a couple of large states, within the U.S. South, that were mostly democratic and contained very large African-American populations.

If this seems like an impossible idea, consider what is happening in Maine, where ever more Northerners feel ignored and disenfranchised.

> Home values in northern Maine are half of those in the South, as are average incomes and education. Many northern Mainers are furious at restrictions on snowmobiles, hunting, logging, and fishing. They are beginning to talk secession.[83] If this becomes a bitter battle, those in southern Maine, who pay most of the taxes, may just say, "Fine keep the Aroostook state."

One of the reasons blacks are having such trouble electing people and feel increasingly alienated is because more and more people from this community have lost the right to vote.

A disproportionate (and record) number of black males go to jail. Human Rights Watch argues:

> "The racially disproportionate nature of the war on drugs is not just devastating to black Americans. It contradicts faith in the principles of justice and equal protection of the laws that should be the bedrock of any constitutional democracy; it exposes and deepens the racial fault lines."[84]

How dare they say this!

Well . . . turns out about 12.9% of black males between 25 and 29 are in jail (versus 1.6% of whites).[85] Many of these folks are in jail for drugs.

Problem is . . . about 72% of drug users are white and 15% are black . . . and blacks are 58% of those in state prisons for drug felonies.[86]

I have a dream, for many, is becoming

I have a fear, or *I have no future.*

(In your twenties? Black? You have a one in three chance of ending up in jail.)[87]

> Think about this for a minute.

If one in three of your kids, your neighbors' kids, your friend's kids ended up in jail, might you begin to doubt the whole system-national myth of equal opportunity, just a little bit?

In many states, felons can't vote, so . . .

One-tenth of African-Americans are disenfranchised.[88]

The U.S. already has one of the highest prison population rate per capita in the world: 686 per 100,000. (Russia, Belarus, and Kazakhstan? 638, 554, 522 . . .)[89]

> Yet year by year more and more end up in jail.

As various paths toward the American Dream are blocked, be they affirmative action or the senate, or voting, frustration mounts. Now various African-American leaders are skipping remedial policies and beginning to demand outright reparations for slavery.

> Reparations are oft ugly words. They bring to mind botched peace treaties. Sometimes payments are so onerous that they can drive countries toward despair, bankruptcy, and extreme nationalism.

> > As occurred with Germany post-WWI.
> > As was avoided in Germany and Japan post-WWII.

But sometimes courts can deem reparations just and overdue, even after centuries. We see this in an increasing number of native Indian and aboriginal cases throughout the world.

Reparations represent financial redress and public acknowledgment of past sins.

Courts are now beginning to consider just how much you should pay someone whose ancestors were kidnapped, transported, enslaved, and sometimes murdered.

Usually the reaction within certain Anglo communities to such claims is: "That was such a long time ago," "Let bygones be bygones," and "Get over it."

> (And sometimes it is a much nastier "Go back where you came from" or "Lazy, good-for-nothing . . .")

> Nevertheless, in 2002 a suit was filed against various corporations, including Fleet Boston and CSX Railroads, on behalf of 35 million African-Americans.[90]

> Accusations included conspiracy, human rights violations, unjust enrichment from their corporate predecessors, and conversion of slave labor into profits.

One poll showed 68% of blacks feel the successors of slave companies should apologize. 32% of whites agree.

55% of blacks feel they are owed cash. 6% of whites agree.[91]

> The suit was thrown out in January 2004 based on an expired statute of limitations.

> Now these suits are moving into international courts. . . .

P.S. If slaves performed $40 million worth of unpaid labor between 1790 and 1860, reparations would be around $1.4 trillion.

Go back to my original question: How many stars will there be in the U.S. flag in fifty years?

How minorities, Hispanics, African-Americans, Native Americans, Hawaiians, Pacific Islanders, and those in some parts of the Caribbean are treated today, what opportunities they have, what insults they recall . . .

will go a long way toward answering this question.

DEMOCRACY + OPEN BORDERS = FOUR MEXICOS?

**"THE REPUBLIC IS A SAND CASTLE,
WHICH THREATENS TO DISINTEGRATE."**[1]

—*President Ignacio Comonfort, 1855*

The great poet Octavio Páz got it right when he wrote:

How many times has Mexico been born?
Mexico is made, unmade, and remade without end.
Each birth different but,
Nevertheless inseparable from other societies
That came before (. . .)
The same and always another.[2]

Just as occurs in the U.S., most Mexicans cannot conceive of their country's borders shifting radically, of losing flag, anthem, coin.

But by now you have read enough to realize just how unlikely continuity is throughout world history.

There are, and have been, many Mexicos.

The notion that Mexico cannot split

Has already been disproved

Several times.

. . . After all, it used to be more than twice as large a country.

Spain-Mexico claimed territory extending from Alaska through Panama.[3]

What happened in the various Mexicos was critical to the U.S. because . . .

As they dissolved . . .

Spanish and Independent Mexicos . . .

Added stars to the U.S. flag . . .

And generated new countries.

And, if there was a really significant future change to the core U.S. border, likely it would depend partly on what happens along the border of Canada or Mexico or both.

Nothing continues to alter the U.S. population as much as continued Hispanic immigration, especially from Mexico.

The single greatest determinant of future U.S. immigration is Mexico.

So it is important to understand what is going on next door.

Not that everyone is paying attention.

When one of the new leaders of the U.S. Congress was asked if he would be traveling abroad during the recess, his response was . . .

"Abroad? No. I have already been there."[4]

Mexico's governments have been such a disaster that the equivalent of one-fifth of the country's total population now lives in the U.S.[5]

These folks are hardworking. They send home $15 billion per year, more than all tourists spend in Mexico and almost equal to total oil revenues.[6]

Mexico remains the largest net exporter of labor in the world.

(#2 is China.)[7]

Mexico's economic outlook has not improved very much.

YEAR	MEXICO'S WORLD RANKING (GDP)[8]
1820	16 out of 24
1900	23 out of 40
1950	28 out of 52
2000	74 out of 100

Consulting firm AT Kearney ranks countries yearly in terms of their attractiveness to foreign investors.

In 2004, Mexico dropped to twenty-second.[9]

Clearly things are not headed in the right direction.

Historically, the great divide between what a country promises and what it actually delivers has meant that not all have wanted to remain Mexicans . . .

Mexico gave birth to the Texan and California Republics, to New Mexico, Arizona, Nevada, and Colorado, as well as Guatemala, Salvador, Honduras, Nicaragua, and Costa Rica.

Nevertheless, Mexico remains the seat and soul of a great culture, one which thrives on both sides of the border. To begin to understand Mexico and its extraordinary regional distinctiveness you have to first understand the country's tortured geography.

This makes Mexico one of the great civilizations of the world, exporting globally an extraordinary variety of food, music, painting, language, and literature.

It also makes Mexico a very challenging place to govern and keep together.

Mario Vargas Llosa once argued "the perfect dictatorship is not communism, nor the Soviet Union, nor Fidel Castro. It is Mexico."

After the great bloodshed of the 1910 Revolution, which killed a tenth of the country's population, Mexico was governed by a single party (PRI) for more than seven decades. There was relatively little extreme repression and no coups. But the system became ossified, corrupt, and atherosclerotic.

By 1997, the average wage of a Mexican worker was 40% lower than it had been in 1980.[10]

But claiming to govern and actually having control over these various regions are two very different propositions. There is a history of violent regional confrontations, demands for autonomy, and secession.

Historians, and Mexicans, often focus on foreign interventions as the key to understanding the country's borders.

But perhaps there is an even more compelling driver of Mexico's fate . . .

Divisions, discord, disagreements between Mexico's various tribes, peoples, parties, and regions.

Of course what happened in the past is not necessarily predictive of the future.

But the past does provide a useful mirror and some lessons. . . .

For much of its history Mexico remained a collection of disparate and rancorous fiefdoms.[11]

Many of these divisions are still alive and well.

As the country comes under increasing pressure, from an expanding population, poverty, and a greater understanding of what others enjoy, some of these old feuds can resurface.

If Mexico were to split, sometime in the future . . .

**It would likely be because its own citizens
chose or allowed this fate.**

**Either by taking the country and its integrity for granted,
or because internal tensions and divisions grew into
irreconcilable differences.**

As happens with so many marriages . . .

And so many countries . . .

There are real questions today as to who can really govern Mexico. Each of the past five presidents has managed some spectacular failures.

Massive devaluations wiped out virtually every major business. The government had to recapitalize industry after industry. Drug violence is ever more an issue.

Fortunately the old, ossified, seven-decade-long, single-party system finally fell apart in 2000, with the election of Vicente Fox, from the conservative National Action Party (PAN).[12]

Unfortunately, expectations were so high, and results so far so meager, that Mexico is undergoing both a rebirth of the PRI and a chaotic transition toward democracy. This is, once again, accentuating regional rivalries and divisions, some of which are centuries old.

Modern Mexico is often seen as three or four major regions.

Two great mountain chains run near Mexico's Atlantic and Pacific coasts. They create a large V that historically isolated various regions.

Many of these key regional differences remain, so it is reasonable, given past Mexican history and present global trends, to at least ask . . .

Could Mexico Breed New Countries? And would these be viable countries? Let's look at four regions:

North, "NAFTA country."

A transition state between the U.S. and Mexico.

A realm where pesos and dollars are interchangeable,

Foreign focused, competitive, powered by agriculture and manufacturing.

A different planet, one with different values and aspirations than southern Mexico.

Central Mexico, capital and heartland.

Home of the not-always-admired Chilango.

(Mexico's equivalent of a New Yorker.)

A region used to centralizing, and ruling.

A region which continues to govern as if it were the old Aztec empire, extracting tribute and expecting its wishes and demands to be catered to . . .

Then Mexico narrows, mountains crash into each other, forming many isolated pockets. Just within the knot of the Isthmus, where Mexico is narrowest, over twelve different groups, including Zapotecas, Populucas, Nahuas, Huaves, Zoques, Mixes, Chontales, Tzotziles, Chinantecos, Mazatecos, and Cholos, live in extreme poverty. In 1997, about 40% lived without electricity and 65% without piped water; 81% lacked drainage.[13]

Indigenous Mexico, beautiful, culturally rich, economically destitute.

Brutal contrasts within an area that produces a great deal of wealth.

(Start with much of Mexico's oil and 80% of its petrochemicals.)[14]

A Divided, angry, proud people.

People used to violence.

Finally, beyond the Isthmus, and a little north . . .

The New Maya,

Once one of the poorest regions in Mexico.

It modernized at a record pace.

Yet despite massive immigration

The Yucatán remains distinctly Mayan.

The Maya have rarely agreed with the taste and views

Of Central Mexico's Aztec-Nahua.

They have a history of rebelling early and often.

In 1842, General Sánta Anna declared Mexico at war
against the Yucatán for seceding and aiding rebel Texans.[15]

Today the Yucatán is a mélange of oil-rich Campeche,
White, colonial cities like Merida,
Desperately poor jungle Mayans,
and nouveau riche Cancuns.

There remain, at least,
Four very distinct
And different
Mexicos . . .

Almost two-thirds of Mexico's states clearly
belong within one of these four regions

NAFTA Country

Heartland

New
Maya

Indigenous

The Four Mexicos

NAFTA COUNTRY	CAPITAL AND HEARTLAND	THE NEW MAYA	INDIGENOUS MEXICO
Baja California	Distrito Federal	Campeche	Chiapas
Baja California Sur	Estado de Mexico	Quintana Roo	Guerrero
Chihuahua	Hidalgo	Tabasco	Oaxaca
Coahuila	Jalisco	Yucatán	
Nuevo León	Morelos		
Sonora	Puebla		
	Querétaro		

There are also twelve transition states, left in white on the previous map, which could end up in one region or another depending on local politics.

> This implies that in the analysis that follows, each of the four Mexicos likely underestimates the potential size and wealth of each entity.[16]

There are real differences and tensions between, and within, regions. . . .

Northern Mexico grows.

Much of the South does not.

The region producing the most children produces the fewest new jobs.

Northern Mexicans are three times wealthier than their southern counterparts.

Three-quarters of all children born in Mexico are born to the poorest 25%.[17] Close to a third of the people in Guerrero live in households with eight or more people. Adult illiteracy is five times higher in the South than in the North.[18] One of four children living in southern Mexico is malnourished.[19]

Ten times more Indians live in the South; comprising 21% of the total population of the region.[20]

Lack of education, income, and skills make the South less Competitive and provides little incentive to Establish entrepreneurial Ventures.

After decades of free-market reforms . . .

Incomes are not converging. . . .

Mexico is not uniting. . . .

In 1993, northern states produced 25.2% of Mexico's manufacturing income; by 2002, it was 28.4%.

Meanwhile, the southern states dropped from 2.8% to 2%.[21]

Poor people from all over Mexico continue to flock toward northern border cities and tourism resorts.

They work hard, but they also generate large shanty towns and place enormous pressure on public services.

(Just as do so many immigrants in U.S. border towns and cities.)

Northerners increasingly blame crime, pollution, and overcrowding on "Oaxacos."

Oaxacos: A catch-all phrase for poor southern migrants.

> Sad because Oaxaca is one of Mexico's most beautiful, diverse, and poor states. It hosts 570 municipalities and at least 16 different languages, plus hundreds of dialects. Food, painting, and handicrafts are among the best in the world.

In an attempt to address these disparities, Mexico's government continues to support large infrastructure projects in the South.

As people flow north . . . .

. . . .

. . . .

. . . . **revenues**
from taxes
flow south.

For every dollar paid in taxes . . .

Mexico City gets thirty-five cents back.

In Northern Mexico, sixty cents comes back.

Those in the Yucatán get more than three dollars.

Southern Mexicans get six dollars.[22]

Not surprisingly, political speeches in Northern Mexico often focus on how much they produce . . .

And how little they get back.[23]

Because of this simmering sense of outrage, seemingly small battles can escalate quickly.

> Throughout 1999–2000 the nightly news focused on an ongoing thriller, Car Wars . . .

In this real-life soap opera, evil bureaucrats from the federal treasury department decided to begin confiscating cars from hardworking Northerners.

(Nothing like a few Federales riding into town to raise hackles.)

Protests spread so quickly that ruling party politicians feared they would be ousted. Chihuahua governor Martinez began supporting the campaign to block the taxman. The governors of Nuevo León and Zacatecas soon joined and began leading street marches.

Always subtle, the central government attempted to bludgeon the region back into submission.

It began stopping bank credits for basic services like water mains.[24]

That was popular . . .

Soon the governors were rallying thousands.

Governor Martinez's position became just a touch tougher:

> *"Chihuahua was never conquered.*
> *It is not anyone's province.*
> *It is a free and sovereign state."*[25]

What began as a trivial battle over car taxes escalated and became a rallying point for autonomy of tax revenues. Regional politicians, from every political party, began trying to outdo each other in lambasting the Feds.[26]

In a panic, Treasury backed down but continued to plot.

That fall, with little warning, Treasury officials decreed any car crossing the U.S.–Mexico border with U.S. plates would post a bond, $400 to $800.

Great move . . .

This infuriated not just northern Mexicans but much of the U.S. Hispanic community. Protests spread across the border, along with boycotts of Mexican products.

> Forty-eight hours after implementing the program, Treasury announced that the car payments would be "postponed."

In the spring of 2000, congress attempted to mediate by simplifying the import process.

> Anyone bringing a car into Mexico could simply pay a fee.

> (Given that close to one-fifth of cars were illegal and that most of these were in the North, this seemed sensible.)

But President Zedillo, adopting the manner of old Aztec emperors, was furious that someone dare challenge His Treasury Department. In a vitriolic speech, he denounced congress for legalizing "contraband" and asked if they were also going to legalize kidnappings and bank robberies.[27]

> Tough speech . . .

> No results . . .

(By 2004, an estimated one million more cars entered illegally, about as many as were sold legally. . . .)[28]

Battles like Car Wars are not a big deal; they do not lead to the breakup of nations . . .

> **As long as they do not reflect systemic rot.**

However, if incidents like Car Wars are a symptom of something much larger . . .

Like a mismatch between what a country promises and reality . . .

Then one might begin to worry about the future of the country.

Small tax revolts can be symptoms of much bigger problems.

(Just ask those who attended a certain tea party in Boston in 1773.)

It is not just Northerners who are furious. . . .

Southern Mexico is also angry.

For decades you rarely saw large-scale public protests in this region. Given the repressive and corrupt nature of many southern political institutions, peaceful protest and ballots are not terribly effective ways of changing unwanted politicians.

> For most of the 20th century, almost no member of the opposition governed in a state in southern Mexico. Protests led to jail, torture, disappearance. Ballots should have carried warnings: "Joining the opposition can be dangerous to your health."

As a result, unlike in northern Mexico, discontent did not tend to be channeled through the political system. Conspiracies and plots festered underground, in clandestine movements.

Guerrilla, paramilitary, and drug enclaves grew in remote mountains. When conflicts did eventually surface, they were often surprisingly sudden and violent.

> October 12, 1992, the five hundredth anniversary of Columbus's "discovery," . . .

A few celebrated.

Many protested.

In San Cristóbal de las Casas, a white bastion in the indigenous highlands of Chiapas, four columns of Indian men marched in from four different places.

> The Indians carried wooden rifles. They tore down the statue of the Spanish conquistador Diego de Mazariegos. Then they dispersed to various corners, picked up all the garbage off the street, regrouped, and left.

Officials in the state government, ever disdainful of the Indians, said finally the "FBI" (the Brute Indian Force) did something useful.[29]

Meanwhile, the protestors were quietly laughing. They had just practiced, in broad daylight, how guerrillas would conquer the town, two years later . . .

On New Year's Eve, 1994, Mexico's president was happily toasting the new North American Free Trade Agreement (NAFTA).

A military aide passed him a little note . . . a rebellion had broken out in Chiapas.

Oops . . .

Turns out the Zapatista rebels had their own ideas on how to commemorate North American integration.

Zapatistas began burning and destroying all arrest, loan, and property records.

Records used by the whites to control and prosecute Indians.

Rebel leader Subcomandante Marcos began answering the mayor's phone . . .

Frightened town folk would call in to report the masked rebels in the streets.

Marcos, with a sense of humor and irony, would calmly assure them that everything was under control.

No worries, mate . . .

Turns out those living in indigenous Mexico had little interest in free trade, capitalism, open borders, and globalization. Harvard's John Coatsworth argues that throughout the continent Native Americans have not fared well during the three great waves of globalization. . . .[30]

The native's first encounter with the rest of the world, Spanish-French-British . . .

Killed most of their peoples.

Then they watched a second wave of globalization/immigration/free markets/trade. . . .

Hundreds of thousands of African slaves.

A third wave of globalization brought foreign investments and concentrated in a few hands land, water, petroleum, mining, and railroads.

Despite economic growth, this resulted in violent conflicts, foreign interventions . . .

And sometimes revolutions.

During these processes, surviving natives often ended up even more isolated and destitute. So in many ways the Zapatista position and logic makes sense.

To them, *free trade* meant foreigners had permission to take gold, oil, trees, and electricity from one of Mexico's richest states while much of the population remained desperately poor.

Throughout southern Mexico, many began saluting a new flag and joining a new army.

The Zapatista Army of National Liberation
(Ejército Zapatista de Liberación Nacional, EZLN) . . .

As violence resurfaced, poverty and insecurity grew. . . .

Many of the most educated left,

Investors went elsewhere,

Southern Mexico fell farther behind.

Southern politicians began demanding ever more . . .

Further frustrating those in the North.

Dividing the country even further.

Rich and poor is not the only fault line . . .

While northern and southern Mexico often disagree on many
things, both tend to agree that Mexico City holds way too much
power. Each region sees itself as the center of its universe,
not as an appendage to the capital.

In Spain, where there are strong pressures for regional
autonomy and secession, regional politicians ingratiate
themselves with their audience by recounting the story
of a famous bullfighter:

A powerful federal politician once asked the torero why he lived
so far away . . . The response was "Seville is where it should be.
What is far away is Madrid."

An anecdote that always brings knowing chuckles and applause.

The regional nationalism prevalent throughout
Spain is just below the surface in Mexico . . .

Much of the territory-cultures of Mexico have been around
over a couple of millennia . . .

The "modern" United Mexican States have existed as such only
since 1810.

Mexico was a Spanish colony for longer than it has been a country.

Mexico's strong culture and history have kept it partly together for a hundred and ninety-odd years, despite a series of crises and, at times, extreme governmental incompetence.

Although many would argue the country only really came together in the bloodbath of the 1910 revolution.

(And some superstitious folk say that given 1810 and 1910, some interesting things could happen circa 2010.)

Existing conflicts are not yet, in and of themselves, enough to drive Mexico apart.

But they are symptomatic of increasing cleavages and polarization.

Northern political campaigns constantly reinforce the stereotype of a hardworking North, a meddling center, and a subsidized and dangerous South.

Some might argue Mexico could never split because its various regions would not be viable as independent states.

Maybe . . .

Except that both past history and small states in Central America and the Caribbean negate this notion. The first time I visited each Central American country, I was stunned by how completely different each country was in almost every aspect.

(Stereotypes abound: tiny Salvador is full of violent entrepreneurs; sleepy Nicaragua sits next to middle-class, bourgeois Costa Rica; much of indigenous Guatemala lives in a different century . . .)

Mexico's regions are more varied, larger, and richer than Central American countries.

If Mexico were to divide up . . .

Into four countries or autonomous regions . . .

They would look like Chile, Poland, Tunisia, and Ecuador.

(In fact, they would likely be larger because transition states would join one block or another.)

Let's begin with the region that generates the most centrifugal tensions, Mexico City. Everything, including the flag, centers around Mexico City and its needs. The central symbol of Mexico's flag . . . a small island on a lake . . . a cactus . . . an eagle devouring a snake . . .[31]

> . . . Is a myth designed to unify the whole of the country around a now defunct lake.

First tribute was levied to continue building on the lake. . . .

> For centuries, when infrastructure was insufficient or governance inefficient, the city would periodically recede beneath floods.

> (In the main square, or zocalo, just to the left of the cathedral, you can still see a column that marks how high the floods were during various years. Many old buildings still show watermarks.)

Eventually Mexico's moneys were used to drain the lake,

> A "clever" decision that left Mexico City the world's only large metropolis far from any major body of water.

Then the capital began extracting a growing water tribute from all its neighbors.

> Massive aqueducts took water from surrounding states in an attempt to soothe the capital's growing thirst.

> Because the central plateau is so high, and water must be fetched from so far away, bringing more water to Mexico City will eventually require as much electricity as consumed by Monterrey, Mexico's second largest city. It costs $1 per cubic meter of water; people are charged 30¢.

Much of Mexico feels it has been feeding the capital and its voracious governments for centuries. Because the central government controls most tax revenues, there is little incentive for the states to tax and send.

Throughout the 1990s, U.S. states collected taxes equivalent to 9.1% of GDP .This allowed them to fund a series of local services like schools.

> Mexico's states collected 3.3%.[32]

Indigenous groups, conservatives, and regional secessionists continue to nurture a shared enmity of Mexico City.

> An enmity and resentment that is centuries old. Otherwise it
> is hard to imagine how 1,519 Spanish conquerors could have
> taken control over Tenochtitlán . . .

> The Spaniards were aided by indigenous groups like the
> Tlaxcaltecas, who were sick of Aztec oppression and having to
> pay tribute to the capital. Unfortunately, Tlaxcala's strategy
> backfired. Instead of devolving power to various regions,
> the devious Spanish conquerors further centralized.

> (And in the late 1990s, Tlaxcala's government launched one of
> the most unfortunate tourism PR campaigns ever conceived:
> "Tlaxcala: A Traditional Host" . . . indeed.)[33]

Regional discontent with Mexico City and its centralized
government also contributed to the loss of half the territory
in the mid-1800s.

> In 1825, even traditional enemies like the Yaqui Indians, the
> Californios, and the New Mexicans created an uneasy alliance
> between local caudillos and indigenous tribes against the
> capital. Something akin then occurred in parts of Texas
> (1835–1836).

But even if much of Mexico walked away from Mexico City,

It would still leave behind a country that looked like a compact Poland.

Central Mexico = A Compact Poland

	Central Mexico[34]	Poland[35]
Area (sq. km.)	173,923	312,680
Population	40,726,992	38,626,349
GDP (in billions)	$251	$241
GDP/Capita	$6,174	$6,090

And like Poland, central Mexico has been engaged in a decades-long struggle to morph from a protected, socialist economy into a quasi-open economy within a much larger trading system.

> Because much of Mexico's government and business headquarters are centralized within the capital, and live off of the periphery, this is likely the one region with the most to lose from a breakup. And thus it is the region most likely to fight tooth and nail for one country, one border.

Meanwhile, northern Mexico is a technology- and maquiladora-driven economy.

But most of its technology is imported from the U.S. or Japan.

Not from Mexico City.

Mexico generates almost no international patents. The fifteen largest producers of knowledge in the country are foreign companies. Most of NAFTA Mexico's products are exported north.

Not to Mexico City.

Most of its inputs come from abroad.

Not from Mexico City.[36]

Mexico City does not guarantee basic services, nor security.

So some now ask, what is the relevance of Mexico City?

During the 1980s and '90s, Mexico's manufacturing jobs stagnated or decreased, with one major exception, the North of the country.

> If one excludes the border, employment in large- and medium-sized manufacturing companies fell 21% (1988–1995).[37]

But along the border, employment flourished.

> In 1980, maquiladoras (in bond industries) employed 113,500 workers. By 1999, employment had risen almost tenfold. Torreón, Coahuila, became the world's blue-jean export capital. Companies like General Electric employed thousands in data-processing operations.[38]

Thousands of people migrated north seeking jobs . . .

> But limited federal investment, a low local tax base, and little
> awareness of the global knowledge economy led to stagnant
> output. Maquiladoras now face formidable competition from
> China and India. China's labor force is three times that of
> Europe and twice that of all of the Americas. India is home to
> 41% of the world's poor and can sell a lot of cheap as well as
> highly qualified labor.

**Between October 2000 and March 2002, maquiladoras lost
278,000 jobs, about 21% of total jobs.**[39]

There is now a good deal of unemployment, crime, and
discontent in the North. Many blame Mexico City, its taxes,
policies, and political squabbling.

Many would like to integrate further with the U.S. Because
when they look at a separate northern Mexico, they realize
it would look a lot like Chile.

Northern Mexico = Chile

	Northern Mexico[40]	Chile[41]
Area (sq. km.)	791,928	756,626
Population	14,314,395	15,498,930
GDP (in billions)	$122	$153
GDP/Capita	$8,549	$10,100

Just as California often anticipates political trends within the U.S., northern Mexico has oft been a bellwether of change.

There is a well-established tradition of dissent in the North, of
going at it first and alone.

(In 1987, a third of those living in the North were willing to engage in
civil resistance to defend democracy, versus less than 10% of those in
central Mexico and 4% of southerners.)[42]

The first major breaks in the governing party (PRI) monopoly occurred mostly in northern states. So in any autonomy debate, one would expect the North to be an early adopter.

Not that it is clear exactly what would happen along the U.S.'s southern border.

Mexico's North is far from being one integrated coherent area.

U.S. - Mexico Border States

Geographically, Tamaulipas, on the bottom right, should be a "northern state."

It is not automatically part of "NAFTA country" in this book because its economy and outlook are quite different from those of neighboring Nuevo León et al. Oil and oil nationalism remain powerful forces within the state, as they are in other Gulf of Mexico states like Veracruz and Tabasco. Tamaulipas has long been seen as a guarantor of "Mexicanness" in an oft-suspect region.

Some claim that Tamaulipas's odd shape, particularly the long thin arm that runs west, along the U.S. border, was intended to cut off its neighbor, a more pro-U.S. Nuevo León . . .

> The growth of maquiladoras within Tamaulipas as well as the decline of the PEMEX oil worker's union may have made the state more NAFTA-centric. On the other hand, the last thing the increasingly powerful drug lords based in Tamaulipas would like to see is greater U.S.-Mexico cooperation. During the first eight days Governor Hernandez was in office, nine mutilated bodies were dumped throughout the state by narcos, including one of the newly appointed police chiefs (January 2005).

The other side of Mexico's complex northern border is also a special case.

With the exception of Tijuana, the Baja California Peninsula is a relatively sparsely populated region, stretching over a thousand kilometers.

Baja is largely isolated from the rest of Mexico.

It is increasingly connected to the U.S.

Driving from Mexico City to Cabo San Lucas, without using a ferry to cross the Gulf, is equivalent to driving from Boston to Las Vegas. You can get from San Diego to Ensenada in a couple of hours. If you start early, you can sleep in Cabo that night.

> It is often cheaper and easier to fly to the tip of Baja from Los Angeles than it is from Mexico City.

It is not easy for foreigners to own land in Baja.

After the Texan and Californian adventures, Mexicans became more than a little wary of foreigners owning a lot of land contiguous to any border.[43] All foreign-owned titles within 100 kilometers of the border and 50 kilometers of the sea have to be held in trust.

Nevertheless,

Many Americans have an interest in the outright ownership of Baja.

More than 70,000 Americans already own homes in trust in Baja.

During the first major modern collapse of Mexico's shaky economy, President Reagan's secretary of the treasury, Don Regan, attempted a massive land purchase. He began demanding Mexico give up Baja in exchange for writing off the foreign debt.

(This would have been very popular with the various California real estate barons that had backed Reagan.)

Horrified Mexican officials decided to default on their debt instead of giving up territory. Faced with a global financial crisis, the U.S. backed off.

Americans kept buying land.

This attempt to take over more of Mexico has been a well-kept secret for decades.[44] No one ever mentioned it to those living in Baja California.

But, even as a Mexican, put yourself in a neutral position for one minute.

To paraphrase philosopher John Rawls's dictum:[45]

You will be born at random into a society.
You do not know where you will end up:
Smart, poor, educated, urbanite, good looking or not . . . random choice.

Which society would you choose?

In this context, dare we ask a very uncomfortable question? Would the average Baja Californian child be better off today if Mexico had accepted Reagan's deal?

(Assuming the existing population was guaranteed U.S. citizenship, and recalling that by the end of the 1990s only one-third of Mexicans felt their kids would end up better off than they were.)[46]

Should Mexico have submitted this proposal to a regional referendum?

What could have been the results?

Almost every Mexican would immediately have said, "No way."

But what about those living in Baja?

Before answering this query, one might wish to recall that the equivalent of one-fifth to one-quarter of Mexico's population has already voted with its feet and lives in the U.S.[47]

Between 1970 and 1995, no country sent more emigrants abroad than Mexico.[48]

This mass migration gutted the countryside. By 2004, more than 85,000 former towns, villages, and rancherias in Mexico had fewer than three inhabited houses. Ghost towns, or towns full of women, are common. Despite many hardships and discrimination, more who migrate are choosing to stay in the U.S. for longer periods of time.

Northern Mexico, or Baja alone, has a far better chance of eventually reaching a European Union type of arrangement with the U.S. than does Mexico as a whole.

(This type of incentive was what first tore apart Yugoslavia and Czechoslovakia.)

It is a choice many richer regions within poor countries have made time and again. The incentive to separate a part of the North increases substantially in the measure that southern Mexico becomes increasingly unstable and poor.

Extreme income inequality and violence could become a matter of national security for the existing Mexican state. And obviously violence and instability in Mexico is also a matter of national security for the U.S. Already there is significant pressure on Mexican officials "to do something about the border."

Violence and immigrants continue to be growing businesses. . . .

Now, let's shift south.

The Yucatán peninsula has always been a separate world.

Yucatecan railroads still have different gauges than those in the rest of Mexico.

The Yucatán is cut off from Mexico by mountains, language, culture, and ethnicity. The peninsula's relative isolation, jungles, poverty, and lack of natural resources (especially silver and gold) provided little incentive to dominate indigenous populations.

> Political prisoners and other undesirables were often banished to the impenetrable jungles of Quintana Roo, where it was almost impossible to communicate or escape. Many were forced to roam the jungle tapping gum trees. Few survived.

Yucatán's indigenous population is twice as high as that of southern states, four times that of the center, and twenty times that of northern Mexico.[49]

Among Mexicans, the Maya are still those most likely to speak their own language.

People are rounder, smile more, wear white clothes, and have a distinctive singsong accent. The music, food, language, humor, and spices are unlike any other in Mexico.

(A Yucatecan restaurant is not your typical Mexican fare; beware of the chilies, they are habaneros . . .)

Many visitors find the Yucatán the most placid and peaceful region within Mexico. But the Yucatán's calm surface hides a complex and violent history.

> Until quite recently, archeologists contrasted the supposed peacefulness of the Maya with the savagery of the Aztecs. Turns out those sweet Maya also liked war, torture, slavery, and human sacrifice. Each Maya village in the Yucatán is still organized into a military-like structure. Every person is assigned to a company, and many village officers have military titles.

> (Just like today's most militarized country . . . Switzerland.)[50]

Yucatecans are Mayans, not Aztecs.

They have traded, and fought, with Aztecs for centuries. White Mexicans and foreigners, both called *dzul*, are not always welcome.

> They represent a different type of human, a foreigner, an enemy.[51]

The Yucatán remained a separate nation for centuries. Spaniards were unable to control most Mayan cities until 1546, a quarter-century after the fall of the Aztec capital.

Thereafter the Spaniards faced periodic uprisings.
Whole areas refused to be conquered.

Nevertheless, a large part of the Yucatán's wealth was taken to Mexico City and Spain. What little was left was poorly distributed, often to carpetbaggers in large haciendas.

Even after Mexico's independence, Yucatecans repeatedly attempted to secede from Mexico.

On May 31, 1841, Yucatán declared itself independent and adopted a flag with stars and stripes . . . red, white, and green.

(Gee, I wonder who inspired this flag . . .)

Yucatán grudgingly rejoined Mexico on August 17, 1848.

The rebel Maya capital, Santa Cruz, was not captured until 1901.

Secessionism reappeared again during Mexico's revolution.

Felipe Carrillo declared Yucatán an independent socialist republic in 1916. In 1923–1924, Mayans again proclaimed an independent Yucatán, with Mayan as the official language.

Through the 1970s, the peninsula remained harsh, even by Mexico's standards of poverty.

The first road connecting the peninsula with the rest of the country is decades old. By then, the main crop, henequen (sisal), had been decimated by artificial fibers.

It would have been hard to argue that the Yucatán could be a prosperous, independent state.

. . . Until quite recently.

But now Cancún, Mexico's most successful tourism resort, is a source of jobs and wealth. The Bay of Campeche holds vast oil reserves. Airports and roads have multiplied. Even maquiladoras flourished.

> (By 1993, mostly due to oil, the Yucatán was the most productive region in the country, almost three-fold that of southern states and 20% more than northern states.)[52]

So the once poor regional cousin has revived its lost empire. It is an economy that looks as viable, in economic terms, as that of Tunisia.

Maya Mexico = Tunisia

	Maya[53]	Tunisia[54]
Area (sq. km.)	166,000	163,610
Population	5,115,691	9,815,644
GDP (in billions)	$31	$63
GDP/Capita	$6,081	$6,500

Most Yucatecans still do not care much for the mores, demands, and customs of central Mexico. Large-scale immigration from other parts of Mexico to the Caribbean resort areas has not stemmed a growing desire for regional autonomy and self-governance.

If anything, immigrants rapidly tend to adopt a Yucatecan's viewpoints vis-a-vis Mexico City.

> So if unchecked, it would not be inconceivable that over the course of five decades the Yucatán would drift closer to autonomy.

Finally, there is the indigenous South. Mexico's southern-Pacific states (Oaxaca, Guerrero, Chiapas) are entirely different from the Yucatán.

Unlike the flat Yucatecan region, mountain and canyons divided the hundreds of different ethnic groups in Chiapas, Oaxaca, and Guerrero.

> The Sunday market in San Cristóbal, Chiapas, resonates with a plethora of languages including Tzotzil, Tzeltal, Chol, Tojolabal, and Lacandon.

Almost every aspect of daily life, from agricultural practices and crops through religious rites and village governance, is different in, and within, the southern states.

This is an isolated, tough, violent, culturally diverse region.

Southern Mexico's exports are less than 0.1% of total exports.[55]

Here, too, one can find a history of fragmentation and secession.

> When Mexican Nationalists discuss the loss of over half of the country's territory, they tend to focus on the perfidious gringos, conveniently ignoring the fact that large losses also occurred along the southern border.

Mexico and Central America were, for centuries, part of the same country. When Mexico began to break off from the Spanish Empire in 1810, it was not clear how much of the Mayan Empire the newly minted Mexican state could claim or keep.

As elites in Mexico City fought the wars of independence, they simultaneously tried to maintain a commercial monopoly throughout Central America and the Yucatán. However, many Central Americans were frustrated with Mexico City's taxes, warlords, poverty, and violence.

Regional strongmen, priests, and farmers began organizing, protesting, and revolting beginning with San Salvador and Nicaragua (1811–1814).

The revolt spread north. By September 1821, Guatemala had left Mexico, taking most of Chiapas.[56] By 1823, most of Central America had abrogated its union treaty with Mexico.

Still . . .
Central Americans vacillated back and forth between independence and Mexico.

Some still argued they would be better off if they became part of Mexico. And in retrospect, maybe they were right.

In 1848, much of the region again voluntarily decided to give up its sovereignty and rejoined the nascent Mexican empire.

Briefly, Mexico became 25% larger than it is today.[57]

Once again, divisions within Mexico's elites prevented the region from unifying.

Central America split off yet again and fragmented.

There have been periodic initiatives to reintegrate various parts of Central America. These range from a common market, to shared airports and highways, and more ambitious global projects. One of Mexican president Fox's first announcements was that he was going to create riches from central Mexico through the top of South America.

Occasionally there has even been talk of merging a couple of nations. But once nations fragment, they are often like Humpty Dumpty. None of these initiatives, some of which are economically rational, has gotten very far.

Some might argue that divisions which occurred, once upon a time, in southern Mexico, could happen again.

But within the southern region left inside Mexico, one finds very different outlooks, languages, priorities, and beliefs from those of the rest of the country. In many ways, Mexico's southern states are similar to, and reflect the rich diversity, pride, conflicts, and divisions of Guatemala, Ecuador, or parts of former Yugoslavia.

Many fear the Zapatista guerrilla movement, with its own flag, borders, and army could attempt to secede.[58] Thus far, the Zapatista rebels have been explicit:

"We do not want the control of territory or the separation of Mexico. We are not betting on destruction . . . we demand the recognition of the rights of indigenous peoples and democracy, liberty and justice for all Mexicans."[59]

However, **where a movement begins and where it ends up is rarely the same point.**

When violent uprisings take place in a geopolitical playground, historic feuds can bury any contemporary political or rebel leadership.

And Chiapas, historically, has always been one of the fault lines of Mexican secessions. The fuel for Zapatista-like movements is centuries of repressed rage. Today's pro- and anti-Zapatista towns reflect the disputes of the 1500s, 1800s, and 1900s.

Centuries ago Mexico's southern states refused to remain subject to the Yucatán Mayan empires.

As Central America rebelled and seceded, Mexico's nascent government desperately attempted to keep Chiapas.

First, Mexico City promised self-determination.

Then a cacique, General Finisola, staged a coup in support of Mexico.

This accentuated divisions and forced people to take sides.

Civil war was quelled with the promise of an open election.[60]

After a bitterly contested referendum, 96,829 Chiapanecans voted to join Mexico.

60,400 voted for Guatemala.[61]

The Soconusco region seesawed between independence, Mexico, and Guatemala through 1842.[62]

And in 1991, Chiapas's governor said: "Chiapas is and will continue to be a state in the Mexican Federation, but Chiapas is also, whether we wish it or not, a Central American country."[63]

This division, this history, is mirrored to date. In the 1820s the most conservative, pro-Mexico citizens of Chiapas lived in Ciudad Real.

> They still do, but their city is now called San Cristóbal de las Casas, and they are still hated by the Indians. They were the first targets of the 1994 Zapatista rebellion. . . .

Secessionists, those who wished to leave Mexico in the 1800s, lived near the Guatemalan border; care to guess where the Zapatistas have the most support? . . . Today's Zapatista municipalities are the same ones that sought autonomy a couple of centuries ago.[64]

Chiapas's centripetal tendencies today are largely due to political ineptness and neglect.

After the favorable 1824 Chiapas vote, Mexico's willingness to tolerate dissent and regional autonomy evaporated.

Within a year, Secretary of State Lucas Alaman argued:

> *"Once members of a society are reunited, there are no referees to decide to separate whenever they want, and in the issues that include all, the minority has to fold to the majority's wish, otherwise the stability of all would be at risk."*[65]

For the next century and a half, the driving logic behind the governance of Mexico's southern-most province was national security.

Unlike neighboring Oaxaca, opposition parties in Chiapas were mostly verboten.

Former dissidents and guerrillas did not become governors; generals and hard-liners did.

Those unhappy with the status quo in southern Mexico were systematically silenced.

Political control was deemed far more important than education, development, and limiting corruption.

But the signs of trouble were there, for anyone who bothered to look. Despite overwhelming dominance by a single party (the PRI), Chiapas's governments were remarkably unstable.

> In twenty-two years, Chiapas lived thorough eleven governors. . . .

> Four would have been normal.

If parts of Chiapas ever decided to leave Mexico, its rationale could well be very similar to that which led the state to leave Guatemala and join Mexico in the first place.

Chiapanecans joined Mexico because, "Guatemala has never given this province science, nor industry, nor any other utility, but has seen it with indifference."[66]

> And, as it turns out, so had Mexico . . .

The poorest indigenous communities in Mexico remain within Chiapas, Guerrero, and Oaxaca.[67]

You can only live on national myths for so long.

After a while, if little turns out to be real.

You may want to leave and generate,

Or revive, myths of your own.

Zapatista demands for municipal autonomy are a symptom.

They are not the fundamental driver of a potential southern split.[68]

The risks to Mexico's southern sovereignty go way beyond the Zapatistas. Chiapas is a country of jungles and mountains, one which is plagued by drugs. Fragmenting and repressing reasonably unified, legitimate, and quasipeaceful indigenous movements could lead to disaster.

> I.e., more power, more governance by those, on the left and on the right, who are tied to drugs.

This implies killing Subcomandante Marcos, and his main officers, does not solve the problem. It may simply create one more iconic martyr figure modeled after Zorro or Che Guevara.

Within poor regions, it is often drug barons who have the resources, organization, and drive to provide employment and income, build schools, and sponsor sports teams. Sometimes those in the drug trade end up running a part of the country, and creating their own autonomous enclave.

> In 1998, the U.S. and the Bolivian government destroyed 80% of Bolivia's coca crop. In 2002, Congressman Evo Morales, leader of the coca growers, was almost elected president. In 2003, Morales set up a press conference, unfurled his flag (a coca leaf), and issued an ultimatum. The new president had one month to improve the lot of the poor.
>
> Otherwise coca growers would lead the same type of street protests that had just ousted the previous president . . .

Proud of being blacklisted by the U.S., Morales is quite explicit in his campaign rhetoric:

> *The coca leaf is becoming the banner of national unity.*
> *A symbol of national unity in defense of our dignity.*
> *Since coca is a victim of the United States,*
> *As coca growers we are also victims of the United States.*[69]

> P.S. Morales is now one of the most popular
> politicians in the country. . . .
>
> In 2005, he had his folks block the streets;
> another president resigned.

Despite its poverty, it is not inconceivable that southern Mexico could someday seek autonomy. If these three southern states were to separate, they would resemble Ecuador.

Southern Mexico = Ecuador

	Southern Mexico	Ecuador
Area (sq. km.)	233,000	283,560
Population	10,439,306	13,212,742
GDP (in billions)	$28	$45
GDP/Capita	$2,740	$3,300

And, like Ecuador, there would probably remain great battles and divisions between the trade/cattle-driven, white lowlands and the corn/coffee-driven indigenous highlands.

The de facto existence of four Mexicos, and the trends toward demanding greater autonomy, lead to a series of tough questions. . . .

If incomes continue to diverge between North and South, is it inconceivable that northern Mexico would wish for more autonomy?

Is a peaceful, Slovakia-like secession completely out of the question?

Could southern Mexico follow the same path as Central America or Ecuador?

Might southern Mexico be better off on its own, controlling its natural resources?

Finally, if Guatemala and Chiapas were part of the same political entity for centuries, is it utterly impossible to imagine them reunited under a Pan-Mayan flag?

Remember, we are talking in fifty or one hundred years, not next month. . . .

These are the kinds of questions Mexico's central government better be asking itself before these questions and issues become even more widespread . . .

And it better be able to provide credible and legitimate answers as to why everyone is better off not changing the status quo.

Bad Governance Can Have Consequences.

You can blame changes in flags, borders, and stars on foreigners all you want.

(Often with reason.)

But likely as not, you might also want to take a look at what has happened within the country itself before autonomy, before secession, became inevitable.

And use these lessons to avoid future pain.

I am not advocating that Mexico split.

I am not saying it would be a good outcome.

I am simply making sure all concerned understand it is possible.

(It has happened once, it has happened twice . . .)

So, faced with these questions . . .
Instead of squawking loudly . . .
Those running Mexico's government today . . .
Or those wishing to govern the country tomorrow . . .
Might want to take these questions seriously . . .
And pay attention to the population's needs.

(Otherwise, they could be surprised by the direction a region like Baja might someday choose.)

Throughout the world, untying is not just increasingly viable; often it leads to success.

In international forums when someone begins to compare Mexico to the Asian Tigers (Malaysia, Taiwan, Singapore, Korea), the response is "they can do it because they are small; Mexico, on the other hand, is a large and complex country."

They are right.

Often Those Living in Small States Do Better.

(As long as they do not depend on natural resources, and if they invest in a competitive education system, establish a rule of law, trust the government, and each other, enough to save.)

> Following World War II, Singapore tried to merge with Malaysia, but it was so poor, it was rejected. Within three decades, a new country, which had to import everything, including fresh water, was producing as much wealth per person as the most developed states in the world.

A large number of the fastest-growing countries over the past three decades are small and natural-resource poor.

By 1996, despite their geographic isolation, Hong Kong, Singapore, Luxembourg, and Switzerland were already considered twice as competitive as the Anglo-Saxon countries, four times more than Asia, almost six times more than the European Union, and seven times more than Latin America.[70]

> Meanwhile, countries rich in things like gold, oil, silver, and diamonds continue to be populated by extremely poor people. Think . . . Congo, Russia, Mexico, Venezuela, and Brazil. [71]

So as one begins to think about the future of Mexico, it is well worth the while of current and future governments to show how the whole remains far greater than the sum of its parts. . . .

P.S. By this point, many may be asking themselves:

> **"What happened to the North American Free Trade Agreement (NAFTA); wasn't this supposed to solve a lot of these problems?"**

Nope.

NAFTA is a trade agreement; it is not a peace agreement, nor a development policy. There is a fundamental distinction between what happened in North America and Europe. The European Union agreement was meant to ensure that, after centuries of brutal warfare, and a couple of world wars, neighbor would quit attacking neighbor.

> (There was good reason to wish this: "on an average day, between September 1939 and August 1945, approximately 25,000 met violent deaths. That comes to one September eleventh, every three hours, twenty-four hours a day, for six years.")[72]

The primary objective of the EU was not economic efficiency, it was peace and security.

NAFTA, the Free Trade Area of the Americas (FTAA), and Mercosur are trade agreements, not security compacts. They are an attempt to keep U.S. and Canadian manufacturing competitive by enlarging markets and by having access to cheap labor.

One agreement is driven by politics, the other by economics.

	EUROPEAN UNION	NAFTA
Key objective	Maintain peace	Improve economic competitiveness
Subsidies for the noncompetitive?	Massive support for sectors like agriculture	Very little subsidy or support across borders
Funds to depressed regions?	Large transfers to poorer states	No funds transfer
Open job market?	Yes, you can work anywhere in Europe.	Little additional legal labor mobility
Common currency?	Yes	No
Shared governance?	Increasing	Virtually none

The EU has improved living standards within most poor regions.

In 1997, Ireland received the equivalent of 4.8% of its GNP in net contributions from the EU, Greece received 4.1%, and Portugal 3.1%.[73] Today Ireland's income per capita is $43,862. The U.S. is $39,991. Britain's is $35,505.(And some Bostonians are seeking EU dual nationality through Irish passports.)

NAFTA has not improved the lot of Mexico's poor very much.

According to some at the World Bank, Mexico had little additional economic growth, wage increases, or poverty reduction because of NAFTA.[74]

NAFTA never really was a "free trade agreement."

A true free trade agreement is one page:
"I agree to trade freely with you as of . . ."

NAFTA is a complex political document, hundreds of pages and annexes detail hundreds of exceptions. Some of the most delicate of these compromises are coming home to roost a decade after signing. Peasants in Chiapas, farming a couple of slash-and-burn acres of corn, had the opportunity to "compete freely" against 2,000-acre, subsidized agribusinesses in Iowa. The price of corn grown in Chiapas was three times that of the world market.

Economic rationalists in Mexico City and D.C., those who have never known hunger, simply say, "These farmers should do something else."

Perhaps they do not realize that, for many, corn is not a commodity?

In case of conflict or economic collapse, corn is insurance against starvation.

(Important given that more than two million Mexican children under five years old are malnourished.)[75]

So given these outcomes, it should not be surprising that, post-NAFTA, the number of economic refugees crossing the border illegally has not decreased.

P.P.S.

Mexico is by no means a weak state.

It is not yet an obvious candidate for untying.

It would surprise few if the four Mexicos were to remain a part of a proud single country.

But this is not a given.

It is worth examining Mexico's trends and challenges because . . .

Other than splits within its own borders, nothing could alter U.S. geography as much as changes within Canada and Mexico.

(After all, Mexico's land has already led to ten or more stars in the U.S. flag.)

And . . .

A majority of the growth of the U.S. Hispanic community was driven by Mexico's political and market failures.

It is not inconceivable that more stars could be added if Mexico were to continue mismanaging its affairs and some in the North or Yucatán got fed up enough.

In this day and age this transition would not involve a war. More likely it would begin with a demand for greater autonomy and self-governance and ever greater integration between border states.

The incentive for the United States, in addition to the enormous real estate development potential, would be to create a richer and hopefully more stable buffer zone.

No other developed country directly borders on a country which is as poor . . .

PART THREE

A

Wide

World

of

Lessons

Learned

7.
EUROPE AND ITS DISCONTENTS
(WHAT IS A COUNTRY, ANYWAY?)

"DEAR ME! . . . WHAT A CHORUS OF GROANS,
CRIES, AND BLEATINGS! WHAT A RAG-BAG
OF SINGULAR HAPPENINGS."

—*Sherlock Holmes*

One of the most disconcerting and disruptive things that ever occurred to U.S. businesses was the rise to power of takeover artists in the 1980s. Long-established conglomerates suddenly came under fire by a bunch of arrogant youngsters who had figured out three things:

- You can borrow a lot of money using the assets of the company you are going to take over as collateral.
- Often separate pieces are worth a lot more than the whole.
- Breaking up can lead to personal riches, power, and freedom.

Suddenly, not even the largest companies, if mismanaged or unprepared, were safe.

Greed, shareholder value, judicial rulings, irreconcilable differences . . . the list of reasons why ITT, ATT, Nabisco, Revlon, Sunbeam, and so many others were carved up like roast turkeys is long and varied. But the bottom line is every CEO today spends a lot of time thinking about how to prevent splits and how to justify staying independent and intact.

Instead of waiting for someone to break it up, GE aggressively and continuously spun out any business in which it could not be #1 or #2.

(Perhaps that is why they nicknamed the CEO "Neutron Jack"?)

Over the past six decades, many of the questions asked of the biggest of businesses were also asked, by citizens, of the biggest of empires. Many a prime minister, president, king has had to respond to two questions: What is the value of the whole? Are the pieces worth more as separate entities?

As region after region figured out it could be freer and perhaps richer if self-governed . . . They began untying.

In country after country, this process continues today. . . .

When Europe entered the 20th century,
there were not a lot of sovereign countries.[1]

After a couple of world wars, the continent broke up
into a myriad of smaller countries.

In 1920,
Europe had
twenty-three
states. By 1994,
it had forty-four.

In part the breakup of states is dictated by huddled masses yearning to break free.

OK.

In part the proliferation of states reflects a global trend and respect for democracy, self-determination, human rights, and multiculturalism. But in part it also reflects a very different economic reality.

The way you generate, and keep, wealth today is very different from what it was a few centuries, or even decades, ago.

In an agricultural economy, if you got up earlier, worked harder, and had better land, you might get a little richer than your neighbors.

But not much richer.

In the 1700s, Western Europe's per capita income was similar to that of Rome in the first century AD.[2]

Politically, this meant the entitled could act like fools or tyrants for generations. To be perfectly blunt, if people were oppressed, tortured, or killed, the basic source of wealth, the gold, the oil well, the land, still remained.

If you were amoral, you could import more serfs, conquer more lands, and remain rich and powerful for countless inbred generations.

Because individuals were not that much more productive in one place or another, through the 1820s, just before the industrial revolution, the income differential between the world's richest and poorest nations was about four to one.

In the 1830s, the rules changed.

Individuals began to use machines to multiply physical labor a thousand-fold.

Those with machines could produce much more.
Those without machines produced the same.
Power shifted fast.

Suddenly the great powers were the industrialized nations, not just the populous nations. How many oppressed folks you conquered mattered less than having entrepreneurial businessmen, inventors, investors, and universities.

Then rules changed yet again, even more drastically. Knowledge began to matter a lot more than manual labor or manufactured product.

In the measure that the global economy shifted from slavery and agriculture toward manufacturing and, eventually, brain power, many colonies and regions began to represent an ever increasing political and economic burden.

Not surprisingly, independence became easier to achieve . . .

Post-WWII, trade grew, as did travel. The world began to reglobalize. A lot of wealth was created by this open system, but there were also political consequences. . . .

As they globalized, sovereign states lost part of their monopoly over border control, employment, trade, currency, and customs.

It became easier for autonomous regions to work through and with other countries. There was ever less dependence on the mother country and its central government. Small countries no longer had to depend on their own minute internal markets for growth.

Integration on a supranational level allows nations trapped within countries a free movement of capital, goods, information, and sometimes labor. It also allows one to protect one's language and governance.[3]

Globalization and open borders sometimes enable small countries and national groups to keep their identity and culture.

(Which may explain why seventeen of today's sovereign countries cover less land than Austin, Texas.)[4]

The untying of Europe began with a couple of obscure coal and steel agreements. Jean Monet understood this type of transnational beginning could be expanded into a far broader European Economic Community.

The original 1957 countries, Belgium, France, Germany, Italy, Luxembourg, Netherlands, gradually let in others to share their umbrella.

Denmark, Ireland, UK joined in 1973. . . .

Greece, in 1981 . . .

Spain and Portugal, in 1986 . . .

By 1992, the European Economic Community had morphed into a more powerful and encompassing European Community–European Union (EU), which was joined by . . .

Austria, Finland, Sweden in 1995 . . .

2004 was a banner year: Cyprus, Czechoslovakia, Estonia, Hungary, Malta, Latvia, Lithuania, Poland, Slovakia, Slovenia.

As borders began to proliferate, they also began to mean ever less.

So there was less at stake when yet one more group began to untie.

Which makes the question we have been asking of the U.S. just as valid for Europe . . .

Just how many stars

Will there be within the E.U.

In fifty years?

In a hundred years?

The EU flag has twelve stars, representing twenty-five countries, so far.

The single greatest administrative expense in the EU? Translators.

As the European Union has grown, so, too, has the number of countries and borders within Europe.

Today's European countries still contain many nations that used to be countries.

We all know the old cliché, history is mostly written by the winners, by those who survive, or at least leave traces of greatness behind.

(Pyramids, paintings, palaces, books, laws, philosophies, religions, science . . .)

It is easy to overlook, under today's nationalist hubris, just how many countries are no more.

After watching the World Cup and Sophia Loren, buying Italian shoes and dreaming of an Italian sports car . . .

It is easy to forget that "Italy" was not a country until 1870.[5]

Italy is a collection of once-great nations, each with its own flag, border, anthem, cuisine, politics, and social mores.

Signs of former sovereignty and greatness are everywhere, for those who care to look. Florence's *Palazzo Vecchio* (Old Palace) was a center of global trade and knowledge. From its Great Hall, the Medicis directed trade, finance, wars. They commemorated their deeds with works by Michelangelo, Leonardo, and Vasari.

But hidden in the back-right-hand corner of this great room is a bittersweet plaque:

In this Hall we witnessed the last year of Florentine independence. After three seconds of silence, the Tuscan representatives affirmed, in MDCCCLIX, the unity and liberty of Italy . . .[6]

Florence, Venice, Sicily, the Papal Estates are no longer the great countries of old. But sometimes long-buried myths and symbols revive and generate new borders. Even today, after a century and three decades, it is still not clear where Italy is heading. Some fiercely defend the *tricolor* flag. Others, mainly in the North, point out that the South is a burdensome region that keeps falling further and further behind. . . .

In 1975, southern incomes were 65% those of northern ones.

By 1995, they had gradually dropped to 56%.

Northern Italians increasingly use elections to protest corruption in business, security, and politics; it is a backlash against immigration and against the Mafia-riddled South.[7]

In 1982, a charismatic leader, Umberto Bossi, founded a local fringe independence movement.

In 1985, what would become the Lega Lombarda/Lega Nord won 2.5% of the vote in one province. In 1987, it got 2.7% of the vote in Lombardy. In the 1989 European election, it got 6.5%. By 1992, it had 20.5% of the national senate election. By 1994, it was a key component of Berlusconi's coalition and obtained 45% of the vote in Lombardy.

As the Lega grew, moved toward the center, entered coalitions, became a part of politics as usual, much of its support eroded. Still supporting Berlusconi, while constantly threatening to leave the coalition, this right-wing party continues trying to create the independent nation of Padania.[8]

Italy is not alone in its struggles to define whether it stays as is or reverts to what was. Most European countries face demands for autonomy and independence.

> Austria, Belgium, Denmark, France, Germany, Italy, Netherlands, Portugal, Spain, United Kingdom . . .

Given that Europe, in 1500, had approximately five hundred political entities,

And that the EU umbrella greatly reduces the cost of independence,

The unwinding of existing countries might continue for a long time.[9]

> Think about what would happen should the Basques become a sovereign country. No need to establish a new currency. They'd keep the euro. Nor would they need to build up a large army. Got NATO to protect them. EU passport allows them to trade, work, and travel anywhere in Europe.

> Not surprisingly, Europeans with separatist agendas, like Basques and the Catalans, tend to be among those most supportive of EU integration.[10] (As are the Quebecois for that matter.)

One of the first things those wishing to untie focus on is achieving membership and support from broad-based trade, defense, and regional organizations.

> One might ask oneself, How far can this proliferation of ministates really go?

> You are beginning to see virtual states. One is based above the Hermès shop in Rome. The Sovereign Military Hospitaller Order of St. John of Jerusalem, of Rhodes, and of Malta has no citizens and no territory.

> > Laughable . . . except it is a sovereignty recognized by eighty-seven countries.

Grand Chancellor Bailiff Ambassador Count Marullo di Condojanni issues passports, license plates, currency. You can even use his stamps, but only if you want to send something to Burkina Faso.

(It is the only country with a reciprocal postal treaty.)[11]

Open borders and broad regional integration challenge every nonrepressive state.

Within the EU, there is ever less leverage vis-a-vis separatists.

In other words,

There is ever more pressure on central governments to justify their existence.

A complex circle, one sees ever more demands for regional autonomy. . . . Autonomous regions demand ever more subsidies and transfer payments. . . . Oft blackmailing already broke central governments with the threat of untying.

As Europe continues to devolve and integrate, two questions come to mind:

So what?
and
What is a country, anyway?

Until recently, you were considered an independent
and sovereign country

If, and only if . . .

You issued and controlled your own currency, . . . Patrolled and
controlled your own borders, . . . Ran your own customs and
established your own tariffs and standards, . . . Determined
when noncitizens could live and work within your borders, . . .
Controlled your own defense, . . . Made your own laws supreme
within the land, etc, etc, etc. . . .

But not much of that is true today for spaceship Europe.[12]

We are long past the point when a country was:

"A closed, impermeable, and sovereign unit, completely separated from other states."[13]

Our parents' borders were very different from ours.

Old Borders	Today
Citizen of . . .	Multiple Citizenships
Have One Lifetime Corporate Identity	Work for Employers Around the Globe
Belong to One Culture	Are Multicultural
Obey National Rights/Duties	Obey International Norms
Import Substitution	Export Promotion
Local Market Key	Global Sales
One Government	UN, NGOs, EU, IMF
War for Territory	War to Prevent War
Fear Other States	Fear Secession
Media Controlled	Global Data Instantly Available
Clear Border	Various Borders
National Currency	Financial Flows That Swamp Any State
U.S. Companies	Multinational Companies
Local Mafia	Global Drug Trade
Guerrillas	Global Terrorists

Sovereignty and control have been devolving for decades.

You cannot build a Great Wall of China or a Berlin Wall and expect to achieve isolation or total control for long. Even Albania broke down, as did Cuba, as will North Korea . . .

But there is a significant difference between U.S. and European stars.

The U.S. is attempting to preserve old borders.

It rejects treaties like Kyoto . . . Refuses to sign international court of justice protocols . . . Rejects international constraints on its soldiers . . . Weakens the UN . . . Establishes global prisons within its army bases . . . Tightens border crossings, issues fewer visas.

Europe has moved far toward a new model.

Attempting a multinational constitution.
Devolving local courts toward international standards.
Strengthening multinational forums in the EU and UN.
Building a multinational army.
Having open borders.

In a sense much of Europe is reacting to WWI and WWII.

Even the "winners" lost place and empire,
plus generations of their youth.

So it is not surprising that Europe would want
to limit the extreme costs of nationalism.

European countries voluntarily control ever less.

(As David Held says, we live in "overlapping communities of fate.")

This can lead to some bizarre scenes. October 25, 2003, in the hall where Florentines relinquished their independence, a group of Italians came together to sing an anthem.[14] But neither words nor tune were those of the Italian national anthem. They sang:

Joy, beautiful spark of the gods,
Daughter of Elysium,
We enter fire imbibed
Heavenly, thy sanctuary.
Be embraced, Millions!
This kiss for all the world!
Brothers! Above the starry canopy
A loving father must dwell . . .

Don't recognize it? It is the European Hymn. The Italians were singing it in German.

(To the tune of Ludwig van Beethoven's Symphony No. 9, 4th movement)

Ambiguous, shared, or devolving sovereignty is not new . . .

In a sense, the breakdown we are seeing in exclusive state sovereignty is similar to that which occurred during the separation of church and state.

Religion used to be the main arbiter of norms and daily life. But as rulers sought defined, exclusive, continuous and contiguous borders, they often came into conflict with this overwhelming supranational authority. Churches gradually lost power, property, sovereignty. The once vast Papal Estates are now 0.44 square kilometers.

More and more countries are ceding legal, commercial, security, and political functions to supranational authorities.

Want to remain completely sovereign?

Do not join the EU
UN
IMF
WHO
WTO
FAO
OAS
APEC
UNESCO
INTERPOL . . .

In coordinating the needs and desires of all of their members, each of these organizations necessarily limits a part of the sovereignty of each member. The more organizations you join, the more sovereign states you choose to coordinate with, the greater the potential for inefficiency and bureau-sclerosis. . . .

> In 2004, the EU's population grew 28%, arable land 40%. Farmers in acceding countries are now subject to 80,000-odd pages of EU laws and regulations on "veterinary, sanitary, animal welfare, and administrative dictums."[15]

Which is OK with both globalists and regionalists since they share a common objective:

Weakening the nation-state.[16]

These trends are documented in various books and articles and point in two directions:

Governments have ever more competitors.

And

Multiple sovereignties overlap and interact.

Coping with various ethnicities is challenging.

> The League of Nations granted Finland sovereignty over 6,500 islands, the Alands, but in exchange its Swedish-speaking inhabitants were granted complete cultural and political autonomy, including control over migration, a flag, and postage stamps.[17]

> Panama's Kuna Indians control who may enter their islands.

> Canada's Hutterites and Mennonites pay income taxes as a group, not as individuals. [18]

> Want to live in Switzerland? First the federal immigration authority must OK you and then you must pass muster with the folks in the canton where you wish to live.

If you were a clothes designer, you might describe varying sovereignties as a gradual transition from colored squares toward tartans.

Scottish clans identify one another through tartans.
Each weave is complex and slightly different.
Verbally describing specific patterns is very hard.
Identifying them by sight is easy.

Sovereignty is constructed from overlapping interests that look like tartans.

Here are the three "tartan rules" of modern sovereignty:

- In viable sovereignties, the base color, the country, its citizens, are dominant.
- The dominant color is crisscrossed, and partly obscured, by other colors.
- Sometimes, too many overlapping patterns make the base color irrelevant.

How dominant inside and outside entities are determines the patterns of sovereignty.

Each country's sovereignty is an individual tartan.

Each country controls, or claims to control, different things, in different ways.

The broad rules established through supranational institutions in turn allow groups to reestablish regional boundaries and primordial identities.

Being Basque is a primordial identity.

Basques are, at the same time, Europeans.

Europe is reestablishing primordial identities under a broad cultural identity.[19]

Primordial Identity	Cultural Identity
Us vs. Outsiders Clearly Defined	Can Join If You Adopt Our Culture
Strict Membership Criteria	Flexible Admissions
Distinct History / Uniqueness	Exportable Model / Invites "Conversion"
Defined by Ethnicity / by Parents	Various Values Adopted
Rigid Politics	Adoptable to Challenges / Various Agendas

Under the primordial distinctions, most Turks will never become true northern Italians or Catalans, but perhaps they could become "Europeans."

Only a few, proud folks are "Marines."
There is only one way to join, one code to follow.
One tribe, you are a member or you are not.

But many are, and can become, "Americans."
There is a much broader umbrella.

The trend toward reestablishing primordial identities, under a protective umbrella and common rules, could lead to an explosion of new stars under the EU flag.

(Or even a break up of the EU)

**A fragmenting EU is highly unlikely to alter the
number of stars in the U.S. flag.**

**But the fragmentation of the EU should
strike a cautionary note for the U.S.**

A series of developed countries, with a lot of shared history,
are breaking up . . .

Part of the U.S.'s strength, so far, has been blending the
criteria for belonging.

> Take, for example, Marie Jana Korbelova;
> you know her as Madeleine Albright.
>
> (Never mind Henry K.)

> But with more and more hyphenated citizenships,
> more entitlements, more reparations for past wrongs,
> it could be difficult to maintain a united country.
>
> African-Americans, Arab-Americans, Cuban-Americans,
> Japanese-Americans, Jewish-Americans, Irish-Americans,
> Italian-Americans, Latinos, Red-Staters, Liberals, Native
> Americans . . .
>
> Today, you have to be very careful how much you
> alienate those within your own border.

**Nativists, immigrant hunters, racial purists,
language police, Anglo-first folk could cause
exactly what they seek to avoid:
the weakening of the country and flag
they so care for.**

So is Europe really a preview of coming attractions?

Is an UNTIED U.S. inevitable?

> **Canada may provide an alternative model,
> yet few pay much attention to Canada.**

Only 14% of American's realize Canada is their largest trading
partner.[20] The U.S. exports more to Canada than to its two next
trading partners combined. No U.S. president even bothered
to visit Canada until 1936.

Many Americans regard Canadians as steady, peaceful, and boring.

(Perhaps many have never seen a Canadian hockey game?)

Few realize just how close the neighbor to the north came to untying.

In less than fifteen years, support for sovereignty surged within Quebec. . . .

18% (1980–1985) . . . 41% (1986–1989) . . . 55% (1990).[21]

> Quebec began acting like an independent state. It opened "representations" that expected to be treated like embassies. For decades the maple leaf was absent from most government buildings in Quebec.[22] It directly admitted French-speaking immigrants.

In October 1995, 94% of Quebec's registered voters rejected secession . . . *by a margin of 0.7%.*

Canada looked like a particularly good candidate for untying.

There were six major reasons for this.

First, there is a long history behind the simmering Francophile anger. In 1839, Lord Durham defined Canada as:

> *"Two nations warring in the bosom of a single state."*[23]

> Through the 1970s, much of Canada attempted to promote English and repress French language, culture, and power. Quebec's population was 80% of French descent, but this group owned less than one-quarter of manufacturing businesses and financial institutions.

Eventually alienation reached a boiling point.

> The Quebec Liberation Front began planting bombs in government offices and mailboxes.

Faced with separatism, Canada's federal government made French and English official languages and began a series of reforms in an attempt to integrate the country.[24]

But Quebec was rapidly heading in the opposite direction. . . .

Bill 101 (1977) made French the only official language in the province. Businesses and provincial government offices were forced to become unilingual.

(Chapter VII, clause 54 of the law: ". . . it is forbidden to offer toys or games to the public which require the use of non-French vocabulary for their operation . . .")

Second, various Canadas are viable. In terms of population and income, an independent West would look like Australia. Quebec alone looks like Finland, but with a lot more land. And even the poor Maritimes are not that dissimilar from New Zealand.

Three Canadas = Australia, Finland, and New Zealand . . .

COUNTRY	POPULATION (in millions)	GDP (in billions)	GDP PER Capita ($)
Western Canada	21.7	661	30,465
Australia	19.7	526	26,632
Quebec	7.5	191	25,471
Finland	5.2	134	25,776
Atlantic Provinces	2.3	55	23,370
New Zealand	4.0	78	19,842

Source: Government of Canada, *CIA Factbook*

Third, Canadian geography is such that if one of the middle parts, say Quebec, separates, it would be hard to keep the rest of the country together.

About 90% of Canada's population lives within a hundred miles of the U.S. border.

(Rumor has it that it is just a little colder up north . . .)

The northern regions, Yukon, Northwest, and Nunavut, are, shall we say, somewhat scarcely populated.

They host 0.003% of the population.

If a central province unties, the others would trade across an independent country. Think about what happens, for instance, to a Maritimes isolated from Canada by Quebec.

They might find it a lot easier to trade and travel north-south instead of east-west.

As was true for centuries.

Canadian
Provinces & Territories

Yukon
Territory

Northwest
Territory

Nunavut
Territory

British
Columbia

Alberta

Saskat-
chewan

Manitoba

Ontario

Quebec

Newfoundland
& Labrador

PEI

Nova
Scotia

New
Brunswick

Through the late 1700s the logic of trade, governance, and culture was north-south, starting in Newfoundland and ending in Florida. The western border was Spain/France.

> There was and is a natural affinity between the Maritimes and New England. In the late 1860s, Prince Edward Island initiated talks with the U.S. on potential annexation. During WWII, more than 100,000 Americans were stationed in Newfoundland. More than 25,000 local women married these soldiers.

> In the 1940s, there was a bitter debate throughout Newfoundland as to whether the region should remain a part of the UK or become part of Canada, the U.S., or an independent country.

> Several Canadian politicians, including Allan Gottlieb, former ambassador to the U.S., and Prime Minister Jean Chretien, have argued that a separate Quebec could lead to a U.S. annexation of parts of Canada.

> Sometimes borders bounce back. . . .

Fourth, untying is legally permissible. After a lot of back and forth over the Quebec issue, the Supreme Court ruled that:

Given a set of specific conditions, the country can legally divide.[25]

Fifth, Canadian national identity is still an odd, and perhaps somewhat fragile thing. Canada did not sever all legal-constitutional ties to Great Britain until 1982. Creating and maintaining the myths surrounding state symbols and sovereignty has been somewhat haphazard.

"O Canada" was not the official anthem until July 1980.

> Canada's proud maple leaf flag is the result of a political compromise.

> > It was designed by a committee and was adopted only in 1965.

> > Canadian children do not pledge allegiance to their flag.

Immigrants pledged allegiance to *"Her Majesty, Elizabeth the Second, Queen of Canada."*[26]

Sometimes Canadians' strongest sense of identity seems to come from what they are not.

"We are NOT Americans."

When asked to describe the difference between the two countries, the first example is "We [Canadians] have health care for all."

Unfortunately, even this once great and generous system is showing ever greater signs of stress. Canada already spends more than any other developed country (OECD) with public health care. But it has fewer doctors and longer waits than most of its European peers.[27] This leads to ever more Canadians to seek treatment in the U.S. . . .

But not everyone in Canada is adverse to closer ties with the U.S.

In a 1991 poll, over one-third of Canadians believed their country would be a part of the U.S. in fifty years. By 2001, almost half of all Canadians believed they would become a part of the U.S. within the next decade.

And not many in the U.S. would be averse to getting close to Canada.

A 2002 poll showed one-third of Americans believed Canada was already just another state.[28]

(See what happens when you cut school budgets . . .)

Sixth, some have significant financial incentives to untie. Canada's rich western provinces spend a lot of money subsidizing the East. First there are direct transfers, "Equalization Entitlements."

Ontario got $0 per person. . . .

British Columbia, $147
Saskatchewan, $464
Quebec, $500
Nova Scotia, $1,223
Newfoundland/Labrador, $1,398
New Brunswick, $1,537
Prince Edward Island, $1,776 . . .

Alberta provides most of the cash. It rarely hears "thank you."

(After all, these are "entitlements.")

By the time you add up the major transfers (CHT, CST, Health Reform, and Equalization), federal transfers per province, per person turn out to be . . .

Prince Edward Island, $2,930
New Brunswick, $2,739
Nova Scotia, $2,455
Newfoundland, $2,449
Manitoba, $2,428
Quebec, $1,757
British Columbia, $1,383
Saskatchewan, $1,332
Ontario, $1,322
Alberta, $1,321

These are direct subsidies and do not include all the things a government does to support failing industries. So late at night, in various Alberta bars, one often hears:

Why do we keep paying Quebec's, and others', bills?

Might we be better off, and richer, alone?[29]

We generate most of the cash.

Politicians and Easterners spend it . . .

It is not just cash that grates; many English speakers resent forced bilingualism.

A majority of Canadians oppose maintaining a distinct, French-speaking society. This is especially true in the West. Opposition to French was 48% in Ontario, 63% in Alberta, and 66% in Manitoba.[30]

(Out West, during the 1995 Quebec referendum, one popular bumper sticker was: "Go, Quebec, Go!")

And finally there is the issue of high taxation with little representation.

Alberta alone has more people than the four Maritime provinces put together, but not the senate votes. The Maritimes, with 7.6% of the population, have almost 29% of senate seats.[31]

According to one study, between 1981 and 1988, Quebec received $27 billion more in taxes than it paid.[32]

(Gee, I wonder why western Canadians are sometimes so sore.)

Some politicians capitalized on this anger. In 1993, the conservative Reform Party promised tax cuts, decentralization, no special status for Quebec. They took 22 out of 26 seats in Alberta and 24 of 30 in British Columbia. By 1997, Reform was the largest opposition party in Canada. In 2000, the party renamed itself Canadian Alliance and took 66 seats, mostly from western States. In 2003, the conservative parties merged with the alliance, further strengthening the western agenda.

If a Canadian untying ever occurred, it is not inconceivable that western Canada could be the first to leave.

Given all six trends, it is surprising Canada remains one. . . .

And this implies we shouldn't just focus on the question "How might Canada split?"

Perhaps a more interesting question is "How has Canada survived and thrived?"

In a world were UN and EU members breed like rabbits, Canada is an important outlier. It is one of the most decentralized federations in the world, one within which many nations, ethnicities, and religions can coexist and thrive.

If an increasingly polarized U.S. wishes to avoid truly wrenching debates and outcomes, as its nations and minorities grow steadily more vocal, it may wish to pay a lot more attention to the mistakes and the successes of its northern neighbor.

There are key lessons to be learned from Canada, including:
Don't be hasty, let everyone vent.

The Quebec issue played out publicly and protractedly. At first, untying seemed OK . . .

> As it began to separate, Quebec begat twice as many MBAs as the national average, a powerful trade union movement, an intellectual elite, and a powerful Liberal party. French Canadians nationalized hydroelectric resources and many English-Canadian—owned businesses.

But strife made staying around unpleasant; ever fewer came to celebrate the new state.

More than 200,000 of the most educated Quebecois emigrated to other provinces.

(Mainly English-speaking Canadians whom Rene Levesque described as "white Rhodesians of Montreal.")

Income tax revenues fell $10 billion.

By 1990, Quebec had the most people living under the poverty line in Canada.[33]

The new and grand Mirabel International Airport never became a hub. It shut down for lack of flights.

(Oops . . .)

All concerned quickly learned that there are substantial hidden costs to sovereignty.

As they say, be careful what you wish for.

> By 2002, after decades of losing brains and business, even the Quebec separatists were in full retreat. Premier Landry was giving speeches in English and standing in front of a Canadian flag. . . .

> Ironically, in the 19th century, French-Canadians were considered the defenders of "Canada." They accused English-Canadians of having divided loyalties because of their British allegiance.[34]

Even during the height of the secessionist fury, 83% agreed that "Canada is the best country in the world to live in."[35]

Respect other languages and cultures.

Recognizing French bilingualism defused a lot of ill will.

Keep enough money handy to leave no one too far behind.

> Transfer payments and subsidies remained a key carrot
> for those who argued for unity.

>> But only countries that manage their finances responsibly
>> can access this instrument on a rainy day.

Have a common competitor/enemy.

Focusing on what could happen to Canada's independence,
should secessionists prevail, generated a common cause to
fight for union.

Force the autonomists to grant what they themselves demand.

Canadians forced Quebec to recognize and deal with its
English-speaking minorities and First Peoples on the
same terms.

Canada may be a model for coping with seemingly irreconcilable differences.

Of course, there is no guarantee in the long run. Canadian
politics remains a contact sport. Things can change very fast.

> Just ask Canadian conservatives. They elected the country's
> first prime minister. They dominated Canadian politics from
> the early 1980s through 1993. Then, in a single election, they
> lost every seat but two . . . in a three hundred–seat parliament.

Over the next five decades, Canada could fundamentally
modify the U.S. flag and border.

One could imagine many different outcomes; here are three scenarios:

While remaining sovereign countries, with their respective flags and borders, Canada and the U.S. could, over the next fifty years, end up with an EU-like border.

After all, if millennial enemies, like France and Germany, can voluntarily and peacefully open borders and share passports, security, currency, and labor markets . . .

Colin Powell, for one, knows just how quickly and drastically things can change: "I have these out of body experiences from my days as a soldier in the Cold War . . . All my former enemies, from my Cold War days, are now my best friends."[36]

Over time, Canadians have warily edged ever closer to their American cousins.[37]

A couple of centuries ago, they explicitly chose not to become Americans (i.e., the War of 1812).

Prime Minister Wilfried Laurier lost his job for proposing free trade with the U.S.

The opposition slogan in 1911?
"No truck or trade with the Yankees."

Post-WWII, P.M. Mackenzie King feared the U.S. would "absorb" Canada and cut off free trade talks.

By 1987, Canada and the U.S. had signed a free trade agreement.

Yet bitter disputes over timber and fisheries flourish.

Nevertheless, somewhat grudgingly, the U.S. and Canadian economies are ever more tightly coupled. Trade, real estate, corporate takeovers, and joint research projects establish ever closer dependency. So ask yourself, Would it be easier for the U.S. and Canada to integrate than for East and West Germany?

Or Puerto Rico and the U.S. for that matter?[38]

This implies each country would remain "sovereign," but crossing the border would be like crossing a state line.

You would not have to change currency. Folks could freely work wherever they wanted. Immigration, customs, and trade policy would be tightly coupled.

A second scenario could involve much more drastic changes:

Many Americans, especially those of the liberal species, have, at times, felt a greater empathy with Canada than with their own government.

> During the Vietnam War (1964–1977), more than 125,000 Americans went to live in Canada. By 1986, over half had chosen to stay permanently.[39]

Twenty-five years ago Joel Garreau wrote *The Nine Nations of North America.* Even back then various U.S. regions had more in common with Canada or Mexico than with each other.

> Those in Vancouver are quite similar to those on the coasts of Washington, Oregon, and California. More conservative Calgary and Edmonton resemble parts of Montana and Colorado . . .

Today the aspirations, politics, and prejudices of Massachusetts and Vermont often seem a lot closer to those of Canadians than they do to those of U.S. red states.

As these divisions grow and ossify, you begin to see maps redrawn and posted on the Internet that look like this:

The notion of Vermont, Massachusetts, Maine, Illinois, Wisconsin, Oregon, Washington, or a chunk of California joining Canada may seem utterly farfetched. But just how alienated those in traditional blue states get, as power shifts south and west, will be a major issue. This is not unprecedented in historic terms; most focus on the South's attempt to untie.

But, in fact, it is the North that has threatened to leave more often.

New Englanders threatened secession early and often:[40]

After Jefferson's Louisiana Purchase, which they claimed was "unconstitutional" and could lead to a perpetual domination of the East by the South and West.

(Maybe they were right after all?)

After Jefferson's 1807 embargo, which stopped all foreign trade.

Because of Madison's War of 1812; no congressman or senator representing states east of Pennsylvania (except Vermont) supported the war. The Hartford 1814 Convention brought together Connecticut, Massachusetts, New Hampshire, Rhode Island, and Vermont in an attempt to establish secession as a constitutional right.

After Texas joined the Union in 1844, New Englanders felt the additional star tipped the balance toward proslavery states.

If the Northeast keeps losing power vis-a-vis the South and the West and if the divisions between liberals and conservatives get bloodier, we could see an old story revive. . . .

> You can no longer send in General Grant to torch the restless. Civility, respect, compromise, and cash keep modern developed countries together. Before the U.S. proceeds too far down the path of "us vs. them" politics . . . It would be well advised to understand some of the carrots and sticks Canada developed as it faced its own bitter challenges.

A third scenario is a Canada that does end up untying. . . .

Canada could conceivably fragment into three or more different countries.

> We have seen that these countries would look like Australia, Finland, and New Zealand.

> Now that there is a lot of gas, there is even a growing nationalist sentiment in Newfoundland/Labrador. Premier Williams was treated "like a hero" when he took down all Canadian flags from provincial buildings during a battle over equalization payments.[41]

Historically, Canadian splits fundamentally altered the U.S. border.

> One of the reasons Americans were able to begin saluting a few stars in their flag was due to French support for the adventure of 1776.[42] Ben Franklin, ambassador to France, carefully enlisted them as an ally against the British.

Quebec could have ended up being a part of the U.S.

> In the 1770s, the English were debating whether to make Quebec the fourteenth Colony. They did not because most Quebecois were Catholics.

And, in fact, a part of Quebec did end up adding stars to the U.S. flag:

> After independence, the U.S. invaded Quebec, laid siege to Montreal, and kept the sections that lay south of the Great Lakes.[43]

Whether it is Quebec, or the West, or the Maritimes, a divided Canada again raises the question of how close each of these entities should be to the U.S. . . .

Perhaps a significant driver of integrating parts of Canada will be the desire, on the part of U.S. conservatives, to expand the size and influence of a U.S. white-Anglo Saxon culture vis-a-vis Hispanics.

American conservative pundit Pat Buchanan has argued all, or part, of Canada should be annexed.

In summary, Canada and Europe are useful ways to think about the questions "What is a country?" And "Does it matter if there are new borders?"

Each has faced demands to untie in very different ways. Each may potentially serve as a model or as a warning to the U.S.

Often, when asked about something one really cares about, it is a good idea to ask someone somewhat more detached to analyze a complex and emotional situation.

In this context, it is interesting to note that when Canadian military officers are asked what keeps them up at night, their response is:

"The biggest threat to Canada is that the United States will collapse on itself. Canada's problems are out in the open, but the degree of turmoil in the U.S. is not admitted."[44]

All species on the planet rise and fall. Even humans.

> It does not matter if you believe in the theory of evolution or
> not. Fact is we began as *Australopithecus*, and gradually
> begat *Homo ergaster, habilis, erectus, neanderthalensis*, and
> now, the perhaps misnamed, *sapiens*.[1] Each humanoid
> species had different talents, adapted, and grew in
> different ways. All but one eventually went extinct. As have
> 99.9% of all species. Only those that evolve survive.

To put this in "scientific terms":

> ### *All life evolves by the differential*
> ### *survival of replicating entities.*[2]

This quote is not just applicable to plants and animals. It is also
applicable to countries. We could state, as a corollary:

All countries evolve by the differential
survival of existing nations.

Old borders reappear, disappear, are redrawn, new countries join the
U.N. (or leave).

The secretary general of the U.N. argued: *fierce new assertions of
nationalism and sovereignty spring up, and the cohesion of states is
threatened by brutal ethnic, religious, or linguistic strife.* His conclusion?

> ### *The time of absolute and exclusive sovereignty*
> ### *has passed; its theory was never matched by reality.*[3]

So, to quote a Native American chief, William Feather:

> *Success seems to be largely a matter of*
> *hanging on after others have let go.*

Throughout history most countries, empires, duchies, and
other fiefdoms have been relatively short-lived.

8.

LIKE YOUR FLAG?
WANT TO KEEP IT?

"IT IS NOT THE STRONGEST OF SPECIES THAT SURVIVE,
NOR THE MOST INTELLIGENT,
BUT THE ONE MOST RESPONSIVE TO CHANGE."

—*Charles Darwin*

In this context, recall that China has been around, evolving and devolving, for over four millennia.[4] By 1600, China's population was greater than that of Europe.

Unlike China, Egypt, India, or Iran, the United States is quite a young country.

The United States has been a sovereign country for about five lifetimes.

(And a small part has been a political entity for eight life times.)

The U.S. could, conceivably, last for millennia.

After centuries of building up power, the U.S. remains a great and powerful place.

> Historian Frances FitzGerald argues the American national myth is "that of creativity and progress, of steady climbing upwards into power and prosperity. . . . Americans see history as a straight line. . . . They believe in the future as if it were a religion."[5]

But one must recall that . . .

> *"Myth grows, spiral-wise, until the intellectual impulse which produced it is exhausted."*[6]

The U.S. will have to adapt continuously to very different circumstances. It will have to nurture and accept very different myths brought forth and cherished by minorities that are now becoming majorities. And, if the U.S. is to remain dominant, these minorities will have to get very good at processing data to create knowledge.

Wealth today comes from managing knowledge. Knowledge is transmitted through code. Problem is, the dominant code keeps changing. . . .

In 1900, you had better have spoken French if you wanted to participate in international diplomacy and German if you wanted to do science. In 1900, you had better have understood English . . .

In 2000, you better know how to use digital code . . .

(E-mail code 0110110001001111010101100110010, reads "I love you." 0110100001000001010101000100101 reads "I hate you.")

Now, life code (A,T,C,G) is becoming ever more dominant

(and perhaps a smattering of Chinese).

Languages, like countries, also grow or disappear. More than 6,000 unique languages survive today. But most are headed toward extinction. Sometimes at a rate of two per week.[7]

Problem is one gets used to one's language, and one begins to assume that today's dominant language has always been and will always be. So many forget to keep learning and, when challenged, become ever more reactionary; they begin to believe the IEWGEFJ faction.

(IEWGEFJ? If English was good enough for Jesus . . .)

Understanding which will be the next dominant language and educating the next generations so that they can apply this new knowledge is nontrivial. There is no clear formula or set of rules.

You can get a sense of the scale of the challenge presented in transitioning from the digital era into that of life sciences by comparing MDs and pilots. Medicine remains a craft-based system. The outcome depends on the skill of the person treating you. There are no uniform quality standards. You pick your doctor carefully. Lifesaving technologies spread slowly and somewhat randomly. Get a second opinion and do some Internet research. . . .

If airlines worked this way, you would interview and look at your pilot's bio before every flight . . .[8]

As the rules keep changing, you have to get literate, stumble along learning, understand new opportunities, and keep changing strategies and investments.

It is an expensive, complex, nonlinear process.

You don't go to college . . . You don't learn the code . . . You cannot maintain a decent standard of living.

A man in his forties who is a college dropout makes $42,000. One who finished college makes $65,000. And it gets worse . . . Three decades ago a man in his fifties with a college degree earned 52% more than someone without a degree. Now the difference is 82%.[9]

This is why Harvard's president Summers argues: *"The most serious domestic problem in the U.S. today is the widening gap between the children of the rich and the children of the poor . . . education is the most powerful weapon we have to address that problem."*

You go to college not to learn something, but to learn to learn. This is essential because the self-evident truths that justify today's economy, religions, science, flags, and borders are confronted time and again by options, challenges, alternative beliefs, new discoveries.

Often the young are the only ones open to change and willing to learn a new code. So you have to keep investing, time and again, in making sure the young learn languages and disciplines that may not have been relevant when you were in school.

(Did you study nanotechnology, bioinformatics, NMR spectroscopy, and brain imaging?)

Historically, those most efficient at gathering, applying, and passing on knowledge to their kids, and getting these kids to learn more, tend to be dominant. Over centuries, no one—not the U.S., not China—remains *the* undisputed winner. The successful eventually quit learning. Or others learn faster.

That is why, when you ask, "Who are the most productive people on earth?"

The answer keeps changing. . . .[10]

TOP FIVE INCOME PER CAPITA						
1820	1870	1900	1913	1950	1973	1992
UK	Australia	UK	Australia	USA	Switz.	USA
Nether.	UK	NZ	USA	Switz.	USA	Switz.
Australia	NZ	Australia	NZ	NZ	Canada	Germany
Austria	Nether.	USA	UK	Australia	Sweden	Denmark
Belgium	Belgium	Belgium	Canada	Canada	Germany	Canada

In 2004, here are the top five: Luxembourg, Norway, Switzerland, Ireland, Denmark.[11]

And for the first time since the 1900s, the U.S. failed to crack the top five. (It was seventh, after Iceland.)

Enoch Powell once said:

All political careers end in failure.

The same is true of countries. . . .

To tell where a country is headed, just ask, "Is it investing in the future or in the past?"

In 2000, the U.S. federal government spent $2,106 per child.

And it spent $21,122 per adult over 65 . . .[12]

There is ever more debt, ever more investment in the old, ever less spent on the young. There are ever more marginalized from the knowledge economy.

What happens to a country over time as many work ever harder and get less?

As many lose their dreams and hope, will they be willing to sacrifice today for future reward?

In this context, take a look at trends in the U.S. minimum wage.[13]

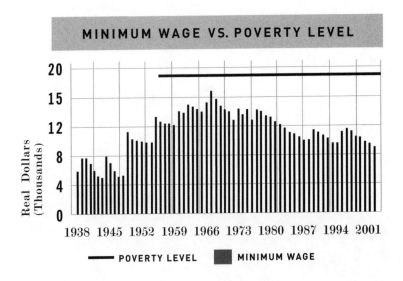

From 1948 to 1968, those at the bottom could see things getting a little better, year after year.

They got worse and worse from 1968 through 2004 . . .

For many, the American Dream is ever more distant.

In 2002, about 11% of U.S. households did not have enough food.[14]

In 2003, 21 million were on food stamps.

Try feeding yourself for a month on $83.91.[15]

It is not just that the purchasing power of the minimum wage has fallen, in constant dollars, from $7.21 per hour in 1971 to less than $5 today. Average weekly earnings also fell.

In 1970, average weekly earnings were $296.
By 2003, they were $279.[16]

Short term, you can use repression, shame, ignorance,
lies, and politics to keep old myths alive. Long term, people
will only believe, pass on national myths, defend borders,
if they provide comfort, wealth, a more stable society, and
a better life.

And today many feel left out.

So ever more borrow, mortgage, scramble to buy a house, to have the
right car, to acquire the right clothes, to afford an extreme makeover.
But as they do so they find it harder and harder. They sleep less.
Worry more. Owe more.

Between 1993 and 2003, the average income of those between 18
and 25 year increased 29%. Housing prices for the same group
increased 39%. The average rent for a one bedroom apartment in
Boston is now $1,800. In Manhattan, it is $2,500.[17] Might there be
a problem in a country where the greatest source of new wealth is
speculating on real estate?

When old myths no longer deliver, they gradually lose legitimacy
and power.

**New generations have to buy into the myth; if not,
religions and countries wither up.**

That wonderful cynic Samuel Butler (1835–1902) once said:

Life is one long process of getting tired.

He was speaking of people.

**But he could have been referring to kingdoms,
principalities, empires, countries.**

What were once upon a time the single most important symbols
of honor now seem quaint and antiquated. Throughout Europe,
people fought, died, to defend the honor of a heraldic shield,
one's coat of arms. Recognize these?

A lot of people used to die for them . . .

But eventually converts flock to other faiths, propagate new myths, raise new flags.

> During the 2004 Greek Olympics,
> spectators cheered for 109 more teams
> than during Tokyo's 1964 Olympics.

True leaders understand you can sometimes lose. They don't just celebrate the wins. They prepare for unavoidable challenges and battles. They recall bitter lessons, as Abraham Lincoln did:

> *"If we first know where we are, and wither we are tending, we could better judge what to do, and how to do it."*[8]

Remember just how much the U.S., Mexican, and Canadian flags have already morphed. So it should not surprise us if they continued to do so in the 21st century.

I am not promoting, nor am I predicting, fewer U.S. states, or a gaggle of Canadas, or four Mexicos within a decade.

I am assuming you, like I, do not seek or want great countries to break up.

> But fifty years is a long time . . .

> One hundred years is close to the half-life
> of the U.S. and Mexico . . .

Often we ignore trends, assume someone else will deal with mounting problems.

We should be paying attention, and worry, about current trends because . . .

Untying is like an avalanche . . .

A few snowflakes accumulate atop a mountain.

Each storm piles on more snowflakes.

Until you get great, compact slabs.

Cornices grow unstable overhangs.

The whole mountain crashes.

If you know what you are looking for, you can sometimes
prevent avalanches by releasing pressure in specific spots.

Another way of thinking about borders?
Lines drawn in the sand . . .
Only constantly redrawn lines survive.

In thirteen months, from November 1990 to December 1991,
the world's second-most-powerful nation-empire, the USSR,
fell to pieces.

**Virtually no one expected the border of the world's other
superpower to shrink overnight to about where it had
been in the 1790s.**

Among the most surprised by these developments: Secretary
General Mikhail Gorbachev, Soviet leaders, and their Western
opponents.

One of those caught unaware by the Soviet collapse was one
of the best-informed people on the planet: General Ervin J.
Rokke.

As military attaché at the U.S. embassy in the Soviet Union
during Gorbachev's presidency, Rokke would wake at dawn,
read every newspaper, and diligently review reams of statistics
on missile throw-weights, steel production, troop readiness,
and leadership strengths and weaknesses.

After endless days and dinners with Soviet officers or political leaders in ornate offices, Rokke would drive home, passing powerful symbols: huge flags, tombs and statues, symbols of Soviet power and ruthlessness.[19]

Despite Gorbachev's reforms, the general remained terrified of the Soviet bear.

It seemed like such a powerful state . . .

**But General Rokke, and almost everyone else,
forgot what makes a strong country.**

When the general got home at night, he rarely listened to his
wife's descriptions of daily life: endless lines, few basic
goods, frustration with a corrupt and incompetent state.

Only after the collapse of the USSR did General Rokke
realize he had missed crucial intelligence, a forecast of the
unthinkable, the disintegration of Soviet borders.[20] He, like
so many others, forgot flags and borders are myths that have
to be constantly supported to survive. He confused symbols
and reality.

> And given conflicts like Georgia vs. Abkhazia and South Ossetia
> or Russia vs. Chechnya, Dagestan, Karachay-Cherkessia, and
> Uzbekistan, there is little evidence the secessionist debate has
> settled.[21]

Governments and societies can fail in so many ways. . . .[22]

Economic collapse . . .
　　　　Political exhaustion . . .
　　　　　　　Intolerance and exclusion . . .
　　　　　　　　　Environmental collapse . . .
　　　　　　　　　　Various pandemics . . .
　　　　　　　　　　　Natural disasters . . .
　　　　　　　　　　　　Excess natural resources . . .

Typically governments go through various stages:

Denial—"Not here."

Minimization—"We have it under control."

Delegitimization—"They are a radical group."

Foreigners—"A plot by X to undermine us."

Not our fault—"We are not liked because . . ."

Unfair—"If not for the U.N., IMF, U.S. . . ."

And finally, **Better off alone anyway** . . .

Various crises can plant divisive seeds. As the seeds of dissent-dissatisfaction-separatism grow, they get harder and harder to trim back.

Sometimes they grow large and high enough to build a new border.

How the U.S., Mexico, and Canada treat folks today, whether they have some hope and a vested interest in the system, will determine what the U.S. borders look like in fifty years.

Countries are based on shared faith, belief, ideals.

(As well as a good dose of economics, logic, reason, realities.)

Time and again the faith, belief, and ideals are shaken up, blindsided, challenged by emerging technologies.

Some adapt, some disappear.

By and large it is a change in technology that enables and defines powerful civilizations.

Whole eras are defined by the most powerful technologies of the time.

(We look at prehistory as stone, bronze, iron ages.
Now we talk of the information age. . . .)

Smart countries never assume, or act, as if they were inevitable, impermeable, and inviolate.

It is not just countries. Once upon a time GM seemed all-powerful. In the 1970s, Russ Fisher, a young insurance man, recognized an unsustainable trend. Health care costs, for some companies, were increasing 30% per year. This did not stop management, nor did it stop autoworkers. Through the mid-1990s, double-digit increases continued.

You can watch, you can warn, as many did in the auto and airline industries. But many countries and companies continue to act like lemmings. In 2005, Russ retired just as U.S. auto companies went into yet another downward spiral.

You may not like the concept, but I hope you are now convinced that basic changes in fundamental symbols, even in the U.S. flag and border, are at least possible. . . .

If not eventually inevitable.

And for all who still disagree, remind yourselves of Galileo's *sotto voce* comment: *"Eppur se muve."*[23] (Although Galileo, when threatened with torture, publicly recanted on the notion that the earth is not the center of the universe, he quietly insisted, "It moves.")

But . . .

Skilled politicians and determined citizens can stave off the inevitable, for a long, long time.

Sometimes success continues a lot longer than one might expect.

Ed Whitlock is a great marathoner. He was 26th, out of 1,690 finishers in the 2004 Toronto Waterfront race (2:54:49). With this time, he would have placed 306th out of 33,000 in the NYC Marathon.

Not bad at age 73.[24]

In a globalized, multisovereignty world, it is ever harder for governments to control all. Countries that can release pressure, adapt, and adopt, avoid leaving various regions behind or isolated, survive a lot longer.

There has been a lot of change and a lot of pressure building up inside the U.S., and Canada, and Mexico.

And most countries in this world for that matter.

Advocates of free trade and globalization are increasingly unelectable.

France has opted out of an EU constitution because it fears losing its standard of living. Germany's Schroeder is also on his way out for the same reasons. Never mind Latin America, where every newly elected leader is from the left.

In the 21st century, most countries will face extraordinary challenges. Keeping big, diverse countries together will be one of them. Particularly in the world's ten most populous countries, which in 2025 will likely be: China, India, U.S., Indonesia, Pakistan, Brazil, Nigeria, Bangladesh, Russia, Mexico.

Many flags continue to disappear into various cupboards and museums.

Today, governments usually have more to fear from within than from without.

Between 1820 and 1945, nine out of ten wars involved border disputes among neighbors.[25]

Now external wars and border disputes take a backseat to internal untying.

From 1945 through 1995, only 35% of eighty wars involved battles between the regular armies of two or more states.

In other words, the majority of conflicts were civil wars or guerrilla insurgencies.[26] (Statistically, developing countries face an 11% chance of having a civil war over a five-year period.)[27]

Increasingly, in both developed and developing countries, it is groups within the state that are asserting their ethnic, religious, linguistic, regional, and/or national identities.

Civil wars and secession can occur without clear religious or ethnic fault lines: Spain, China, Russia, USA, Panama.[28]

Even a country as ethnically and geographically unified as Japan could someday face major challenges. Three prefectures, Tokyo, Osaka, and Aichi (Nagoya), pay for most of the other forty-four. They subsidize the farm sector and traditional businesses. Less than 13% of Japan's workers were engaged in very competitive industries. Many of the lead sectors of the economy, particularly cars and electronics, have been relocating abroad.[29]

Someday, those living within Japanese cities, whose vote counts a fraction of someone living in the countryside, may rebel against high taxes and little influence.

Untying occurs to rich and poor.

To Catholic, Protestant, Buddhist, Muslim . . .

It is happening in Asia, Europe, and Africa.

Odd thing is . . . not yet in the Americas.

But demands for greater autonomy and secession throughout the Americas could prosper today even though they did not do so for the past two centuries.

It is ever harder for illegitimate institutions to arbitrate regional disputes and secessionist claims.

Canada's travails remained mostly orderly because many political parties reacted moderately to extreme demands and most respected rulings by the constitutional court.

> As the U.S. Senate threatens to cut off filibusters, it becomes less important to consult and to compromise. Otherwise, Judges and Senators could come to represent ever more polarized factions. Particularly when House Majority Leader Tom DeLay threatens, again, to ignore the separation of powers: "We will look at an arrogant, out of control, unaccountable judiciary . . ."

> It is a fragile middle keeping things together.

As each side turns toward ever more extreme rhetoric, the credibility of most central governments and major institutions has been eroding since the late 1950s. The percentage of Americans who say they trust Washington only "some of the time" and "almost never" increased steadily from 30% in 1966. . . .

> In 2003, it was 71%.[30]

If government and business are seen as one, both may become increasingly illegitimate. In 1964, around 29% felt government was run by a few big interests looking out for themselves. By 1984, it had risen to 55%. In 2004, it was 64%.[31]

(Similar trends, albeit at different rates, in Canada, Europe, and Japan.)

This coziness between government and big business has been a concern for a long time.

In one of the first U.S. science-fiction books, the hero falls asleep in 1887 and wakes up to a world dominated by mega corporations in 2000. Author Edward Bellamy feared a 20th-century dominated by soulless machines, insatiable greed, gigantic scale, concentration, and wealth undreamed of. He understood some of the costs and the benefits of where the U.S. was heading.

"Oppressive and intolerable as the regime of the great consolidation of capital, even its victims, while they cursed it, were forced to admit the prodigious increase in efficiency, which had been imparted to the national industries, the vast economies effected by the concentration of management and the unity of the organization. . . . To be sure this vast increase had gone chiefly to make the rich richer."[32]

A vacuum in trust and in the rule of law can have severe consequences.

(It is like entering the Taklimakan Desert; if you go in, it is hard to come out.)

Trust in Major U.S. Institutions[33]

	Three Decades Ago	End of 1990s
Government	75%	25%
Medicine	73%	29%
Universities	61%	30%
Major Companies	55%	21%
Journalism	29%	14%

As trust in legislators, presidents, and courts erodes, few leaders maintain the personal and institutional legitimacy required to resolve increasingly bitter disputes. So, staying in power becomes a matter of building and maintaining a fundamentalist base.

Direct mail, targeted ads, and push polls are sometimes used to reinforce prejudice and suspicion, or, as some explained during the 2004 U.S. presidential campaign, "to mobilize the core base."

The U.S., in turn, becomes increasingly polarized by religion-politics-race-class; issues like abortion, right to die, flag burning, and gay marriage further stir the pot.

The other side is oft portrayed as "evil."
Politics becomes ever more personal and divisive.

Political parties reinforce these divisions, exploiting and promoting lack of trust in and hatred in others. (Paul Krugman argues that the 2004 election was about keeping America safe from married gay terrorists.)

Words such as *change, openness, foreigner,* and *compromise* become dirty words. Moderates are increasingly reviled by all sides.

> Many are targeted by those within their own party. The Club for Growth put $2 million behind a conservative challenger against Sen. Arlen Specter in the Republican primary. (Perhaps one of the reasons senators like Olympia Snow, Lincoln Chafee, John McCain, Susan Collins, Arlen Specter, and George Voinovich are endangered species. Never mind extinct species like Rockefeller Republicans.)

There is ever more talk of impeaching whoever is president, governor, mayor, judge. The political environment becomes more bitter, fundamentalist, nativist, regionalist.

> "[Nationalism/tribalism] is the cheapest and most reliable means for a politician without anything else to offer to rise to prominence."[34]

In April 2005, the senate majority leader joined Christian conservatives in a series of national telecasts. They denounced Democrats as opponents of "people of the faith." Meanwhile, DeLay argued the judiciary is too liberal and hostile to Christianity.[35]

If this was merely a problem of leadership, or politics, or big business, it would not be a fatal flaw.

> It is when people, when communities, stop trusting each other that there is real trouble. And it seems Americans trust one another less and less. Four decades ago, 58% of Americans believed "most people could be trusted." In 2003, only 35% did.[36]

(Perhaps part of the problem is that, in a society increasingly divided by riches and the lack thereof, the word *trust* has been hijacked to mean "monopoly, inherited wealth, lawyer-led asset protection"?)

It is not that people are more evil today than they were in your grandparent's generation. More likely, this sense of unease as to "who can I trust" reflects the overwhelming pace and magnitude of change. Nothing seems stable.

> How many times has your bank changed because of mergers?
> Do you still buy your parents' favorite make of cars?
> Does e-mail make you work shorter hours?
> Does your world seem safer, calmer, more prosperous?
> Do you live where you were born?

New companies, new industries, new technologies . . .
a few thrive, but most feel at least some unease with the rate of change.

> In 1991, there were bitter debates over whether to allow commercial applications over the Internet. In 1993, you could drive to almost every website location in the world. They were housed either on Sand Hill Road in California or near MIT in Massachusetts.[37]

> In 2005, you can carry out more than 360 trillion calculations (Teraflops) in a single computer. In 2005, the Venter Institute generated 100 million letters of new gene code every day.

As technology charges ahead, many countries fail to upgrade infrastructure and people.

A train could easily transport you from Boston to New York at 300 mph . . . but only if the right track has been laid. If not, then the trains run at the same average speed as they did a century ago . . .

Which is exactly the case today.

Many fail to invest and evolve. They spend everything trying to protect what they have today.

> Just playing defense leaves you ever further behind. U.S. car companies are increasingly overwhelmed, even at home.
> The U.S. is 14th in the world in broadband access.

In an attempt to create order, stability, and certainty,
many attempt to surround themselves with those they know . . .

People gate their communities, join ever more powerful churches, which function as all-purpose town halls and social centers. They focus on the region, and religion, not the nation. Daniel Bell picked up on these trends; back in 1978, he argued:

> *The nation state is now too small for the*
> *big problems of life*
> *And too big for the small problems in life.*[38]

Over and over countries are overwhelmed by globalization.

Countries are untying and "resizing."

It is a global phenomenon . . .

Countries Where Some Wish to Untie[39]

Africa	Asia/Pacific	Europe	America	Middle East
Rwanda	Georgia	Macedonia	United States	Iraq
Angola	Indonesia	Moldova	Chile	Iran
Nigeria	Russia	Albania	Argentina	Syria
Tanzania	Papua New Guinea	Rumania	Canada	Israel
Ethiopia	Bangladesh	Yugoslavia	Mexico	Turkey
Eritrea	Philippines	France	Colombia	Lebanon
Djibouti	Ukraine	Slovakia	Brazil	Saudi Arabia
Uganda	China	Poland	Honduras	
Ghana	Myanmar	Sweden	Nicaragua	
Mali	India	Finland	Bolivia	
Nigeria	New Guinea	Portugal	St. Kitts and Nevis	
Algeria	Azerbaijan	Germany	Peru	
Cameroon	Afghanistan	Spain	Ecuador	
Zambia	Pakistan	United Kingdom		
Equatorial	Japan	Italy		
Guinea	Uzbekistan	Denmark		
Senegal	Solomon Islands	Belgium		
Sudan	Vietnam	Netherlands		
Yemen	Malaysia	Switzerland		
Chad	Australia	Slovenia		
South Africa		Croatia		
Kenya		Serbia		
Zimbabwe		Cyprus		
D. R. Congo		Norway		
Morocco		Austria		
Ivory Coast				
Togo				
Benin				

Ever larger and more powerful global networks control trade, currency, and security.

(GATT, NATO, EURO, OECD, and other four-letter words . . .)

Which, in turn, allow the dividing into smaller and smaller political units under an umbrella of broad alliances and rules. Countries are now emerging at a rate comparable only to those after World War I and the decolonization of the 1960s. These are the new flags of the 1990s:

(Kind of reminds you of that line in a song: *"Pledge allegiance to the flag . . . whatever flag they offer . . .*)[40]

Within the next five decades . . .

We might conservatively expect to see fifty new flags surrounding the United Nations.

Some broadcast their plight and seek recognition through the Unrepresented People's Organization (UNPO). Former members have achieved full independence, including Armenia, Palau, Estonia, Georgia, Latvia, and East Timor. Fifty-plus members hope to follow these examples.[41]

The U.S. remains an outlier. Despite all current foibles, it is a very powerful nation, one whose flag, bucking almost every international trend, could continue to grow. John McArthur, a smart Canadian, dean of the Harvard Business School for fifteen years, argues that:

Most of those who have bet against the United States, in military, political, or financial terms, have consistently lost.

And will likely continue to lose.

It would not be surprising, in fifty years, to read a newspaper that described a larger, more powerful United States, a stronger Mexico, a greater Canada. There are several scenarios under which there are more U.S. stars, real or virtual.

Some still believe, as Senator Beveridge did back in the late 1800s, that: "We are enlisted in the cause of American supremacy, which will never end until American commerce has become the lord of civilization; and the stars and stripes the flag of flags throughout the world."[42]

If the U.S. flag were to expand dramatically, much of this growth would probably come from its overseas territories and its contiguous borders.

Parts of Canada or of Mexico could join or confederate. Short term, seems unlikely. But even societies that traditionally invaded and expressed great fear of one another, like the various Italian states, sometimes end up together. France and Germany now share currency, jobs, and military without one or the other winning an all-out war.

The answer to the first question in this book, "How many stars do you think will be in the U.S. flag in fifty years?" is by no means foreordained.

It will be primarily up to the citizens and quasi-citizens of the U.S., of Canada, and of Mexico to answer that question.

They can change the outcome by succeeding.

They can change the outcome by failing miserably.

Current flags, borders, anthems, and currencies are lagging, not leading, indicators of what is to come.

They strengthen after something is created.
They disappear long after most is lost.

Do not confuse symbols and myths with reality. One of today's red meat, conservative issues is defending the Pledge of Allegiance. Particularly after a lawsuit sought to take out the words *under God.* How dare someone today contravene the founding fathers? Except . . .

> The Pledge was written for a Boston magazine as a one-off stunt just over a century ago, in 1891. The author, Francis Bellamy, was not a conservative; he was a Baptist preacher kicked out of his church for his socialist views. Its objective was to get people to focus on serving their country instead of on getting rich. In other words, it was intended as a manifesto against "the atomizing effects of industrial capitalism."

Ironically, the right now often ends up doggedly defending what was once sacred to the left.

> Today's source of bitter contention, the words *under God,* do not originate from either the founding fathers or even from the original pledge. They were added in 1954 as a way to set the United States apart from the atheistic Soviet Union."[43]

The No Child Left Behind Law is another example; it recognizes what all see. There is a significant achievement gap in test scores between Whites/Asians and Blacks/Hispanics/Native Americans.

The law forces schools to report the differences between ethnic groups and to do something about them. Teachers and principals can be fired; schools can be taken over. One would think those on the left, long advocates of desegregated schools, would be those most in favor. Yet they are often the most opposed (especially teachers unions). Ironically "liberal" politicians end up blocking extra tutoring, standards, testing, and real results.[44] (While knowing full well education is the only thing that really closes wealth gaps.)

It is what you build or reject today that will determine what your country will look like tomorrow.

A former president of Brazil wisely argues:

In Latin America we are still waiting for a miracle.

We have to understand that miracles are no longer available.[45]

Only countries that maintain a strong sense of community and invest in the future, rather than the past, will be able to postpone centrifugal tendencies.

Growing intolerance, declining educational standards, inability to attract talent, growing disparities in wealth can end up splitting societies and eventually countries.

Post-9/11 Chinese Ph.D. and postdoc applications dropped 50% at many Ivy League schools.

Eventually fewer brains means less growth.

Less growth means fewer jobs.

As it becomes ever more of a burden to take care of those who have been left behind, all sides become ever more resentful of giving too much or of not getting enough.

As we celebrate the 75th anniversary of the theory of relativity, perhaps it is time to apply Einstein's knowledge to countries and sovereignty:

> *"The world we have created today has problems*
> *which cannot be solved by thinking about them the way*
> *we thought about them when we created them."*

I.e., neither the founding fathers nor the Bible hold all the answers. . . .

So let's assume you like where you live. You like the flag, learned the anthem, understand the borders and those who live within.

And you would like your kids and grandkids to feel the same way.

What do you have to do? What should you watch out for?

Time and again you see examples of great countries that fail to adapt and grow. They systematically quit learning, shut down research, refuse to change.

Around the first millennium, China was run by the Sung Dynasty. They were producing as much steel as Europe would produce five to six hundred years later.[46]

There is little question who really ran the world in the 1200s, 1300s, 1400s. It wasn't the Europeans, it was the Chinese. They were so far ahead, no one could really compete.

Scholars completed the world's greatest encyclopedia, 4,000 volumes.

So ask yourself . . . Self . . . , "Why aren't we all speaking Chinese yet?"

In 1421, a bolt of lightning burned down the Forbidden City and a superstitious emperor took it as a divine sign. China retrenched and began reducing trade, exploration, tribute, and learning from the outside world.[47] Europe kept learning, gathering knowledge, growing, while China stagnated for centuries. But even through 1820, after centuries of Mongol hoards and lousy governance, China and India were still the two dominant players in world commerce, producing 45% of the world's output.

China survived bad leadership but not the industrial revolution and techno-illiteracy.

Today, despite extraordinary growth, China and India account for only 5.8% of global trade.[48]

It is not a Godgiven right for any country to exist forever.

(Even if in God it trusts.)

Robert D. Kaplan, a smart man and bestselling author, who has seen a lot of countries, argues:

> *"The existence of the United States*
> *should never be taken for granted."*[49]

It is going to take a lot of political skill and communication to mend existing rifts. (And a lot of sacrifice to pay mounting debts.)

But, it is ever harder for Republicans and Democrats (or Independents, for that matter) to put aside differences and just go out for a beer after work.

One of Donald Rumsfeld's maxims is: "A friend in Washington is someone who stabs you in the chest" . . .

It did not used to be that way.

House Speaker Tip O'Neill was once visited by a very excitable freshman congressman. The young one asked Tip how he dealt with "the enemy."

Tip leaned back, smiled, and asked, "And just who is the enemy?"

"Why, the Republicans, of course, . . ." said the freshman.

Tip gathered himself up and said, "Young man, the Republicans are the opposition. . . ."

"The Senate is the enemy."[50]

When politicians lose the ability to talk to many of their colleagues, when many of your fellow citizens come to represent evil, it will get harder and harder to work together to overcome the inevitable challenges that all countries face.

I wrote this book hoping to start a serious debate, one that points out that all nations untie and therefore begins by examining the seemingly impossible . . .

Could
It
Even
Happen
to
the
U.S.?

Hopefully you now understand how some of the decisions and actions taken today will determine the answer to this question fifty years hence. . . .

And will choose to do something about it.

CONCLUSION:
WHAT IS YET
TO BE DONE?

January 21, 2008, 8:00 A.M. The White House. The Oval Office.

Faced with an ever more complex agenda, the new president and her chief of staff began their first official meeting a little stunned, concerned, and overwhelmed. They had never thought they would be sitting there having to make these choices, having to sort out these priorities. The anti-campaign had started out as a lark.

A series of mothers got together because they were sick of the endless squabbling, accusations, filibusters, deficits, and radical positions that increasingly guided both parties.

(In 2005, the head of the Democratic National Committee argued "many Republicans had never made an honest living in their lives." In 2005, some prominent Republican leaders were denouncing Democrats as Godless people.)

The Mother's Crusade, inspired by Thomas Paine, was called Common Sense. It was a group that disliked Woody Allen and Michael Jackson. It was also sick and tired of Tom DeLay and the holier-than-thou crowd.

It was a group that did not remotely like or approve of abortions, but it also knew that daughters make mistakes and should not be forced into back alleys.

It was a group that believed in God and in science and thought both should be a part of everyday life. Many had elderly parents who needed more and more care, but they were facing horrid choices in terms of limiting school budgets and mortgaging the kids' future to pay for this care.

Above all, it was a crew that was furious at having to sacrifice retirement savings, jobs, and schools, to fund tax cuts for the very wealthiest, for the top 1,000[th] of the pyramid.

(The recent Bush tax cuts mean those earning more than $10 million per year pay a smaller percentage of their income in taxes than those making $100,000 to $200,000 per year.)[1]

What started as a lark, as a protest, as a cry for change, rapidly grew into a national movement, one that tore traditional political parties apart.

Overwhelmed by divisive and vindictive politics, tired of the stream of body bags coming back from Iraq and Afghanistan, of husbands losing jobs to better-educated Chinese, more and more women were joining. The movement grew. The media paid attention, played up their positions, forced the traditional candidates to address their concerns.

But no one, including the parties, the candidates, the media, or even the members of Common Sense, saw this movement as a real challenge, as a true campaign.

Then came the crash.

China, tired of saber-rattling over Taiwan, over trade deficits, over pressure to revalue the Yuan, over North Korea, made a very deliberate political calculation. They could, within an authoritarian system, take a lot more political pressure and pain than could an American administration. So they gradually quit buying treasury bills and began investing in gold, silver, platinum, diamonds, oil, and commodity futures.

The dollar began to drop.

Interest rates began to rise.

Other countries diversified out of dollars.

Many Middle Eastern governments, having felt bullied for years, joined in, dumping their vast reserves.

Because many Americans were so highly leveraged and so dependent on real estate, the resulting rise in interest rates had a cascade effect. Faced with the new and draconian personal bankruptcy laws, many decided to sell immediately and salvage part of their capital. But because so many of the recent condos, developments, apartments, lofts, golf homes, and time shares were bought on the basis of speculation, there was little real demand.

Home values fell fast.

Because most people's wealth and savings were in their homes, this crash hurt people far more than the NASDAQ/S&P 500 collapse of 2000.

People despaired.

Tired of politics and business as usual, the voters began looking for alternatives.

Previous third party candidacies had languished: in Ross Perot's eccentricities, in Pat Buchanan's hatreds, in a modest and decent John Anderson. So no one expected that a new movement, one initiated by housewives, would go anywhere.

Except it did.

Years of grass roots organizing for kids' car pools, soccer games, Tupperware, Mary Kay cosmetics, PTA, safe streets, church bake sales, and corporate retreats generated a series of vast networks that understood most people were working harder and making less.

It was a group that was sick of bravado and few results.

A group sick of too much testosterone and too little civility.

Common Sense membership exploded; it was a group of folks who when asked, "Would you vote for Mr. XXX on the right or Mr. YYY on the left?" would tend to answer, "Really and truly none of the above." Soon the movement grew far beyond what any of the founders expected. They decided they need professional leadership for Common Sense.

They began recruiting, but shunned politicians.

Eventually they found a smart, tough CEO. One who had run a growth business, not one dependent on political largesse. Still no one expected a political tsunami. Their aspiration was simply to make a statement.

But most voters were so exasperated with politics as usual that when they stepped into the voting booth, their vote turned into a protest vote.

(To quote American poet Nikki Giovanni, citizens decided to "remove from your life those who offer you despair and disrespect.")[2]

Independent candidates, running on third-party platforms, did very well at every level, and an outsider won the presidency.

The heretofore behemoth governing party came close to disappearing . . . in a single election.

(Before you totally discount this type of scenario, realize it has already occurred in places such as Canada, Peru, Mexico, Spain, and Japan.)

So it came to be that on January 20, 2008, the new president of the United States of America faced a daunting task, how to keep a great nation from untying, from tearing itself apart through hatreds and growing divisions.

She set a few priorities during her first day in office . . .

Give people an incentive to create real wealth.

If you can make more money buying, selling, and flipping real estate, why bust a gut studying bioinformatics, nanotechnology, and building a startup? Not enough remain disciples of Thomas Alva Edison who once said, "Opportunity is missed by most people because it is dressed in overalls and looks like work."

The new president proposed a series of radical revisions to the existing tax code. One could deduct interest payments and thus receive a government tax subsidy on one's first home. But one could no longer deduct a series of real-estate-related transactions, including second homes, most rentals, homes over $3 million.

If these changes were passed, despite the violent and virulent opposition of various and sundry inhabitants of the Gucci Gulch lobbying teams, people would really begin to assess whether they were buying a home to live in, whether renting a second home made economic sense, if the vacation home was really worth it . . .

Supply and demand might begin to align.

To counter the political pull of the elderly vote, the new president proposed taking the notion of one person/one vote to its logical conclusion.

Each person, regardless of age, should have a vote.

Before age eighteen, parents would have one proxy vote per child. If the two parents could not agree, the vote would be nullified or one parent would agree to vote for one of the children. This policy began to moderate the extraordinary political influence of the senior vote and provided cover for those wishing to invest in the future.

During the brutal campaign and upheaval that led to a third party candidate, California voters had characteristically placed a radical proposition on the ballot. Many were tired of having to choose, in election after election, between bad and worse candidates. Too many were voting for someone because they disliked someone else even more. Now they had decided to do something about this.

The same folks that organized to recall Governor Grey Davis were now demanding that each ballot, in each election, also have an option that read:

"None of the above."

The organizers proposed that, in any given election, if this were the option chosen by the greatest number of voters, then no one would be elected. Instead, a special election would be scheduled, and none of the candidates who had been on the original ballot would be allowed to run for that specific office for five years.

California voters, tired of manipulated primaries, many dominated by the most radical groups within their party, passed the proposition overwhelmingly.

Now the new president decided, as a part of her agenda for reform and renewal, to strongly endorse this proposal and try to make it national.

(The SEC soon followed up and proposed to place the same type of provision on all corporate board ballots.)

The president began stressing that tax cuts and debt are one and the same. If you cut taxes today but national debt goes up, you and your children will eventually pay a lot more.

By changing national accounting to include net taxes paid per family plus net debt per family, people could keep a more realistic scorecard. An administration would only be considered successful if net wealth increased, not if payments were postponed.

Recruiting those willing and able to defend the U.S. had become harder and harder. The new president realized that either the U.S. had to severely reduce foreign involvement or it had to recruit more people into military service.

It was not just that the chances of ending up injured or dead in Iraq were about as high as those in Vietnam in 1966, it was the lies; it was the uncertainty. Recruits were tired of bait and switch, of having tours of duty extended and home leave canceled. So were parents. In August 2003, 43% of parents felt they could support their children joining the military. By November 2004, this figure had fallen to 25%.[3]

Short term, the only way for the U.S. to maintain current entanglements, without more recruits, was to begin rebuilding international networks. Increasingly, the country would have to send foreign troops, from ally countries or from the U.N., to various hot spots.

Long term, the only way to maintain dominance and strength was through technological leadership, which means learning.

Schools and academics became a matter of national security.

In a technology driven world, the U.S. overall achievement on international science and math tests is in the high teens.

Just as a varsity sport requires talent, toughness, and twice-a-day practices, competing economically with Japan, Korea, China, Finland, Singapore, and so many others requires outstanding scholarship.

The president trusted her fellow citizens enough to bet that smart countries and smart people reconcile moral beliefs and learning.

> Science doesn't necessarily shut down religion and vice versa. Various translations and interpretations of the Bible, the Torah, the Koran, and every other holy book have proven one thing time and again: We keep learning. We discover an ever more complex and vast universe. And therefore, humans should never place a period where God has placed a comma . . .

Treating science the way one used to treat sex in the 1950s is not smart.

> Libraries and schools used to burn and ban books that tangentially addressed sex. To celebrate the new millennium and the greatest explosion of data and knowledge ever seen, many U.S. schools have been busily banning or burying evolution, Darwin, fossils, the age of the Earth. . . .

A festival to ban books and articles related to various aspects of science? We have seen this picture before. When the feeling that "we know enough already and do not have to learn or teach a lot more" permeates a society, declines soon follows.

> (i.e., Egypt 1200s, China 1300s, Spain 1490s, Japan 1600s, Mexico 1800s, France 2000s)

Still, the new president realized that technology was moving so fast and changing so many parameters of what humans could or could not do, that many felt hopelessly left behind.

> This was a particularly sore issue among the poorest Hispanics, blacks, and whites. And soon this group will represent more than 40% of America.

The president, faced with overwhelming challenges during her first days in office, did understand that there was one overarching priority:

Make it unrewarding and uncomfortable for anyone, in the mainstream, to promote untying.

> The president was convinced entertainers, actors, and pundits may engage in amusing or outrageous discourse, but no reasonable politician should follow this route, nor should they incite citizens toward bitterly divisive discourse and behavior. She did not believe that this is a country where most resemble, or think like, either Howard Stern or Rush Limbaugh.

The idea was not to outlaw free speech, but it was to continuously question and expose the issues and to make people understand the consequences of demonizing large sectors of their fellow citizens.

Over the few weeks that followed, the deteriorating overall economic situation forced a series of draconian cuts and reallocations of federal and state budgets.

Many blamed immigrants and imports for the lack of jobs and income. Open borders got a lot tighter.

But the president realized that the primary reason for having to face such painful choices and adjustments lay primarily within.

The country, companies, and individuals had for years mortgaged the future through debt, had endorsed various and sundry tax cuts while attempting to fund and fight a couple of wars, and had neglected the only thing that powers today's countries in the long term: education and brains.

Faced with many on the far left and the far right pushing differences, hatred, divisions, the president knew she had to take control of the agenda, to provide a space for moderation, compromise, and shared pain.

So when suffering extreme attacks for attempting to unite, restructure, and rebuild a sustainable future, the president began answering with a shorthand phrase:

"Are you seeking to untie?"

This is a book written out of love and respect for Mexico, for the U.S., for Canada, Thailand, Australia, Britain, Nepal, Bhutan, Argentina, Brazil, Ecuador, Peru, Singapore, Malaysia, China, Japan, Costa Rica, France, the UK, Italy, U. A. E., and so many other places that have been so kind to me as I have crisscrossed the globe. These trips have reminded me time and again of a few great lines of Alfred, Lord Tennyson's "Ulysses": *"Much I have seen and know,—cities of men/ And manners, climates, councils, governments/ Myself not least, but honor'd of them all,—"* My desire is not to have these countries fight, split, or disappear. My desire is simply that citizens in each realize what they have, what they are doing, and what they might do differently if they wish to avoid what so many have already gone through.

Many people helped me understand the world. I am particularly indebted to Rodrigo Martinez, a good friend and colleague who helped with the first two versions of this book. Gaye Bok, Alison Sander, Jane Delgado, Louie Cabot, and Caleb Winder were full of thoughts, knowledge, and research. Bill Moore, Ann Schneider, James Cabot, and Lisa Goldberg helped going over data, digging up facts, providing ideas. Chris Meyer and I began to explore the world of deficits together. Many people helped clear up errors and inconsistencies, strengthening arguments and questioning assumptions. John Schneider, Mary Schneider, Paul Davis, Oscar Arguelles, Enrique Marquez, and Luis Sanchez helped redirect and rationalize the book by carefully commenting on the manuscript. I hope the book reflects their hard work.

I was inspired by great teachers, mentors, and colleagues: Bruce Scott, George Lodge, Jorge Dominguez, Ray Goldberg, Jonathan West, Mala Htun, Linda Bilmes, John Coatsworth, Jack Womack,

Otto Solbrig, Lubna al Qasimi, John McArthur, Craig Venter. Special thanks to Barbara Rifkind, who first as an agent and then as a friend made this a reality.

Many authors and journalists helped me understand and see the world in a different way. Some I have met and consider friends, others I have just read and learned from. They include Alejandro Junco, Larry Rother, Phil Bennet, Robert Kaplan, Benjamin Barber, Rysard Kapuchinsky, Ramon Alberto Garza, Farred Zacharia, Tim Golden, John Ellis, Chris Anderson, Andres Openheimer, Julia Preston, and Mari Carmen Vergara. Moises Naim helped me start down this road by publishing some early thoughts about countries and their destinies in *Foreign Policy.*

Helen Reese, my agent, brought *As the Future Catches You* and this book to an extraordinarily talented and patient editor, John Mahaney, and his talented assistants, Shana Winghert and Lindsay Orman. Together they steered a great team of designers, photo and text editors, as well as fact checkers. Toby Greenberg did a wonderful job with images and clearances.

Various activists continue lonely battles to bring the plight of their region or ethnic group to the attention of the majority. Foremost among these are folks like Mike Graham and Lucas Benitez. They taught me to see a lot of wrong. Fortunately, a series of businessmen also taught me how to build things and have the resources to set things right. They include David Rockefeller, Bill Harmon, Sam Bodman, Ken Burnes, and John Cabot.

John and Elizabeth Moors Cabot taught me from a very early age, the importance of diplomacy and of understanding why others think and act the way they do. Lessons were reinforced after Antonio Enriquez Savignac became secretary general of the World Tourism Organization and began sharing hundreds of anecdotes and lessons from every corner of the Earth.

And, of course, my greatest thanks to Mary, Diana, and Nico, for their patience and love.

CHAPTER 1: HOW DARE YOU . . .

1. For this and other useless but fun trivia, visit http://www.econ. iastate.edu/classes/econ355/choi/rank.htm.
2. Pete Peterson, *Running on Empty* (New York: Farrar Strauss & Giroux, 2004).
3. N. Gregory Mankiw, chairman of the Council of Economic Advisers, December 2, 2004, speech, Washington, D.C.
4. David Walker's January 23, 2004, speech was widely reported, including the *Post Gazette.* See "Top Fiscal Watchdog Delivers Stinging Attack on Deficit," www.postgazette.com/pg/04023/ 264717.stm.
5. Newt Gingrich, speech for Chatham Institute (Dana Point, California, November 5, 2004).
6. George W. Bush, "Strengthening Social Security," January 11, 2005. Needless to say, statements as strong as this one and Karl Rove's "The current system is heading for an iceberg" have been catalysts for bitter debates. Most agree that spending is out of control, but the root causes and solutions are still hotly contested. Some feel tax cuts have nothing to do with budget deficits. Some believe privatizing Social Security will bring about a stock market boom and higher returns. Daniel Gross in "Social Security Bashing: A Historical Perspective" (*New York Times* January 16, 2005, p. 6) points out that predictions of fiscal doom surrounding Social Security and Medicare have been around even before the programs were launched. But of course the question remains, to quote Malcolm Gladwell, Is there a tipping point? Are we close to it?
7. Alan Greenspan, European Banking Congress 2004 (Frankfurt, Germany, November 19, 2004). Robert B. Reich quote from *Locked in the Cabinet* (New York: Knopf, 1997), p. 65.

8. Dennis Cauchon and John Waggoner worked with the Urban Institute and produced a great series, "One Nation Under Debt" for *USA Today*; October 4–5, 2004. They focused on hidden liabilities and how costs for current programs escalate, along with debt. http://www.usatoday.com/news/nation/2004-10-03-debt-cover_x.htm.

9. Edmund L. Andrews wrote a brutal dissection of the budget: "In Plan to Reduce Deficit by Half, Bush Administration Turns to Old Projections," *New York Times*, January 2, 2005, p. 14.

10. Elizabeth Becker, "Trade Gap Widens on Record Imports," *New York Times*, March 12, 2005, p. B1. In January 2005 the U.S. imported $159.10 billion and exported $100.83 billion.

11. U.S. Bureau of Labor Statistics. Court Smith, Oregon State University has put up some worrisome graphs on this trend: http://oregonstate.edu/instruct/anth484/minwage.html.

12. Issue Brief, "Fiscal Policy in Campaign 2004: Electing the First President of the Senior Boom," *Concord Coalition*, October 21, 2004, p. 9. Editorial, "The Social Security Crisis," *Asian Wall Street Journal*, December 17–19, 2004, p. A7.

13. Data from Brookings Institution and the Congressional Budget Office. Reported in Jonathan Weisman, "Aging Population Poses Global Challenges," *Washington Post*, February 2, 2005, p. 1.

14. "Key Questions Voters Should Ask the Candidates About the Budget, Social Security, Medicare," *Concord Coalition*, 2004.

15. Gov. Haley Barbour. Medicaid now covers 60% of the country's total nursing home bill and is 40% of the revenue of hospitals that cater to the poorest folks. See Sarah Lueck, "Surging Costs for Medicare Ravage State, Federal Budgets," *Wall Street Journal*, February 7, 2005, p. 1.

16. Floyd Norris, "Is It Time to Stem Asia Deficits With a Weak Dollar?" *New York Times*, October 22, 2004, p. C1.

17. Emmanuel Todd, *Après l'Empire: Essai sur la Decomposition du Systeme Americain* (Paris: Editions Gallimard, 2002).

18. "America's Privilege: World Worry?" *Economist*, November 8, 2004.

19. By 2004, the U.S. government owed $817 billion to Japan, $600 billion to China, $235 billion to Taiwan, and $193 billion to South Korea. James Brooke and Keith Bradsher, "Dollar's Fall

Tests Nerves of Asia's Central Bankers," *New York Times*, December 4, 2004.

20. It is useful to recall the collapse of the previous great era of globalization, the 1870s through World War I, and the seeds of nationalism/depression/war this planted. See, for example, Harold James, *The End of Globalization: Lessons From the Great Depression* (Boston: Harvard University Press, 2002); Kevin O'Rourke and Jeffrey Williamson, *Globalization and History: The Evolution of a Nineteenth-Century Atlantic Economy* (Boston: MIT Press, 1981 reprint).

21. "America's Privilege: World Worry?" *Economist*, November 8, 2004.

22. Greg Ip, "Dollar's Fall Risks Plunging U.S. Economy Into Crisis," *Wall Street Journal Europe*, January 18, 2005, p. 1.

23. Nick Carver et al, poll by Central Banking Publications, reported by Chris Gilles, "Central Banks Turn From U.S.," *Financial Times*, January 24, 2005, p. 1.

24. Interview with Linda Bilmes, Kennedy School of Government, Cambridge, Mass., March 2005.

25. Roger Lowenstein, *When Genius Failed: The Rise and Fall of Long-Term Capital Management* (New York: Random House, 2000); Jill Treanor, "Hedge Fund Warning as HBSC Posts Record Profit," *The Guardian*, August 3, 2004.

26. Nanette Byrnes, "The Coming Pension Crunch," *Business Week*, September 15, 2004, http://www.businessweek.com/bwdaily/dnflash/sep2004/nf20040915_8863.htm.

27. Alan Greenspan, testimony, Senate Banking Committee, February 24, 2004.

28. http://financialservices.house.gov/media/pdf/100604ba.pdf.

29. Commerce Department News Release, "Personal Income and Outlays," December 1, 2004, *http://www.bea.gov/bea/newsrel-archive/2004/pi1004.htm*. Calculation covers personal income as a percent of disposable personal income.

30. Dennis Cauchon and John Waggoner, "$84,454 Is Average Household's Personal Debt," *USA Today*, October 4–5, 2004.

31. Shawn Tully, "Is the Housing Boom Over?" *Fortune*, September 20, 2004. He bases the data on Fidelity National Financial and HSBC analyst reports.

32. Data from LoanPerformance Inc. and National Association of Realtors, Motoko Rich, "Boom in Prices Brings Investors to Home Sales," *New York Times*, March 1, 2005, p. 1.

33. PMI Mortgage Insurance Co., *Winter 2005 Risk Index.*

34. Alex Chadwick, "Health Care Costs Lead to Personal Bankruptcies," NPR Special, February 3, 2005.

35. Alan Cowell, "Personal Debt Surges in Britain," *New York Times*, September, 3, 2003, p. W1.

36. Gabrielle Gelati, "Why Has Global FX Turnover Declined? Explaining the 2001 Triennial Survey," *BIS Quarterly Review*, December 2001.

37. George Soros and Geoff Shandler, *The Crisis of Global Capitalism: Open Society Endangered* (Boulder: Public Affairs, 1998). One measure of how globalized the world has become is that Hans Tietmeyer, president of the Bundesbank, decided to speak at the *Wall Street Journal*'s Americas Conference, New York City, October 2, 1998. Among his comments: " 'Globalization should be stopped' is a simplistic strategy but there are legitimate questions regarding the current management of markets."

38. Lewis, a high school dropout whose father was an English pub owner, is fanatic about his privacy. His first newspaper interview was granted to Timothy L. O'Brien and published in the *New York Times*, "Into the Lair of a Currency-Trading Tiger," May 10, 1998, p. 1.

39. Eugene Linden, "Asia: How to Kill a Tiger. Speculators Tell the Story of Their Attack Against the Bath," *Time International*, March 11, 1997, p. 24.

40. Stephen F. Frank, "Harvard Puts Losses From Investments at $1.3 Billion Since Beginning of July," *Wall Street Journal*, September 1998. Most of this capital was later recuperated in subsequent market swings.

41. The standards of what makes a particular individual powerful and successful are constantly changing. When Pheidippides ran from Marathon to Athens, he died of exhaustion. In the first modern Olympic games, in 1896, only one foreigner finished the race. In April 1999, more than twelve thousand ran in the Boston Marathon.

42. Gregory Millman, *The Vandal's Crown: How Rebel Currency Traders Overthrew the World's Central Banks* (New York: Free Press, 1995).

43. Thomas L. Friedman argues this point convincingly in *The Lexus and the Olive Tree* (New York: Farrar, Straus & Giroux, 1999).

44. Federal Reserve Bank of New York, *The Foreign Exchange and Interest Rate Derivatives Markets: Turnover in the United States*, April 2004, p. 2.

45. Speech by Carlos Gomez y Gomez, XII International Symposium of Public Accountants (Monterrey, California. October 14, 1998). Also see speeches by Alfonso Romo Garza.

46. Speech to President Zedillo by Eugenio Clariond (Consejo Mexicano de Hombres de Negocios, March 11, 1999), reported in Mariel Zuniga, "Exige IP a Zedillo Dollarizar," *Reforma*, March 12, 1999.

47. Poll done by Monitor de La Manana, Mexico City, 1998.

48. See, for example, "Mexicans Quietly Mull Tying Peso to Dollar," by Jonathan Friedland, *Wall Street Journal*, September 28, 1998, p. 1.

49. William Finnegan wrote a tough, bitter article against the Washington Consensus: "The Economics of Empire," *Harpers*, May 2003, pp. 41–54.

50. Thomas Fleming, "America's Crackup," *National Review*, July 28, 1997.

51. CNN/AP, "Killington Residents Vote to Secede from Vermont," March 14, 2004; Carolyn Handy, "Ludlow Listens as Killington Talks Secession," *Rutland Herald*, August 17, 2004.

52. Peter Overby, "We're Outta Here! Modern Political Secession Movements in the U.S.," *Common Cause*, Winter 1992.

53. Associated Press, "Senators Want Eastern Washington as 51st State," February 23, 2005.

54. Frederick Wehrle, *Le Divorce Tchecoslovaque* (Nonette: Editions Creer, 1991).

55. Pascal Boniface, "The Proliferation of States," *Washington Quarterly* 21, no. 3 (Summer 1998), p. 116. See also Paul Grande, *Vie et Mort de la Yugoslavie* (Paris: Fayard, 1992).

56. Paul Collier, "Economic Causes of Civil Conflict and Their Implications for Policy," *World Bank Paper 2000*, p. 10.

57. If you want to put this in social-scientese . . . "Countries, and the notion of sovereignty, are social constructs and therefore subject to changing interpretations." Samuel Barkin and Bruce Cronin, "The State and the Nation: Changing Norms and the Rules of Sovereignty in International Relations," *International Organization* 48, no. 1 (Winter 1994), p. 108. There are some who argue that sovereignty is far more stable and absolute. See, for instance, Stephen Krasner, "Sovereignty: An Institutional Perspective," *Comparative Political Studies*, April 1988, pp. 66–94. Most heads of state prefer to believe this later interpretation. History tends to prove them wrong.

58. James Robertson, *American Myth, American Reality* (New York: Hill and Wang, 1980). He continues: "Myths are the patterns— of behavior, of belief, and of perception—which people have in common. Myths are not deliberately, or necessarily consciously, fictitious" (p. xv).

59. The British Empire map is courtesy of the Victoria and Albert Museum, London/Art Resource, New York. Empires do love their maps. You can collect beautiful debris of this hubris at places like Martayan Lan in New York or Jonathan Potter in London. The wonderful maps of the 1500s, 1600s, and 1700s are reminders of just how often old borders disappear and then reappear.

60. Calculation based on *The Historic and Modern Atlas of the British Empire* (UK: Methuen & Co., 1905) and *Britannica Almanac 2003*.

61. Based on questions posed in an excellent book by Robert H. Jackson: *Quasi-states: Sovereignty, International Relations, and the Third World* (UK: Cambridge University Press, 1990), p. 13. It provides a good overview of the conditions necessary to maintain a sovereign state.

62. http://www.dailyrepublican.com/constitution-test.html. The test is due to change in 2006. Bureaucrats have been rewriting it since 2001. . . .

63. Marvin Virgil Stenhammar testified before the U.S. Senate Judiciary committee on July 8, 1998. Nat Hentoff wrote a very powerful op-ed explaining these ideas, "Worshiping the Flag," *Washington Post*, September 12, 1998, p. A19.

64. Raymond Lindquist, pastor, Hollywood Presbyterian Church, California. According to Guru.net, Lindquist said: "Every great preacher had better be manic-depressive. He or she needs to be high at 11:00 on Sunday morning, preaching with all the confidence of divine authority. And that preacher had better be low by 2:00 on Sunday afternoon, or he will be impossible for his wife to live with the rest of the week."

65. Designed by technocrats, the flag brought together a blue crescent representing Islam, two blue lines representing the Tigris and Euphrates rivers, and a yellow stripe recognizing the Kurdish minority. Within minutes of unveiling, some began comparing the color and design with the flag of Israel and that was the end of that. . . . You can follow one thread of reaction to the new symbol on the BBC's Web site: http://news.bbc.co.uk/2/hi/middle_east/3660663.stm.

66. To simplify a complex debate, this book will use the terms *state* and *country* interchangeably. Lawrence Ziring, Jack C. Plano, and Roy Olton in *The International Relations: A Political Dictionary* define *state* as "a social group that occupies a defined territory and is organized under common political institutions and an effective government." Some add that the group must be willing to assume the international legal obligations of statehood. Any given country may contain several distinct nations within or across its borders. A *nation* is a "distinct race or people, characterized by common descent, language, or history" per the *Shorter Oxford Dictionary* (Oxford: Clarendon Press, 1998).

67. Some of the most common explanations include foreign invasion (all ex-colonies), extreme corruption (Zaire); religious/ethnic differences (Afghanistan, Algeria, Yugoslavia, India); drug wars (Colombia, Laos, Myanmar); civil war (Angola, Cambodia, Liberia, Sierra Leone); mismanagement and repression (Iraq, East Germany, North Korea, USSR); lack of education and overpopulation (Haiti); and ideological warfare (South Vietnam).

68. See, for example, the great atlases by Abraham Ortelius (Antwerp, 1570/1603) and Gerard Mercator/Jodocus Hondius (Amsterdam, 1609).

1. J. Scott Moody, "Federal Tax Burdens and Expenditures by State," *Special Report No. 124* (Washington, D.C.: The Tax Foundation, July 2003); Sumeet Sagoo, "Federal Tax Expenditures by State," *Special Report No. 132* (Washington, D.C.: The Tax Foundation, December 2004).

2. Sumeet Sagoo, "Federal Tax Expenditures by State," *Special Report No. 132* (Washington, D.C.: The Tax Foundation, December 2004); Certificates of Ascertainment and Certificates of Vote Sent to the Archivist of the United States in December 2004, www.archives.gove/federal_register/electoral_college/index. html, cited on the Web site "Presidential Election of 2004, Electoral and Popular Vote Summary," http://www.infoplease.com/ipa/A0922901.html.

3. The Environmental Working Group has built an extraordinary database that allows you to search how much each person and each farm gets, per state, per crop, http://www.ewg.org/farm/; Timothy Egan, "Big Farms Reap Two Harvests With Subsidies and a Bumper Crop," *New York Times*, December 26, 2004.

4. Arthur Ochs Sulzberger quoted in Anthony Bianco's "The Future of The New York Times," *Business Week Online*, January 7, 2005, www.businessweek.com.

5. Rick Lyman, "Some Bush Foes Vote Yet Again With Their Feet, Canada or Bust," *New York Times*, February 8, 2005.

6. Bill Bishop, "The Great Divide. Where We Live. What We Think. How We Vote," *Austin American Statesman*, April 4, 2004. Richard Louv, "The New Segregation," *San Diego Union Tribune*, April 11, 2004.

7. Robert David Sullivan, "Beyond Red & Blue 2004: An Election Analysis" (from the Website CommonWealth: http://www.massinc.org/commonwealth/new_map_exclusive/ post_election_update_2004.html). This is a really interesting and detailed look at some of the political divisions that lie beyond and between state borders. It was important in framing the thinking of the U.S. part of this book. Politbureau quote is from U. Penn Law School's Nathaniel Persily.

8. Dan Brown, *The Da Vinci Code* (New York: Doubleday, 2003). It might amuse you to see the various books that have been put out to refute this book and the review in the *National Catholic Reporter* of four of the eleven books put out so far to counter the claims in the Brown book. http://ncronline.org/NCR_Online/archives2/2004c/091004/091004q.htm.

9. Tim LaHaye and Jerry Jenkins, *Left Behind: A Novel of the Earth's Last Days* (Carol Stream, Ill.: Tyndale House, 1995). This book is merely the first of twelve. . . . And there have, of course, been books negating the entire concept of apocalyptic rapture as something invented in the 1830s by British evangelical John Nelson Darby. See Barbara R. Rossing, *The Rapture Exposed: The Message of Hope in the Book of Revelation* (New York: Westview Press, 2004).

10. Juan Enriquez Cabot, "Interpretar a Dios," *Reforma*, June 16, 2003.

11. Krebs's maps have gotten more sophisticated. Take a look at the latest: http://www.orgnet.com/divided.html.

12. Jon Gertner, "Our Ratings/Ourselves," *New York Times Magazine*, April 10, 2005, p. 40.

13. For example, L. Brent Bozel III, Michael Moore, Ann Coulter, Clyde Prestowitz, David Corn, James Hirsen, and Arianna Huffington.

14. Karl Popper expounds the extreme version of this in *The Open Society and Its Enemies* (1945): "the very thought that natural elements such as nation, linguistic, or racial groups do exist is simply a fabrication."

15. Edmund Burke, *First Letter on a Regicide Peace*, 1796. A great piece, here is an excerpt: "Individuals are physical beings, subject to laws universal and invariable. The immediate cause acting in these laws may be obscure: the general results are subject of certain calculation. But commonwealths are not physical, but moral essences. They are artificial combinations, and, in their proximate efficient cause, the arbitrary productions of the human mind. We are not yet acquainted with the laws which necessarily influence the stability of that kind of work made by that kind of agent. There is not in the physical order (with which they do not appear to hold any assignable connection), a distinct cause by which any of those fabrics must necessarily

grow, flourish, or decay; nor, in my opinion, does the moral world produce anything more determinate on that subject than what may serve as an amusement (liberal, indeed, and ingenious, but still only an amusement) for speculative men. I doubt whether the history of mankind is yet complete enough, if ever it can be so, to furnish grounds for a sure theory on the internal causes which necessarily affect the fortune of a state."

16. Kevin Roberts, CEO of Saatchi and Saatchi, describes the process as generating lovemarks. "A Lovemark is a brand that has created loyalty beyond reason; it's infused with mystery, sensuality and intimacy, and that you recognize immediately as having some kind of iconic place in your heart" (http://www.pbs.org/wgbh/pages/frontline/shows/persuaders/interviews/roberts.html).

17. This is a simplification of a complex process; see Charles S. Maier, *Dissolution: The Crisis of Communism and the End of East Germany* (Princeton: Princeton University Press, 1997).

18. R. Norman Matheny, *Christian Science Monitor*, www.csmonitor.com/durable/1999/11/09/p7s1.htm.

19. Philip Gerard, "Why Extending Soldiers' Time in Iraq Could Prove Dangerous," *History News Network*, http://hnn.us/articles/4974.html; Michael S. Foley, "Can We Really Get by Without a Draft," History News Network, http://hnn.us/articles/5197.html.

20. Susan Crean and Marcel Rioux, *Two Nations: An Essay on the Culture and Politics of Canada and Québec in a World of American Preeminence* (Toronto: James Lorimer & Company, 1983), p.10.

21. As with most everything, this is a more complex story. . . . Turns out there was no one U.S. Confederate flag. There were at least three major iterations of this flag. And the last confederate general, Stanhope Watte, surrendered using a five-star flag that represented the "Cherokee Braves," an alliance of Seminoles, Choctaws, Chickasaws, Cherokees, and Creek Indians. See William M. Grimes-Wyatt and Gregg Biggs, http://images.google.com/imgres?imgurl=fotw.vexillum.com/images/u/us!c128a.gif&imgrefurl=http://fotw.vexillum.com/flags/uscsap1.html&h=216&w=323&prev=/images%3Fq%3DU. S.%2BFlag%2BConfederate%26start%3D20%26svnum%3D1

o%26h1%3Den%261r%3D%26ie%3DUTF8%260e%3
DUTF-8%26sa%3DN.

22. When Ireland joined the EU in 1973, it was the poorest state. By 2004 its GDP per capita was second only to Luxembourg. However, because so much of this belonged to foreign businesses, the GNP was substantially lower. Enterprise Ireland, "Ireland Economic Profile," September 2004, http://www.enterprise-ireland.com/NR/rdonlyres/E35A9AF1-99FE-400F-92D9-8860455DC3E7/0/EconomicProfleSept04_new.pdf.

23. Andrew Kohut, Pew Research Center, Pew Global Attitudes Project, poll taken between February 19 and March 3, 2004.

24. Texas Ordinance of Secession, February 2, 1861, This passed by 166 to 8.

25. Not that the Texas comptroller would have anything more useful to legislate. . . . http://www.window.state.tx.us/comptrol/eyeontex/081803.pdf.

26. *Texian* is what the early inhabitants of Texas were called, particularly those from the Independent Republic. Someday this nickname may resurface. . . .

27. Daniel Miller and Lauren Savage, *Texan Arise: The Republic of Texas, Past, Present, and Future* Frankston: Texas National Press, 2004; Simon Romero, "In Small Town, the Fight Continues for Texas Sovereignty," *New York Times*, February 13, 2005, p. 14.

28. Ernest Gruening, *The State of Alaska* (New York: Random House, 1954), p. 1.

29. Mikhail Dmitrievich Tebenkov, *Atlas of the Northwest Coasts of America: From Bering Strait to Cape Corrientes and the Aleutian Islands* . . . (Kozma Terentov, engraver, 1852).

30. Fareed Zakaria, "The Myth of America's 'Free Security' (Reconsiderations)," *World Policy Journal*, June 22, 1997.

31. Claus Naske and Herman Slotknick, *Alaska: A History of the 49th State* (Grand Rapids, Mich.: William B. Eerdmans, 1979), chap. 3, "The Americanization of Alaska." Of course no native was ever asked if they wished to change before it was a fait accompli. . . .

32. Clarence Hulley, *Alaska 1741–1953* (Portland: Binefords & Mort, 1953), p. 206.

33. Buying the territory required support from two-thirds of the Senate. Out of 45 senators, 27 Ayes, 12 Nays, 6 Absent.

34. Ernest Gruening, *The State of Alaska* (New York: Random House, 1954), pp. 15, 63, and 94.

35. Despite huge herds, apparently only one naturalist, Georg Steller, ever observed and described the sea cow. Ernest Gruening, *The State of Alaska*, pp. 15, 94.

36. Clarence Hulley, *Alaska 1741–1953*, p. 292. Ernest Gruening, *The State of Alaska*, p. 363.

37. Elizabeth Peratrovich, *A Recollection of a Civil Rights Leader* (compiled by central council of Tlingit and Haida, August 1991). This extraordinary woman fought time and again against discrimination in Alaska. She rebutted the senate attacks by coming to the floor and arguing: "I would not have expected that I, who am barely out of savagery, would have to remind gentlemen with five thousand years of recorded civilization behind them of our Bill or Rights" You can read more about her: http://www.alaskool.org/projects/native_gov/recollections/peratrovich/Elizabeth_1.htm.

38. Ernest Gruening, *The State of Alaska*, pp. 356, 368.

39. They based this on the Wheeler-Howard Act (1934), which gave the secretary of the interior the power to incorporate tribes. As Indians began to vote, their power increased. By the 1940s, Klawock Frank Petrovich, Sitka Andrew Hope, Kake Frank Johnson, and Eskimos Percy Ipalook and William Beltz had been elected to the local legislature.

40. 102 Ct. Cl. 209; 1944 U.S. Ct. Cl. Lexis 26, Oct. 2, 1944 (Court of Claims decision).

41. David H. Getches, Charles F. Wilkinson, and Robert A. Williams, *Cases and Materials on Federal Indian Law*, 4th ed. (St. Paul, Minn.: West Publishing Company, 1998), p. 906. Supreme Court decisions confirming that tribal property, fishing, and other rights continued unless the U.S. Congress explicitly extinguished them. Beginning in the 1960s, Inuit and other tribes sued the U.S. Government for their territory (approximately 365 million acres or most of the State of Alaska). The U.S. passed the Alaska Native Claims Settlement Act (ANCSA), with the Alaska Natives receiving $963 million and the right to select 44 million acres to keep in exchange for giving up their claims to most of the state of Alaska. The money

and title were distributed to native-owned corporations chartered under state law and the settlement actively extinguished the natives' hunting, fishing, and water rights.

42. Delegate Anthony J. Diamond, House of Representatives 5205, 73rd Congress, 2nd Session, April 11, 1934, p. 11.

43. Claus Naske and Herman Slotknick, *Alaska: A History of the 49th State* (Grand Rapids, Mich.: William B. Eerdmans, 1979), ch. 7, "Alaska's Rocky Road to Statehood."

44. William R. Hunt, *Alaska: A Bicentennial History* (New York: W.W. Norton, 1976), p. 182.

45. You can see what these secessionist characters are up to in the far North at http://www.akip.org.

46. Richard J. Sweeney, McDonough Business School, Georgetown University, "Secession and Expulsion: Lessons for the EU from United States History 1789–1861," LEFIC Working Paper, pp. 2003–12.

47. Richard Drinnon, *Facing West: The Metaphysics of Indian-Hating and Empire Building* (Minneapolis: University of Minneapolis Press, 1980), p. 313. Much of this Philippines material comes from Deborah Berman Santana's excellent article "*No Somos Unicos:* The Status Question From Manila to San Juan," *Centro* Special Issue: 1898–1998 Part 2, XI:1 (Fall 1999). This is an overview of the differences and difficulties facing all those who live under the U.S. flag but have very different rights and privileges.

48. Ironically, no Panamanian ever signed the treaty granting the canal zone in perpetuity to the U.S. A Frenchman, Phillipe Buneau-Varilla, seeking to protect his investment, signed "on behalf" of Panama (Hay-Buneau Treaty).

49. The basis for this is article 9 of the Paris treaty and the U.S. constitution's treatment of territories. The U.S. Supreme Court ruled in 1980 that Puerto Rico is governed under the territorial clause of the constitution.

50. San Juan Mayor Sila M. Calderon quoted in "Marking a Puerto Rican Anniversary," *New York Times,* July 26, 1998, p. 24.

51. Poll done by *El Nuevo Dia,* 1996. In the 1998 plebiscite, 50.3% voted for continuing the commonwealth status quo and 46.5% for statehood.

52. Josh Levin, *Slate*, "The 2004 Olympics: A Dialogue on the U.S.–Puerto Rico Basketball Game," August 15, 2004, http://slate.msn.com/id/2105188/#ContinueArticle.

53. Jorge Duany, *The Puerto Rican Nation on the Move: Identities on the Island and in the United States* (Chapel Hill: University of North Carolina Press, 2002), p. 238.

54. About 3.4 million Puerto Ricans live on the mainland vs. 3.9 million on the island. Deborah Ramirez, "A Voting Block Just Waiting to Happen," *South Florida Sun-Sentinel*, January 26, 2002, p. 19A.

55. Jorge Duany, *The Puerto Rican Nation on the Move: Identities on the Island and in the United States*, p. 31.

56. Much of this section on Puerto Rico reflects a discussion that took place at the Kennedy School of Government on April 29, 1998. Two papers were particularly relevant: former Attorney General Dick Thornburgh's "Constitutional Framework for Self-Determination in Puerto Rico" and Harvard's Tax Program Director Glenn Jenkin's and J. Thomas Hexner's "Puerto Rico: An Economic and Fiscal Briefing." See also Alexander Odishelidze's "Puerto Rico at a Crossroads."

57. The Northwest Ordinance of 1787 allows territories with a population of 5,000 adults to elect a local legislature and send a nonvoting member to congress. After reaching a voter population of 60,000, the territory can petition for statehood.

58. Ted Miller, "American Football, Samoan Style," ESPN, May 28, 2002, http://espn.go.com/gen/s/2002/0527/1387562.html.

59. Deborah Berman Santana wrote a good overview of the differences and difficulties facing all those who live under the U.S. flag but have very different rights and privileges. "*No Somos Unicos:* The Status Question From Manila to San Juan."

60. USCIS "Announces New Work Authorization Requirements for the Citizens of the Federated Republic of Micronesia," press release, July 2, 2004, http://uscis.gov/graphics/publicaffairs/newsrels/Micronesia07_02_04.pdf.

61. *The New York Times Almanac 1998* (New York: Penguin Putnam, 1997), p. 205.

62. http://www.cia.gov/cia/publications/factbook/geos/cq.html.

63. And by the way, there are even areas that are "unorganized American territories." They have no citizens and are administered by the secretary of the interior. Even these can lead to conflict. The U.S. has controlled Navassa, a small island just off Haiti, for 140 years, but Haiti has also claimed the rock since its independence in 1804. The U.S. wants to preserve the island as a biological reserve while Haiti wants to mine guano and mythical deposits of gold and uranium. See Larry Rother, "Whose Rock Is It Anyway? And, Yes the Haitians Care," *New York Times*, October 19, 1998, p. A4.

64. James Brooke, "China Sees Chances for Fun and Profit Offshore," *New York Times*, November 25, 2004.

65. This is just looking at what is already within the U.S. borders. Never mind those on the fringe deliberately plotting additional expansion. There are groups, like the Expansionist Party of the United States. Their ambitions go beyond the already-held territories in the Caribbean and Pacific. They advocate merging with places like Britain, Australia, New Zealand. And they claim to be working with foreign counterparts in places like Taiwan, Israel, and Canada. *http://members.aol.com/xpus/index.html.*

66. Resident Representative Juan N. Babauta, Commonwealth of the Northern Mariana Islands, spoke before the House Resources Committee regarding Enforcement of Federal Law in the CNMI on September 16, 1999. He argued: "Here in the third century of our democracy there remain four million U.S. citizens who are denied the right to vote for the laws that govern them or the right to vote for the President who administers those laws simply because those citizens live in American Samoa and Guam and Puerto Rico, the Virgin Islands and the Marianas. Why even US citizens living in foreign countries can vote for members of Congress and the President. Only those of us in America's "territorial" enclaves are denied this fundamental right of citizenship."

CHAPTER 3: TECHNOLOGY AND RELIGION'S BRUTAL MARCH

1. "Tech Centers' Political Swing Reflects Growing Split in U.S.," *Austin American Statesman* (Texas), December 22, 2002; Bill

Bishop and Mark Lisheron, http://proquest.umi.com/pqdweb, January 7, 2003, p. 2.

2. Instituto Brasileiro de Geografia e Estatistica, MEC, Lucent report.

3. UNDP statistics cited in Kristian Heggenhougen, "Human Rights and Health in Latin America," *DRCLAS News*, Spring 1998, p. 11.

4. Data from Achieve Inc., a nonprofit, nonpartisan group established by the National Governor's Association.

5. Want to scare yourself a little? Go to www.GlobalSecurity.org.

6. John H. Coatsworth, "Economic and Institutional Trajectories in Nineteenth-Century Latin America," in John H. Coatsworth and Alan M. Taylor, eds., *Latin America and the World Economy Since 1800* (Cambridge, Mass.: Harvard University DRCLAS, 1999).

7. Victor Alba, *Nationalists Without Nations: The Oligarchy Versus the People in Latin America* (New York: Praeger, 1968), p. 57–58.

8. John H. Coatsworth, "Economic and Institutional Trajectory in Nineteenth-Century Latin America," in John H. Coatsworth and Alan M. Taylor, eds., *Latin America and the World Economy Since 1800*, pp. 26, 43.

9. Angus Maddison, *Monitoring the World Economy 1820–1992* (Paris OECD, 1995), p. 23.

10. Peter Lyman and Hal R. Varian, "How Much Information," 2000. From http://www.sims.berkeley.edu/how-much-info.

11. Lee Gomes, "Miniaturization Is Key to Computer's Growth, But Parts Sure Are Tiny," *Wall Street Journal*, February 7, 2005, p. B1.

12. Kenichi Ohmae, *The End of the Nation State* (London: Harper Collins, 1995), p. 8.

13. "Internal Strains Forecast for China; U.S. Aid Chief Cites Income Disparities and Ethnic Tensions" *International Herald Tribune*, March 3, 2005.

14. Chris Buckley, "Let a Thousand Flowers Bloom: China Is a Hotbed of Research," *New York Times*, September 13, 2004, p. C1.

15. James Robertson, *American Myth, American Reality* (New York: Hill and Wang, 1980), pp. 280–294.

16. Patricia Devaney from Stanford University's Office of Science Outreach wrote a devastating critique of the state of science education in the U.S.: http://www.stanford.edu/group/oso/mission.html, March 1, 2004.

17. Luis Fernando Ramirez and Juan Enriquez were able to study Korea in the summer of 1996 thanks to the help of Dal Ho Chung, Steve Bloomfield, Prof. Young-Jin Kim, and the Weatherhead Center Fellows Program.

18. World Bank, *World Development Indicators 1997*, pp. 284–287.

19. Cornelia Dean, "A New Screen Test: It's Bible vs. the Volcano," *New York Times*, March 18, 2005.

20. William J. Bernstein, *The Birth of Plenty* (New York: McGraw-Hill, 2004), p. 110.

21. David J. Elkins, *Beyond Sovereignty; Territory and Political Economy in the Twenty-First Century* (Toronto: University of Toronto Press, 1995), p. 13.

22. Bernard Lewis has written extensively on this phenomenon. See, for example, *What Went Wrong? The Clash Between Islam and Modernity in the Middle East* (New York: Perennial, 2003). Income calculation vs. OECD was done by Bruce Scott. See also Juan Enriquez and Helen Quigley, "Will Life Sciences Be a Driving Force of the 21st-Century Economy? Challenges for Arabic-Speaking Countries," *Harvard Business School Working Paper 03-114* (2002).

23. William J. Bernstein, *The Birth of Plenty* (New York: McGraw-Hill, 2004), p. 33.

24. If you wish to ruin your breakfast, you can read the rest of this most unpleasant document: http://www.jrbooksonline.com/ALHAMBRA_DECREE.htm.

25. John H. Eliott, *The Decline of Spain, Past and Present, no. 20* (Nov. 1961), quoted in William Bernstein, *The Birth of Plenty* (New York: McGraw Hill, 2004).

26. Maureen Dowd, "Sacred Cruelties," *New York Times*, April 7, 2002.

27. CBS News poll, March 23, 2005. Maureen Dowd wrote a devastating column, "DeLay, Deny and Demagogue," *New York Times*, March 24, 2005, p. A 23. Ellen Goodman also wrote a powerful piece, "Death and Politics," *Boston Globe*, March 24, 2005, p. A15.

28. Sheldon Alberts, "A Death with Little Dignity," *National Post*, April 1, 2005, p. A4.

29. John Danforth, "In the Name of Politics," *New York Times*, March 30, 2005.

30. Hay palabras *"que tienen sangre en las silabas."* Pablo Neruda,

Confieso que he Vivido: Memorias (Chile: Universidad de Chile, 1994), p. 30.

31. The *New Advent Catholic Encyclopedia* describes this scene: "Naturally there were trials to be endured and obstacles to be overcome. Some of these obstacles arose from the jealousy of the Jews, who vainly endeavoured to imitate Paul's exorcisms, others from the superstition of the pagans, which was especially rife at Ephesus. So effectually did he triumph over it, however, that books of superstition were burned to the value of 50,000 pieces of silver (each piece about a day's wage). This time the persecution was due to the Gentiles and inspired by a motive of self-interest. The progress of Christianity having ruined the sale of the little facsimiles of the temple of Diana and statuettes of the goddess, which devout pilgrims had been wont to purchase, a certain Demetrius, at the head of the guild of silversmiths, stirred up the crowd against Paul. The scene which then transpired in the theatre is described by St. Luke with memorable vividness and pathos (Acts, xix, 23–40). The Apostle had to yield to the storm." http://www.newadvent.org/cathen/11567b.htm.

32. Andrew Jacobs, "Georgia Takes on Evolution," *New York Times*, January 30, 2004. The measure was partially repealed by outraged parents, but in Cobb County, textbooks still carry a warning label, "Evolution is a theory, not a fact." Andrew Ward, "Atlanta's Way Ahead Battles for Survival With the Old South," *Financial Times*, December 13, 2004, p. 4.

33. Neela Banerjee, "Christian Conservatives Press Issues in Statehouses," *New York Times*, December 13, 2004, p. 1.

34. In a 2004 Gallup Poll, 45% preferred the creationist view while 35% believed Darwin.

35. Rodrigo Martinez, Juan Enriquez, and Jonathan West, "DNA Space. The Geography of the Genome," *WIRED*, June 2003, p. 160.

36. Nucleic Acids Research, 2005. You can access all these databases through http://nar.oupjournals.org/cgi/content/full/33/suppl_1#TBL1.

37. Juan Enriquez, *As the Future Catches You* (New York: Crown Publishing, 2001).

38. The map was researched by Rodrigo Martinez and Juan Enriquez as part of the Harvard Business School's Life Science Project.

39. Zhu Xiao Di, "Million Dollar Homes and Wealth in the United States," Joint Center for Housing Studies, Harvard University, January 2004 (W04-1).

40. Stephen D. Krasner, "Sovereignty," *Foreign Policy*, January/February 2001, p. 26. Stanley A. Renshon, "Dual Citizens in America: An Issue of Vast Proportions and Broad Significance," Center for Immigration Studies, July 2000, http://www.cis.org/articles/2000/back700.pdf.

41. Sam Dillon, "US Slips in Status as Hub of Higher Education," *Bangkok Post*, December 22, 2004, p. 10.

42. Here is how countries ranked in education in 2003: http://nces.ed.gov/timss/Results03.asp?Quest=3.

43. Donald G. McNeil Jr., "The Last Time You Used Algebra Was . . ." *New York Times*, December 12, 2004, p. 3.

44. National Science Foundation, *2004 Science and Technology Indicators* (May 2004), Appendix 2-33.

45. 3% refers to Hispanics who have a BA or more in science and related fields, per Patricia Devaney, Stanford University, Office of Science Outreach, http://www.stanford.edu/group/oso/mission.html, March 1, 2004.

46. Valery A. Tishkov, Conflict Management Group, "Nationalities and Conflicting Ethnicity in Post-Communist Russia" (Working Paper Series, 1993), p. 40.

47. Gary Orfield, "Commentary on the Education of Mexican Immigrant Children Chapter" in Marcelo Suarez Orozco, ed., *Crossings* (Cambridge, Mass.: Harvard University Press, 1998), p. 276. He further argues that the programs that might help incorporate this growing population are being cut back or eliminated, including affirmative action, reasonably priced state school systems, test prep help, government scholarships, minority small business programs, voting rights enforcement, and various civil rights protections (p. 278).

CHAPTER 4: EXCUSE ME . . . I WAS HERE FIRST

1. http://www.theramp.net/kohr4/HEROES.html.

2. Judge George W. Folta, October 7, 1952 (107 Fed. Supp. 697).

3. Joe Titone, "Resolution Would End Tribal Sovereignty,"

Spokesman Review, July 3, 2000. You can read Fleming's side of the story at http://www.parr1.com/Fleming/FlemingArti cleNO12.txt. Clearly, he does not understand the concept that there are sovereign states within the U.S. You might also want to look at a few of the additional complaints Native Americans have; you might be surprised . . .
http://www.theramp.net/kohr4/interestingfacts.html.

4. Press Release, Office of the Mayor, "Mayor to Repeal Indian Imprisonment Act of 1675," November 24, 2004, *Nipmuck Newsletter*, Summer 2003, http://www.cityofboston.gov/news/pr.asp?ID=2387.

5. Urban Institute Survey commissioned by HUD, reported in Genaro C. Armas, "Indians Face Bias, Study Says," *Boston Globe*, November 19, 2003, p. A16.

6. Charlie LeDuff, "Tension Over Who Prospers in Indian Country," *New York Times*, July 18, 2003, p. A11.

7. There seems to be a trend in countries where legal systems are based on English common law. For instance, native Canadian demands that negotiations take place government to government forced a national referendum on whether to establish a "third order of government." Had it been approved, this agreement would have created another layer of government in addition to the federal, provincial, and local levels. The referendum was rejected in October 1992, but the issue continues to smolder. David J. Elkins, *Beyond Sovereignty; Territory and Political Economy in the Twenty-First Century* (Toronto: University of Toronto Press, 1995), p. 208. In Australia, after more than a hundred years of having their lands appropriated, native Australians began to fight back through the courts. In 1971, they lost an important case before the Supreme Court of the Northern Territory (*Milirrpum v. Nabalco Pty, Ltd* 17 F.L.R. 141 [NT Sup. Ct.]) that rejected the notion of aboriginal title. However, subsequently a more sympathetic Australian government came to power and sponsored the Woodward report recommending transfer of Northern Territory tribal lands to aboriginal ownership. In 1976, Australia passed the Aboriginal Land Rights Act, which among other things, established a way for aboriginal peoples to acquire land through a system of land trusts. In 1981,

the Land Acquisition Act was passed to force sales of land to meet aborigine claims. David H. Getches, 4th ed. (St. Paul, Minn.: West Publishing Company, 1998). *Federal Indian Law,* Charles F. Wilkinson and Robert A. Williams, *Cases and Materials,* pp. 1022–1023.

8. Stan Pelczynski, "The Australian High Court Recognition of Native Title—The Mabo Judgement and Its Implications," http://www.innu.ca/mabo.html, July 27, 1993.

9. Initially, the Spanish empire, empowered by Pope Alexander VI's 1493 bulls directing Spain to "colonize, civilize, and Christianize," conquered the American Indians Land through purchase or conquest. Initially it was enough to read out a *Requerimiento* informing the natives that their lands were given to the King and Queen of Spain. However, in the mid-sixteenth century, Spanish legal theory incorporated the notion that the natives had natural rights, but that their unfamiliarity with the European Law of Nations required that they have a "civilized" nation serve as their guardian. Getches et. al., *Federal Indian Law,* p. 46–51.

10. David H. Getches et al., *Federal Indian Law.* J.G.A. Pocock, "Law, Sovereignty, and History in a Divided Culture: The Case of New Zealand and the Treaty of Waitangi," The Iredell Memorial Lecture, Lancaster University, UK, October 10, 1991.

11. *The Treaty of Waitangi (State Enterprises) Act of 1988.*

12. Richard T. Price, "New Zealand's Interim Treaty Settlements and Arrangements—Building Blocks of Certainty" in *Speaking Truth to Power: A Treaty Forum* (British Columbia: Law Commission of Canada, 2000), pp. 135–163.

13. *Haida Nation v. British Columbia (Minister of Forests),* 2004 SCC 73 and *Taku River Tlingit First Nation v. British Columbia (Project Assessment Director),* 2004 SCC 74 were adjudicated jointly. They do not establish clear land title, but in a 7–0 decision they require that Indians be consulted over land use even if they are not clear current owners but claim ancestral land rights. "Haida Launch Aboriginal Title Case in BC Supreme Court," *Tribal Drum,* March 6, 2002. Clifford Krauss, "Natives' Land Battles Bring a Shift in Canada Economy," *New York Times,* December 5, 2004, p. 3.

14. Some citizens of Connecticut are furious at the notion of separate sovereignty. For instance, http://www.connecticut-alliance.org/.

15. Joseph Rosenbloom, "The Big Gamble," *Boston Globe Magazine*, October 19, 2003.

16. For this section I relied extensively on David H. Getches et al., *Federal Indian Law*, particularly pp. 46, 51, 59, and 63.

17. Much of this section draws on an excellent book by Vine Deloria Jr. and Clifford M. Lytle: *The Nations Within: The Past and Future of American Indian Sovereignty* (Austin: University of Texas Press, 1998). It is a brief overview of an area that remains one of the most complex issues of U.S. federal law involving hundreds of treaties, thousands of statutes, and hundreds of thousands of administrative rules.

18. Yale Law School has collected the texts of the key treaties and promises through its Avalon Project. Read them and weep. http://www.yale.edu/lawweb/avalon/ntreaty/ntreaty.htm.

19. Here is one version of what happened thereafter: http://www.rootsweb.com/~pamiffli/indian.html.

20. The Royal Proclamation of 1763 served as a model for the U.S. Constitution. States agreed that "The Congress shall have power . . . to regulate Commerce with foreign Nations, and among the several States, and with the Indian Tribes." See U.S. Statutes at Large, 7:13. See also U.S. Constitution Article 1, Section 8, Clause 3 and the Marshall Trilogy (*Johnson* v. *McIntosh*, 1823; *Cherokee Nation* v. *Georgia*, 1831; and *Worcester* v. *Georgia*, 1832). Among other things, these decisions reinforce "the original inhabitants were admitted to be the rightful occupants of the soil, with the legal as well as the just claim to retain possession of it, and to use it according to their own discretion." Getches et al., *Federal Indian Law*, p. 144.

21. David H. Getches et al. *Federal Indian Law*, p. 152. Over the intervening period, treaties had created more and more reservations that the House of Representatives had to fund, but they were not part of the ratification process. Therefore, they put an end to treaty making with the Indian tribes. From 1871 until 1919, congress gave the president power to create reservations through Executive Order. After 1919, all changes had to be via

an Act of Congress. See, for example, the Elm Tree Treaty. John Gilmary Shea, *The Story of a Great Nation* (New York: Gay Brothers & Company, 1886). http://etc.usf.edu/clipart/5600/ 5614/elm_tree_treaty_1.htm.

22. Angie Wagner, "Hanging on to Heritage," *San Diego Union-Tribune*, May 23, 2004.

23. This Sioux example comes from http://sorrel.humboldt.edu/ ~go1/kellogg/federalrelations.html: "A Brief Historical Overview of the Relationship Between the Federal Government and American Indian: From Colonial Times to the Present." This is an interesting page with several useful links.

24. In the mid-1970s, a growing market for uranium (found on Sioux reservation land) and desire for control over their own lands, prompted the Ogallala Sioux to declare their independence and cited the Fort Laramie Treaty of 1868. Eventually, the U.S. Court of Claims found that no valid agreement had been concluded in 1876 to cede the Black Hills to the U.S., and, after years of court battles, the U.S. government settled on paying $122 million to the tribe as compensation. By the time of settlement, a majority of the Sioux sought for retaining their land rather than accept monetary compensation. Attorneys whose contracts had expired negotiated a final settlement, and the Sioux have yet to accept this compensation, Getches et al., *Federal Indian Law*, p. 285.

25. *Native American Church of North America* v. *Navajo Tribal Council*, 272 F.2d. 131, 134 (10th Cir., 1959).

26. U.S. American Indian Policy Review Commission, *Final Report*, May 17, 1977 (Washington, D.C.: U.S. Government Printing Office, 1977).

27. Donna Lee Van Cott, "Explaining Ethnic Autonomy Regimes in Latin America" (Latin American Studies Association, March 16–18, Miami, Florida).

28. United Native America News. "Origin of the Names of 28 U.S. States: From the Native American Community." Posted January 10, 2005. Like all names from the past, there will be many alternative interpretations and origins. But the point is that the Americas as a whole are covered with Native American names because the Native Americans were there first.

29. Tim Giago wrote a column on this atrocity for *USA Today* in December 1990 to commemorate the hundredth anniversary of the massacre. It is reprinted every year in the *Lakota Times, Indian Country Today,* and the *Lakota Journal.* Lakota march every December 29 to commemorate the massacre and are attempting to get the Medals of Honor revoked.

30. James Robertson, *American Myth, American Reality* (New York: Hill and Wang, 1980), p. 20.

31. There are several sites that describe the revered founding fathers and their successors in slightly different terms from those of your average high school textbook. For instance: http://www.theramp.net/kohr4/HEROES.html, http://www.bluecorncomics.com/uncivil.htm#reagan, and http://www.unitednativeamerica.com/aiholocaust.html.

32. Wolfgang Meidier wrote an extraordinary chapter on "The Only Good Indian Is a Dead Indian: History and Meaning of a Proverbial Stereotype," http://www.dickshovel.com/ind.html. He attributes the Roosevelt quote to Hermann Hagedorn, *Roosevelt in the Bad Lands* (Boston: Houghton Mifflin, 1921), p. 355.

33. There are, of course, two sides to every story, and this is a complex one. Minnesota's Governor Ramsey had sought to kill 303 people. Lincoln negotiated this down to 39. For one version of this story, see http://www.unitednativeamerica.com/issues/lincoln.html.

34. Trevor Hughes, "Council: So Long Chivington," *Daily Times-Call,* December 30, 2004.

35. This is a good Web site to review how many Indians view history: http://www.humboldt.edu/~go1/kellogg/federal relations.html.

36. Henry F. Dobyns, "Estimating Aboriginal American Population: An Appraisal of the Techniques With a New Hemispheric Estimate," *Current Anthropology,* 1966, a paper that is still leading to brutal debates. These controversies were reviewed in an article by Charles C. Mann, "1491," *The Atlantic Monthly,* March 2002, pp. 41–53. See also Alfred W. Crosby, Jr., *The Columbian Exchange: Biological and Cultural Consequences of 1492* (Westport, Conn.: Greenwood, 1972); Henry F. Dobyns, *Their Number Become Thinned: Native American Population Dynamics in Eastern*

North America (Knoxville: University of Tennessee Press, 1983); Russell Thornton, *American Indian Holocaust and Survival: A Population History Since 1492* (Norman: University of Oklahoma Press, 1987); and James Wilson, *The Earth Shall Weep: A History of Native America* (New York: Grove Press, 2000).

37. Ann Coulter, "Not Crazy Horse Just Crazy," February 17, 2005, www.anncoulter.com.

38. UNA-News, "Ann Coulter's racist remarks towards American Indians," February 29, 2005.

39. The Cherokee Tobacco Case 78 U.S. 616, 20 L.Ed. 227, 11 Wall. 616 (1870) began impinging on native sovereignty through taxes in 1879. Then the Seven Major Crimes Act of 1885 continued this trend, as well as the Dawes General Allotment Act of 1888. The Wisconsin Judicare's Indian Law project has put together a summary of seminal Supreme Court cases regarding Indian law cases since 1800, http://www.judicare.org/sct.html. You can see trends first limiting Indian sovereignty and then gradually expanding it. You can see more recent battles in Timothy Egan, "New Prosperity Brings New Conflict to Indian Country," *New York Times*, March 9, 1998.

40. Deloria and Lytle. p. 238.

41. You can read the full text of S.J. 37, 108th Congress, the "Apology Resolution" at http://www.unitednativeamerica.com/issues/res37.html.

42. In 1997, Eric Nadler, Deborah Nelson, and Alex Tizon wrote a great series on HUD and Indian tribes for the *Seattle Times*. Their first article was on the Muckelshoots. Their reporting was awarded a Pulitzer, http://www.pulitzer.org/year/1997/investigative-reporting/works/1-3/.

43. A summary of "Key Issues," *United Property Owners Update*, December 2004, pp. 1–2.

44. Want the conservative take on these issues? See Jan Golab, "The Festering Problem of Indian Sovereignty," *The American Enterprise*, September 2004.

45. www.epa.gov/region09/air/_maps/r9_tribe.html.

46. Kirk Johnson, "A Tribe, Nimble and Determined, Moves Ahead With Nuclear Waste Storage Plan," *New York Times*, February 28, 2005, p. A15.

47. Joseph J. Kolb, "Growing Meth Use on Navajo Lands Brings Call for Tribal Action," *New York Times*, February 7, 2005, p. A19. There was no law to criminalize sale, possession, or manufacture of meth. So tribal police had to treat offenses as federal offenses and have the FBI come in for every case they wished to prosecute.

48. http://www.pbs.org/wotp/tribes/wampanoags/.

49. See Frank B. James et al. Petitioners V. William P. Clark, Sec. of the Interior et al. Petition for Writ of Certiotare. U.S. Supreme Court No. 83-623. Available at www.usdoj.gov/osg/1983/sg830125.txt. This is just one of many issues being negotiated between the federal government and the Wampanoags, www.mvy.com/wpinfo.html.

50. If you would like a glimpse into the legal battles, and particularly the personalities of some of the lawyers involved, take a look at Joseph Rosenbloom's article: "The Big Gamble," *Boston Globe Magazine*, October 19, 2003.

51. James Dao, "Anxiety Growing Over Indian Claim in New York State," *New York Times*, January 13, 1999, p. 1.

52. Kirk Semple, "Tribe Lays Claim to 3,100 Square Miles of New York, But Will Settle for a Clean Lake," *New York Times*, March 11, 2005, p. A14.

53. http://factfinder.census.gov/home/aian/aian_list.xls.

54. Tim Vanderpool, "Border Crackdown Hits Tribes Hard," *Christian Science Monitor*, March 3, 1998, p. 4. In 2003, Arizona Democrat Rich Grijalva pushed a bill that would grant automatic citizenship to members of the tribe whether born in Mexico or the U.S. Dave Wagner, "Southwest Tribe Struggles With Border Woes," *Boston Globe*, April 27, 2003, p. A6.

55. Timothy Egan, "Indians Win Round in Fight on Trust Funds," *New York Times*, February 23, 1999, p. 1.

56. This may just be a preview of coming attractions; see, for example, Billee Elliott McAuliffe, "Forcing Action: Seeking to 'Clean Up' the Indian Trust Fund: Corbell v. Babbitt, 30 F. Supp. 2D 24 (D.D.C. 1998)," *Southern Illinois University Law Journal 25*, no. 3 (Spring 2001).

57. *Cobell* v. *Babbitt* became *Cobell* v. *Norton*, http://doc.narf.org/cases/index.html. See, for instance, Bill McAllister, "Norton

Convicted of Civil Contempt; Judge Lambasts Interior Chief, Aide Over Trust," *Denver Post*, September 18, 2002.

58. Johnnie P. Flynn, "If You Can't Beat Em, Cheat Em," *Indian Country Today*, p. 1.

59. Olga Kharif, "Native Americans Stake a High Tech Claim," *BusinessWeek* on-line, November 26, 2001.

60. Pamela White, "In Search of Justice: Indians vs. the Cavalry Once More," *Boulder Weekly*, April 4, 2002. The article notes that the *Wall Street Journal* has compared the actions of Interior Department officials to those of Enron. . . .

61. John Files, "U.S. Is Ordered to Tell Indians Before Selling Trust Property," *New York Times*, October 4, 2004, p. A17.

62. Pamela White, "In Search of Justice."

63. American Indian Policy Research Institute, "Fundamental Principles of Tribal Sovereignty," www.airpi.org/st98fund.html.

64. UNA-News, "Cobell v. Norton—Structural Injunction Reissued," February 25, 2005.

65. Jeff J. Corntassel and Tomas Hopkins Primeau, "The Paradox of Identity: A Levels-of-Analysis Approach," *Global Governance* 4 (1998): 144.

66. Census 2000 PHC-T-18, "American Indian and Alaska Native Tribes in the United States: 2000. Table 1. American Indian and Alaska Native Alone and Alone or in Combination Population by Tribe for the United States: 2000." In part this reflects the possibility of self-identifying as a member of more than one race in the 2000 census.

67. Tony Horwitz, "Apalachee Tribe, Missing for Centuries, Comes Out of Hiding," *Wall Street Journal*, March 9, 2005, p. A1.

68. http://www.winnememwintu.us/. Environmental Justice Sub-Committee Meeting, California Bay Delta Authority, Sacramento, California. July 9, 2004, http://calwater.ca.gov/BDPAC/Subcommittees/Environmental Justice/EJ_Meeting%20_Notes_7-9-04.pdf; Dean E. Murphy, "At War Against a Dam, Tribe Returns to Old Ways," *New York Times*, September 14, 2004, p. A13.

69. To get a sense of how broad and sophisticated these webs are becoming, take a look at the People's Paths Homepage, http://www.yvwiiusdinvnohii.net/resource.html.

70. Chargoggagoggmanchauggachaubunagungamaugg is the longest place name in the U.S. It reflects past boundaries: "English knifemen and Nipmuck Indians at the boundary or neutral fishing place." Pam Belluck, "What's the Name of That Lake? It's Hard to Say." *New York Times*, November 20, 2004, p. A1.

71. Paula Mitchell Marks, *In a Barren Land: American Indian Dispossession and Survival* (New York: William Morrow, 1998).

72. Speech by Arvol Looking Horse, Keeper of the Sacred Calf Pipe for the Lakotas, Nakota, and Dakota, on behalf of the Sioux Nation. Unrepresented Nations and Peoples Organization (UNPO), The Hague, Netherlands, January 1995.

73. www.un.org/esa/socdev/unpfii/.

74. Lia Zanotta Machado, "Indigenous Communitarianism as a Critique of Modernity and Its Judicial Implications," in Willem Assies and A.J. Hoekema, eds., *Indigenous People's Experiences with Self Government*, IWGIA no. 76, Copenhagen.

75. Donna Lee Van Cott, "Explaining Ethnic Autonomy Regimes in Latin America" (Latin American Studies Association, Miami, Florida, March 16–18).

76. Some Native Americans responded to the apology with a brutal parody, announcing the creation of the Bureau of White Affairs (BWA). If you want to begin to get a sense of how the shoe might fit if it had happened to you . . . http://www.unitednativeamerica.com/bureau/index.html.

77. Timothy Egan, "New Prosperity Brings New Conflict to Indian Country," *New York Times*, March 9, 1998.

78. You can read the amazing original sleazy e-mails at http://www.indian.senate.gov/exhibits.pdf and then look at a few of the articles they inspired, such as editorial, "Sleaze in the Capitol," *New York Times*, January 2, 2005, p. 8; Susan Schmidt, "Papers Show Tribe Paid to Try to Sway Bill," *Washington Post*, November 18, 2004, p. A1; Susan Schmidt, "Ex-Lobbyist Is Focus of Widening Investigation," *Washington Post*, July 16, 2004, p. A19; Andrew Ferguson, "A Lobbyist's Progress: Jack Abramoff and the End of the Republican Revolution," *Weekly Standard*, December 20, 2004.

79. UNA News, Re: Red Lake Shooting, messages posted on Yahoo news report, March 23, 2005. These comments come from

different individuals. Together they create a stream of hate.

80. *Native Hawaiians Study Commission*, vol. 1, pp. 87–88.

81. Eventually the UK ended up taking Australia, Christmas Islands, Cook Islands, Ellice Islands, Fiji, Kiribati, New Hebrides, New Zealand, Niue, Ocean Island, Papua, Rotuma, Solomon Islands, and Tonga. France took Maiao, Marquesas, New Caledonia, Tahiti, Tuamotus, and Wallis. Germany took the Bismark Archipelago, Carolinas, Marianas, Marshall Islands, New Guinea, Solomons, and Western Samoa. The U.S. took Alaska, East Samoa, Guam, Hawaii, Midway, Phillipines, and Wake.

82. And they had support. U.S. Secretary of State James Baline wrote President Harrison on August 10, 1891: "I think there are only three places that are of value enough to be taken that are not continental. One is Hawai'i and the others are Cuba and Porto (sp.) Rico." Ralph S. Kuykendall, *The Hawaiian Kingdom, vol III, 1874–1893, The Kalakaua Dynasty* (Honolulu: University of Hawaii Press, 1967), p. 486.

83. In 1898, the Republic of Hawaii expropriated 1.8 million acres of crown and government lands and ceded those lands to the U.S. Under the Newlands Joint Resolution of 1898 that annexed Hawaii as a U.S. territory, congress gave control of those acres to the territorial government. By the 1920s, the native Hawaiians were mostly relegated to urban slums. Congress created the Hawaiian Home Commission (42 Stat. 108, chapter 42) and redirected 203,500 of the original 1.8 million acres to be used for Hawaiian homesteads. In 1959, the "Act to provide for the admission of the State of Hawaii into the Union (Public Law 86-3; 73 Stat. 4) ceded 1.2 million acres of public lands to the state to be held in trust for the benefit of native Hawaiians, as well as to benefit Hawaiians generally. The act also made the state (vs. the federal government) responsible for administering the homestead lands. See S.344, 108th Congress, 1st Session, February 11, 2003, findings, pp. 3–9 in http://thomas.loc.gov/ cgi-bin/query/C?c108. In 1978, Hawaii redrafted its constitution and provided for 20% of the revenues from ceded lands to go specifically to native Hawaiians and to be administered by a newly created Office of Hawaiian Affairs

(OHA). The trustees for the OHA were to be elected by native Hawaiians.

84. Rachel Salazar Pareñas, "White Trash Meets 'the Little Brown Monkeys,'" *Amerasia Journal* 24 no. 2: 115–34; Deborah Berman Santana, *"No Somos Unicos:* The Status Question From Manila to San Juan," *Centro* Special Issue: 1898–1998 Part 2, XI:1 (Fall 1999).

85. Want to read an interesting book on the power of naming things and renaming things? Houston Wood, *Displacing Natives: The Rhetorical Production of Hawai'i* (Lantham, Md.: Rowman & Littlefield, 1999), p. 11.

86. http://www.hawaiischoolreports.com/symbols/seal.htm.

87. Houston Wood, *Displacing Natives,* pp. 130–38.

88. This, of course, was pre-9/11. Many within the military felt completely betrayed. Their assumption was that Chief of Staff Karl Rove had given in to New York's Puerto Rican votes. You can get a sense of their anger in http://www.newsmax.com/archives/articles/2001/6/14/160231.shtml. Read Spanish? Here is the report to the secretary of defense, recognizing the problems but explaining why Vieques is vital: http://www.defenselink.mil/news/Oct1999/viqs_101899.html. Or see Jack Spencer, "The Importance of Vieques for Military Readiness," Heritage Foundation Backgrounder # 1411, February 2001.

89. www.hawaii-nation.org/turningthetide-6-4.html, December 1993.

90. S.J. Res. 19, 1993. See also what is known as the "Apology Resolution," Public Law 103-150 (107 Stat. 1510). Signed by President Clinton on November 23, 1993, it "apologizes to native Hawaiians on behalf of the people of the United States for the overthrow of the Kingdom of Hawaii on January 17, 1893, with the participation of agents and citizens of the United States, and the deprivation of rights of native Hawaiians to self-determination." It also states, "The indigenous Hawaiian people never directly relinquished their claims to their inherent sovereignty as a people or over their national lands to the United States, either through their monarchy or through a plebiscite or referendum." See Eric M. Kapono, "Hawaiians Accused of Trespassing on Their Land," *News From Indian Country,* March 31, 1998.

91. The group seeks sovereignty over the ceded lands and has allegedly threatened state and federal officials. Mark Matsunaga, "Nation of Hawaii Warns U.S., State Judges: Kanahele Group Cites 'War Crimes,' " *Honolulu Advertiser*, June 28, 1995.

92. Reuters, "Hawaiians Vote to Begin Sovereignty Process," September 11, 1996. Perhaps more surprising, in 1999 a survey "showed that more than 43% of Hawaiians—evenly split among natives and nonnatives—either favored or partly favored the idea of sovereignty in principle. And 41.8% of nonnative residents (compared with 35.4% of native Hawaiians) thought that natives should manage the ceded lands. Kim Murphy, "In Hawaii, a Lesson in Racial Disharmony," *Los Angeles Times*, August 18, 2002.

93. See *Rice* vs. *Cayetano*. Take a look at the detailed arguments and dissent on this decision in http://supct.law.cornell.edu/supct/html/98-818.ZS.html.

94. The suit was dropped after the school and the student's family reached an agreement, but Judge David Ezra was still making up his mind. See http://search.yahoo.com/search?p=kamehameha+Judge+David+Ezra&ei=UTF-8&fr=my_top&n=20&fl=0&x=wrt.

95. Akaka Bill, S344 IS, 108th Congress, 1st Session, February 11, 2003, p. 6, taken from http://thomas.loc.gov/cgi-bin/query/C?c108.

96. The Akaka bill is a source of great discord within the Hawaiian community, many of who want to pursue independence and reassert the full sovereignty enjoyed by Hawaii prior to 1893.

97. Ehu Kekahu Cardwell, "Aloha March This Weekend," e-mail, October 15, 2003.

98. Want more detail? Take a look at http://www.hawaiination.org/.

99. "How a Freer Quebec Could Shape the Continent," *Business Week*, July 9, 1990, p. 40.

100. Indian Act 1927 (Section 141). Discussed in B. Titley, *A Narrow Vision: Duncan Scott and the Administration of Indian Affairs in Canada* (Vancouver: University of British Columbia Press, 1986).

101. Andree Lajoie, "What Constitutional Law Doesn't Want to Hear About History" in *Speaking Truth to Power: A Treaty Forum* (Ottawa: Law Commission of Canada, 2000), pp. 27–28.

102. And various UN bodies have heard Cree and Inuit objections to large hydroelectric projects in James Bay. After all, Article 35 of the Constitution Act, 1982 reads: "The existing aboriginal and treaty rights of the aboriginal peoples of Canada are hereby recognized and affirmed."

103. *Delgamuukw* v. *British Columbia* (1997) 3 S.C.R. 1010.

104. John Borrows details how each of these claims has been thrown out in "Questioning Canada's Title to Land: The Rule of Law, Aboriginal Peoples and Colonialism" in *Speaking Truth to Power*, p. 36. These doctrines of land tenure gradually eroded through *Report of the Royal Commission on Aboriginal Peoples: Looking Forward and Looking Back* (Ottawa: Supply and Services Canada, 1996); *Island of Palmas Case United States* v. *Netherlands* (1928), 2 R.I.A.A 829; *Western Sahara Case* (1975) I.C.J Rep. 12. *Mabo* v. *Queensland* (1992) 107 A.L.R. 129. Status of Eastern Greenland Case (*Denmark* v. *Norway*) (1933) 3 W.C.R. 148.

105. John Borrows, "Questioning Canada's Title to Land: The Rule of Law, Aboriginal Peoples and Colonialism" in *Speaking Truth to Power*, p. 52. As a basis for this he cites among others *Logan* v. *Styres* (1959), 20 D.L.R. (2d) 416 (Ont. H.C). British Columbia, *Papers Connected With the Indian Land Question 1850–75* (Victoria Government Printer, 1875); S. Milloy, *A National Crime: The Canadian Government and the Residential School System 1879–1986* (Winnipeg: University of Manitoba Press, 1999); *R.* v. *Sylboy* (1929) 1 D.L.R. 307 (N.S. Co. Ct.), *Simon* v. *The Queen* (1985) 24 D.L.R. (4th) 390 (S.C.C); *R.* v *Marchall* (1999) 2 S.C.R 456; *Thomas* v. *Norris* (1992) 2 C.NL.R. (B.C.S.C.); *Guerin* v. *The Queen* (1984, 13 D.L.R (4th) 321 (S.C.C); *Kreuger* v. *The Queen* (1985) 17 D.L.R. (4th) 591 (F.C.A); *Canada (A.G.)* v. *Lavell* (1974) S.C.R. 1349; *Qualification and Registration of Voters Amendment Act*, 1872.

106. You can get a sense of the debate from "The Power of Governance," *Aboriginal Times* 5, no 11 (October 2001). Also S. Venne, *Our Elders Understand Our Rights: Exploring International Law Regarding Indigenous Rights* (Penticton, B.C.: Theytus, 1998) and J. Anaya, *Indigenous Peoples and International Law* (New York: Oxford University Press, 1996).

107. Talk by Prof. Richard Simeon, Harvard Law School (Cambridge, Massachusetts, December 15, 1998).

108. Premier Gordon Campbell, Throne Speech, British Columbia, 2003. This could have significant consequences because the province ignored the 1763 directives that required land treaties be signed by native Indians, and, as of February 2003, only one treaty had been finalized. Reuters, "British Columbia Apologizes to Its Indians," February 11, 2003.

109. Peter DeMarco, "Ceremony Marks Anniversary of Harvard's Indian College," *Boston Globe*, April 9, 2005, p. B3.

CHAPTER 5: BORDERS BOUNCE: DO YOU *HABLA ESPAÑOL*?

1. Diana Washington Valdez, "Oñate Statue May Land at Airport," *El Paso Times*, October 4, 2003.
2. Census Bureau 1996; National Research Council 1997.
3. Survey by David Hayes-Batista, director of the Center for the Study of Latino Health and Culture, University of California at Los Angeles, February 2003.
4. Hispanics make up almost three-quarters of all K–12 students within the Los Angeles Unified School District. Macelo and Carola Sanchez Orozco have done extensive work on this phenomenom. http://www.lausd.k12.ca.us/lausd/offices/Office_of_Communications/Fingertip_Facts_2004_2005.pdf.
5. Miriam Jordan, "As Border Tightens, Growers See Threat to Winter Salad Bowl," *Wall Street Journal*, March 11, 2005, p. A1.
6. Samuel Huntington, "Jose, Can You See?" *Foreign Policy*; March/April 2004. Cover Story. The article itself is titled "The Hispanic Challenge." Huntington expands and sharpens these arguments in *Who Are We: Challenges to America's National Identity* (New York: Simon & Schuster, 2004). Some of these arguments, however, have been around for a while. See, for example, Peter Brimelow, *Alien Nation: Common Sense About America's Immigration Disaster* (New York: Random House, 1995).
7. Zogby Poll, "American Views of Mexico and Mexican Views of the United States," conducted May 25 and 26, 2003. 28% of respondents disagreed. 14% did not know, published in "Harper's Index," *Harper's*, May 2003, p. 11.
8. http://www.indiana.edu/~jah/mexico/images/pop1824.jpg.

9. Hearings on this deportation issue were launched in California in 2004. The final report is due July 2007. See Sen. Lou Correa, Mexican Repatriation Commission, SB 227, http://info.sen. ca.gov/pub/bill/sen/sb_0401-0450/sb_427_cfa_20040606_ 122736_asm_comm.html.

10. *Castañeda v. State of California*, California Supreme Court, July 15, 2003. If you want to see just how fast this debate can get politicized, nasty, and bitter, check out the conflicting reader reviews of Balderrama and Rodriguez's book *Decade of Betrayal: Mexican Repatriation in the 1930s*, http://www.amazon.com/ exec/obidos/tg/detail/-/0826315755/ qid=1100583621/sr=1- 1/ref=sr_1_1/104-0778551-3019960?v= glance&s=books.

11. Eric Roy, "Righting an Old Wrong: Repatriated Mexican Americans Ask California for Reparations and an Apology," *VOA News*, September 28, 2003.

12. Stephen L. Klineberg, *Houston's Ethnic Communities* (a report, Department of Sociology, Rice University, Houston, 1996).

13. http://www.census.gov/population/www/documentation/twps 0029/tab0029.html and http://factfinder.census.gov/ servlet/DTTable?_bm=y&reg=DEC_2000_SF4_U_PCT174: 001&ds_name=DEC_2000_ SF3_U&-CONTEXT=dt&-mt_ name=DEC_2000_SF3_ U_PCT019&-mt_name=DEC_ 2000_SF3_U_PCT063A& mt_name=DEC_2000_SF3_U_ PCT063H&-redoLog=true& geo_id=01000US&-format= &-_lang=en.

14. Zanguill produced a play called *The Melting Pot* in 1908 on how immigrants become Americans launching the myth of the melting pot. Now, of course, in the age of hyphenated citizenship, people are reverting toward the African-American, Irish-American, Native American. . . .

15. Susan Gonzalez Baker, Frank D. Bean, Agustin Escobar Latapi, and Sidney Weintraub, "U.S. Immigration Policies and Trends: The Growing Importance of Migration From Mexico" in Marcelo Suarez Orozco, ed., *Crossings* (Cambridge, Mass.: Harvard University Press, 1998).

16. In 2000, the census bureau counted 34,658,190 African-Americans and 35,305,818 Hispanics and Latinos. Mixed races complicate this picture even more. See Elizabeth M. Grieco and

Rachel C. Cassidy, "Overview of Race and Hispanic Origin," Census 2000 brief, March 2001.

17. Deborah Sontag, "A Mexican Town That Transcends All Borders," *New York Times*, July 21, 1998.

18. Robert Suro and Jeffrey S. Passel, "The Rise of the Second Generation: Changing Patterns in Hispanic Population Growth" (Pew Hispanic Center Study, October 2003).

19. U.S. Census Bureau, http://www.census.gov/population/ socdemo/hispanic/ppl-165/slideshow/2.

20. Ramah McKay, http://www.migrationinformation.org/US focus/display.cfm?ID=122.

21. The U.S. quota limits applications to 65,000 per year, which was met the first day of the fiscal year. This led to howls from Microsoft, HP, Intel, TI, Micron. . . . See http://www. microsoft.com/issues/essays/2004/11-16visas.asp.

22. http://www.census.gov/prod/2000pubs/cenbr003.pdf.

23. You can read the heart-rending tales of two unfortunates in Deborah Sontag, "In a Homeland Far From Home," *New York Times Home Magazine*, November, 16, 2003.

24. Surveys conducted by the U.S. Mexico Studies Center UCSD in 1983 and 1996. Data excludes "do not know" and "non" respondents.

25. This is part of a trend toward longer stays and more permanent residency which began in the 1970s, and has now accelerated. In part it has to do with the recurring financial crises in Mexico and the increasing disparity in wages between the two nations. U.S. employment needs also changed toward permanent rather than seasonal jobs. And finally, changes in U.S. immigration law and enforcement that made continuous crossings more difficult. The great scholar in this field is Wayne Cornelius. See, for example, Wayne Cornelius, "From Sojourners to Settlers: The Changing Profile of Mexican Migration to the United States" in Jorge Bustmante, Clark Reynolds, and Raul Hinojosa, eds., *U.S.-Mexico Relations: Labor Market Interdependence* (Stanford, Calif.: Stanford University Press, 1992), pp. 155–193; Wayne Cornelius, "The Immigration Issue in U.S.-Mexico Relations: A Structurally Determined Irritant," presented at the conference "Mexico and the

United States in the Next Decade. May 11, 1998," La Jolla, California.

26. Surveys conducted by the U.S. Mexico Studies Center UCSD in 1983 and 1996. Data excludes "do not know" and "non" respondents.

27. http://www.census.gov/prod/2001pubs/c2kbr01-3.pdf.

28. There is general agreement Bush did better among Hispanics in 2004 than in 2000. But how much better is a matter of bitter dispute. The William C. Velazquez Institute claims he got 33% of the vote. New media exit polls show 44%. The Anneberg Poll estimates 41%. John F. Harris, "Bush's Hispanic Vote Dissected," *Washington Post*, December 26, 2004, p. A6.

29. William A. V. Clark, *The California Cauldron: Immigration and the Fortunes of Local Communities* (New York: Guilford Press, 1998) p. 178, and NALEO Primary Election Profile 2004.

30. Christopher McCaleb, CNN.com, April 6, 2000, http://www.cnn.com/2000/ALLPOLITICS/stories/04/06/bush.calif/.

31. James Crawford, http://ourworld.compuserve.com/home pages/JWCRAWFORD/langleg.htm#.

32. The U.S. Supreme Court struck down the Arizona law on January 11, 1998.

33. Ian S. Lustick, Dan Miodownik, Roy J. Eidelson, "Secessionist Movements in Multicultural Status: Does Sharing Power Prevent or Encourage It?" *American Political Science Review* 98(2): pp. 209–30.

34. David G. Gutierrez, "Migration, Emergent Ethnicity and the 'Third Space' : The Shifting Politics of Nationalism in Greater Mexico. Rethinking History and the Nation State: Mexico and the United States," *Journal of American History*, Special Issue, 1999, p. 28.

35. Facundo Cabral wrote haunting words: *"No soy de aquí, ni soy de allá/. No tengo hogar ni porvenir/y ser feliz es mi color de identidad."*

36. Timothy J. Dunn, *The Militarization of the U.S.-Mexico Border 1978–1992* (Austin: University of Texas Press, 1996).

37. Pub. L. 104-208 Illegal Immigration Reform and Immigrant Responsibility Act of 1996/SEC. 101.

38. According to a Department of Justice survey carried out in

mid-1996, the INS had a greater budget than the FBI and more employees than the Departments of State or Labor. The INS's federal agent force had 12,403 agents, more than the bureau of prisons (11,329) or the FBI (10,389).

39. Marlise Simons, "More Dutch Plan to Emigrate as Muslim Influx Tips Scales," *New York Times*, February 27, 2005, p. 7.

40. Take a look at the primary document http://www.epic.org/privacy/terrorism/hr3162.html.

41. Steven E. Flynn wrote a prescient article on just how hard it is to seal borders: "Beyond Border Control," *Foreign Affairs*, November/ December 2000, pp. 59–68. "U.S. DEA Chief Says Arrest of Key Mexican Drug Lords Hasn't Increased Street Price of Drugs," *Associated Press*, August 19, 2003.
"Anti-Kingpin Strategy: Should Drug, Terror Wars Target Organizational Leaders?," *ABC News*, September 29, 2002, http://abcnews.go.com/sections/nightline/DailyNews/drugs_terror_similarities020929.html.

42. L. D. Johnston, P. M. O'Malley, & J. G. Bachman, "Ecstasy Use Falls for Second Year in a Row, Overall Teen Drug Use Drops," University of Michigan News and Information Services, December 19, 2003, www.monitoringthefuture.org. This wonderful headline fails to mention that overall use, after a decade of brutal incarcerations and billions spent on drug wars, is up about 16% from 1991.

43. This is a story filled with layers of irony. It turns out the Taliban may have been more effective than U.S. troops at reducing poppy production. "In 2000 . . . Afghanistan was the world's leading opium/heroin producer with 65,510 hectares of opium cultivation. In 2000, the Taliban, governing Afghanistan at the time, controlled over 96 percent of the area where opium poppy was cultivated. Afghanistan managed to reduce its production levels by 97% from 2000 to a record low of 1,685 hectares in 2001." http://www.whitehousedrugpolicy.gov/publications/international/factsht/heroin.html.

44. Judy Aita, "UN Report Urges International Aid for Afghan Drug Control," International Information Programs, U.S. Department of State, October 29, 2003; Eric Schmitt, "Afghans Gains Face Big Threat in Drug Traffic," *New York Times*, December 11, 2004, p. A1.

45. John W. Gonzalez, "Danger Won't Halt Border Crossings," *Houston Chronicle*, 2003, http://www.chron.com/cs/CDA/ssistory.mpl/special/deadlycrossing/1910631.

46. Jeff McDonald, "Death and 10 Years of the Border Fence," *San Diego Tribune*, October 3, 2004.

47. Just to give you a sense of what this might mean, take a look at http://www.lawg.org/docs/fence%20points.pdf.

48. http://www.nationmaster.com/country/mx/Economy.

49. It all depends on how you want to define *poverty* and compare it with that of the U.S. In 2002, 34.6% of Mexicans earned two minimum wages or less (less than $8/day) and 30.9% earned between two and four minimum wages (less than $16 day), http:// www.ine gi.gob.mx/est/contenidos/espanol/tematicos/mediano/med. asp?t=mingo2&c=3314. (Pesos were converted at 10 P = 1 $.)

50. Marjorie Valbrun, "Florida Tries to Keep Down Flow of Immigrants by Working to Improve Quality of Life in the Islands," *Wall Street Journal*, July 27, 1998, p. A16.

51. Booth William, "One Nation Indivisible: Is It History?," *Washington Post*, February 22, 1998, p. A1. This is the first in a series of excellent articles on America's racial and ethnic divides done by the *Post*. You might want to read the series: http://wa shingtonpost.com/wp-srv/national/longterm/ meltingpot/ melto222.htm.

52. Modern Language Association, reported by AP's Deb Riechmann, October 10, 1996. Elizabeth B. Welles, "Foreign Language Enrollments in the United States Institutions of Higher Education, Fall 2002," *ADFL* Bulletin 35, no. 2 (Winter 2004).

53. "Spanish in the Senate," *Washington Times*, February 3, 2005, p. A7.

54. The Planning & Development Department, City of Houston, *Demographic & Land Use Profile for Houston, Texas*, June 1992. *The Wall Street Journal Almanac 1998* (New York: Down Jones, 1998), p. 677.

55. Edward Hegstrom, "History Gets More Difficult / Looking at Both Sides of San Jacinto's Story Rewrites Texas' Past," *Houston Chronicle*, April 21, 2002, p. A1.

56. Simon Romero, "Welcome to THE-jas, Land of the Alamo and the Cowboy," *New York Times*, January 2, 2005, p. 10.

57. William A.V. Clark, *The California Cauldron*, p. 19.

58. http://www.dss.cahwnet.gov/research/res/pdf/GENtrends/
     CAethnicity2000.pdf.

59. Carol Ness and Erin McCormick, "Hispanics Now Make Up
     Third of Californians/ Race: Whites No Longer a Majority," *San
     Francisco Chronicle*, March 30, 2001, p. A1.

60. Speech by Ernesto Zedillo, National Council of La Raza
     (Chicago, Illinois, 1997). The head of Mexico's INS was even
     more blunt; when interviewed after ninety Mexicans died trying
     to cross the California desert, he said: "At no time will we take
     any action that could discourage Mexicans from emigrating to
     the United States. That is because these are people who leave
     their families and their homes with the legitimate goal of bet-
     tering their lives." Anthony DePalma, "Border Deaths Don't
     Change Mexico's View of Crossings," *New York Times*, August 24,
     1998, p. A4. And now that we are on the subject, even the bor-
     ders themselves were in dispute until quite recently. In 1963,
     one could stand on 600 acres of land, known as Chamizal, and
     confidently say one was in Texas. By year-end the same plot was
     part of Mexico. In 1864, a series of floods shifted the Rio
     Bravo/Rio Grande. A part of Mexico suddenly ended up on the
     U.S. side. This led to a bitter dispute, which was not settled until
     1963 when a new canal returned the river to its original course.
     But this did not solve all issues. In November 1997, Mexico
     signed a treaty establishing the mari-time limits of the U.S. and
     Mexico in the Gulf of Mexico and the Pacific. Presidents Carter
     and Lopez Portillo had almost settled the dispute in 1978, but
     the U.S. Senate had not approved the deal.

61. Tex-Mex version of "The Night Before Christmas" posted by
     Jim and Nita Lee, http://www.hamline.edu/~math/wnk/
     humor/mex_nite.html. Others attribute this to Lalo Guerrero
     (1956), http://lmri.ucsb.edu/pipermail/reformanet/1998-
     November/003819.html.

62. An illustrative example of the friendly greetings some
     Floridians launched at President Bush just after he announced
     a new amnesty plan for undocumented workers, West Palm
     Beach Gardens, Associated Free Press 9 published in
     La Jornada, January 2004.

63. Digital History, "The Roots of American Economic Growth; Immigration Begins 1820–1860," http://www.digitalhistory. uh.edu/database/article_display.cfm? HHID=613.

64. David M. Kennedy, "The Price of Immigration," *Atlantic Monthly*, November 1996, p. 58. Nicholas Kristof wrote an interesting article entitled "At This Rate We'll be Global in Another Hundred Years" when the foreign-born population was 8%, in the *New York Times*, May 23, 1999, p. 5. But things change fast; by 2002, it was 11.5%, of which 52.2% was from Latin America, http://www.census.gov/prod/2003pubs/p20-539.pdf.

65. Stuart Anderson, "The Contribution of Legal Immigration to the Social Security System," National Foundation for American Policy, February 2005, http://www.nfap.net/researchactivi ties/studies/SocialSecurityStudy2005.pdf.

66. Kaiser-Pew Poll, "The 2004 National Survey of Latinos: Politics and Civic Participation," April 21, 2004, to June 9, 2004, covered 2,288 Latino respondents, including 1,166 registered voters, http://www.kff.org/kaiserpolls/pomr072204nr.cfm. These trends have been true since at least 1993. See Rodolfo O. de la Garza, Chris F. Garcia, and Louis DeSipio, *Latinos: Remaking America: Mexican, Puerto Rican, and Cuban Perspectives on American Politics* (Boulder, Col.: Westview Press, January 1993), p. 407.

67. U.S. poll was carried out in April 1998 among 755 Hispanics. It was carried out by Michael Deaver and Marc Penn and paid for by Univision.

68. Elena Lopez, "Supporting Latino Families: Lessons and Exemplary Programs," Harvard Family Research project, Graduate School of Education, 1997, *http://www.census.gov/population/socdemo/hispanic/ppl-165/slideshow/15.*

69. Gary Orfield, *Dropouts in America: Confronting the Graduation Rate Crisis* (Cambridge, Mass.: Harvard University Press, 2004).

70. Educational Attainment by Race, 1960–95 and U.S. Department of Commerce, Bureau of the Census, U.S. Census of Population, 1960, vol. 1, part 1; *Current Population Reports*, Series P-20 and unpublished data; and John K. Folger and Charles B.

Nam, "Education of the American Population" *1960 Census Monograph*, from U.S. Dept. of Education, National Center for Education Statistics, *Digest of Education Statistics 2002*, http://www.infoplease.com/ipa/A0774057.html.

71. Rachel Swarns, "Hispanic Mother Lagging as Others Escape Welfare," *New York Times*, September 15, 1998, p. 1.

72. Many Hispanics begin by working illegally, come from poor backgrounds, have little time to focus on education. This creates a negative cycle. Kids work low-skilled, low-paid jobs to help their family. Still, it frustrates me no end that the leaders in the Hispanic community keep forgetting the message in the film *Stand and Deliver*.

73. Tony Judt, "Is There a Belgium?" *New York Review of Books*, December 2, 1999, pp. 49–53.

74. From the Welsh Language Board, http://www.bwrdd-yr-iaith.org.uk/en/cynnwys.php?cID=1&pID=127.

75. Lizette Alvarez, "Land Reforms in Scotland Give Big Estates the Jitters," *New York Times*, February 23, 2003, p. 4.

76. Richard Barrett, "Descendants of Slaves Back in Their Place," November 7, 2003, http://www.nationalist.org/alt/2003/nov/place.html.

77. Want to see a fancy Web page by a racist-secessionist organization? http://www.alalos.org/index2.

78. In 1870, California and Oregon opposed the fifteenth amendment because they feared that the right to vote regardless of "race, color, or previous condition of servitude" might include not just blacks but also Chinese. You can read about some of the extraordinary obstacles Asians faced in http://www.apa.si.edu/ongoldmountain/gallery2/gallery2.html. The South Carolina debate? http://www.cnn.com/ALLPOLITICS/stories/1998/11/03/election/ballots/interracial.marriage/index.html.

79. Ariel Hart, "Fight in Alabama on Segregationist Language," *New York Times*, November 12, 2004, p. A19.

80. Jesse Jackson and Craig Palast, "Black Voters Disproportionately Disenfranchised," *Seattle Post-Intelligencer*, January 25, 2005.

81. U.S. Census Bureau, "Texas Moves Closer to Majority-Minority States," press release, September 30, 2004.

82. You can get a much more sophisticated view of what is really going on in elections by looking at the maps made by Michael Gastner, Cosma Shalizi, and Mark Newman at the University of Michigan: http://www-personal.umich.edu/~mejn/election/.

83. Sarah Schweitzer, "Maine's Split Personality," *Boston Globe*, February 27, 2005, p. B1. Household incomes in the Aroostook State are $28,837 (versus $43,630 in York, a southern town). Home values, $60,200 vs. 122,600. College degrees, 14.7% vs. 22.9%.

84. The data and notes on this page regarding black incarceration are taken from "Race, Prison, and the Drug Laws," *Drug War Facts*. If you want to get the complete story, go to http://drugwarfacts.org/racepris.htm and *Key Recommendations from Punishment and Prejudice: Racial Disparities in the War on Drugs* (Washington, D.C.: Human Rights Watch, June 2000), http://www.hrw.org/campaigns/drugs/war/key-reco.htm.

85. Paige M. Harrison and Jennifer Karberg, *Prison and Jail Inmates at Midyear* (Washington, D.C.: U.S. Department of Justice, April 2003), p. 11, Tables 13, 14.

86. Substance Abuse and Mental Health Services Administration, *National Household Survey on Drug Abuse: Summary Report 1998* (Rockville, Md.: Substance Abuse and Mental Health Services Administration, 1999), p. 13; Bureau of Justice Statistics, *Sourcebook of Criminal Justice Statistics 1998* (Washington, D.C.: U.S. Department of Justice, August 1999), p. 343, Table 4.10, p. 435, Table 5.48, and p. 505, Table 6.52; Allen J. Beck, PhD, and Christopher J. Mumola, Bureau of Justice Statistics, *Prisoners in 1998* (Washington, D.C.: U.S. Department of Justice, August 1999), p. 10, Table 16; Allen J. Beck, Ph.D., and Paige M. Harrison, *Prisoners in 2000: U.S. Dept. of Justice, Bureau of Justice Statistics* (Washington, D.C.: U.S. Department of Justice, August 2001), p. 11, Table 16.

87. M. Mauer and T. Huling, *Young Black Americans and the Criminal Justice System: Five Years Later* (Washington, D.C.: The Sentencing Project, 1995); Thomas P. Bonczar, *Prevalence of Imprisonment in the U.S. Population, 1974–2001, NCJ197976* (Washington, D.C.: U.S. Department of Justice, August 2003), p. 8.

88. Thomas P. Bonczar, "Study Suggests Black Male Prison Rate

Impinges on Political Process," *The Washington Post*, January 30, 1997, p. A3. Over 1.46 million black men out of a total voting population of 10.4 million have lost their right to vote due to felony convictions. Jamie Fellner and Marc Mauer, *Losing the Vote: The Impact of Felony Disenfranchisement Laws in the United States* (Washington, D.C.: Human Rights Watch and The Sentencing Project, 1998), p. 8. Election statistics cited are from the U.S. Census Bureau, "Voting and Registration in the Election of November 1996," July 1998.

89. Roy Walmsley, *World Prison Population List, Fourth Edition* (London: Home Office Research, Development and Statistics Directorate, 2003), p. 1, from the Web at http://www.home ofice.gov.uk/rds/pdfs2/r188.pdf, last accessed April 29, 2003.

90. Peter Viles, "Suit Seeks Billions in Slave Reparations," CNN, March 27, 2002, http://archives.cnn.com/2002/LAW/03/26/slavery.reparations/index.html.

91. CNN/USA Today/Gallup. The poll should be seen as an indicator of general opinion, not as statistically significant numbers because the black population polled was quite small; 1,001 adults were surveyed, 820 whites, 146 blacks on February 8 to 10, 2002 (error rate plus or minus 9 percentage points for blacks).

CHAPTER 6: DEMOCRACY + OPEN BORDERS = FOUR MEXICOS?

1. *Carta de Ignacio Comonfort a Manuel Doblado. 19 de Noviembre 1855*, from Genaro Garcia, "Los Gobiernos de Alvarez y Comonfort Según el Archivo del General Doblado," *Documentos Inéditos o Muy Raros Para la Historia de México* (Mexico Distrito Federal: Porrua, 1974), p. 416. This was apparently a common feeling throughout Mexico in parts of the nineteenth century. Juan Alvarez also argued the *"el país iba desmoronándose como arena"* in 1854. Quoted in Anselmo de la Portilla, *Historia de la Revolución Mexicana Contra la Dictadura del General Santa Anna 1853–1855* (Mexico Distrito Federal: INEHRM, 1987), Appendice p. XLIII. For a full discussion, see Fernando Escalante Gonzalbo's excellent *Ciudadanos Imaginarios* (Mexico Distrito Federal: El Colegio de Mexico, 1992).

2. *Cuantas veces ha nacido México? / México se hace, deshace y renace sin cesar. / En cada nacimiento ha sido distinto y, / No obstante es inseparable de otras sociedades Que lo han precedido (. . .)/El mismo y siempre otro,* 1992. Ironically, this passage was used by the Ministry of Foreign Affairs of Mexico to celebrate the cultural diversity of Mexico.

3. Mexico's viceroy sent expeditions to claim Alaska in 1774, 1777, 1778, and 1790.

4. Anecdote witnessed by Larry Summers and retold at the DRCLAS/HAA Meetings, Mexico City, March 2, 2005.

5. The census bureau estimates that there were 25.1 million people of Mexican descent living in the U.S. in 2003, http:// www.census.gov/population/socdemo/hispanic/ppl165/ slideshow/4.

6. Report by Dilip Ratha, World Bank, reported in R. Gonzalez, J. Carson, and D. Brooks, "Cifra Record por Remesas: 15 MMD," *La Jornada,* October 9, 2004, p. 1. Oil price equivalent income is calculated at normal levels, not $53 per barrel.

7. The single greatest source of immigration to the U.S. is from Mexico. Of those admitted legally in 1994, 106,995 came from Mexico; 53,976 from China; 53,501 from the Philippines; 51,047 from the Dominican Republic; 41,344 from Vietnam; 34,873 from India; 28,020 from Poland; 21,010 from the Ukraine; 17,353 from El Salvador; and 17,251 from Ireland. Of these, 43.8% resided in California or New York. http:// uscis.gov/graphics/shared/aboutus/statistics/Immigs.htm.

   Of those admitted legally in 2002, 219,380 came from Mexico; 61,282 from China; 51,308 from the Philipines; 22,604 from the Dominican Republic; 33,627 from Vietnam; 71,105 from India; 12,746 from Poland; 21,217 from the Ukraine; 31,168 from El Salvador; and 1,425 from Ireland. http://uscis. gov/graphics/shared/aboutus/statistics/IMM02yrbk/IMMEx cel/table3.xls.

   There is some evidence that up to 800,000 Mexicans tried to cross; some succeeded, some were caught and processed, others were simply sent back unofficially, Bertha Fernandez, *"Deporta EU Anualmente a mas de 800,000 Mexicanos," El Universal,* April 13, 1997. Although the single greatest source of immigration to the U.S. is Mexico, per capita, the Philippines is greater. (In the Philippines, 4.2 million work abroad. That is more than 15% of its total workforce.) The 5,165,734 Mexicans working in the U.S. (in 2000) make up about 10.9% of the total Mexican workforce. American Immigration Law Foundation, http://www.dfw.com/mld/dfw/news/world/7121890.htm.

8. http://www.nationmaster.com/country/mx/Economy.

9. Miriam Pasada Garcia, "México Cayo del Tercer Lugar al 22 en Interés Para Inversionistas Extranjeros," *La Jornada,* October 12, 2004, p. 31.

10. Enrique Dussel Peters, "Recent Structural Changes in Mexico's Economy: A Preliminary Analysis of Some Sources of Mexican Migration to the United States" in Marcelo Suarez Orozco, ed, *Crossings* (Cambridge, Mass.: Harvard University Press, 1998), pp. 69–70.

11. Only during the twentieth century was there a large-scale migration and intermingling of people across the whole of Mexico, mainly driven by the ebb and flow of violence during the revolution, and by rapid urbanization. But even during the revolution, the agrarian South had little to do with the political revolt in the North. Much of Mexico remains a collection of disparate regions and customs.

12. Jorge Domínguez, one of the great scholars of Latin American politics, economics, and history, provides an overview of these trends in "México, Hoy y Mañana" (Octava Conferencia Anual Francisco Fernández Ordóñez, Casa de América, Madrid, November 6 2000).

13. Nemesio J. Rodriguez, "*Istmo de Tehuantepec: de lo Regional a la Globalización*" (Instituto Nacional Indigenista, 1997).

14. See the human rights organization report "Miguel Angel Pro," *La Violencia en Oaxaca,* May 25, 1997.

15. The decree reads in part: "[as long as Yucatán] does not denounce its shameful alliance with the adventurers called Texans, whom they are helping with money . . . the Department of Yucatán will be considered an enemy of the Nation as long as it does not break with the Texas rebels." Published as "*Decreto Formal del General Santa Anna Nulificando los Tratados,*" May 7, 1842, in Serapio Baqueiro, *Las Revoluciones de Yucatán Desde*

1840 Hasta 1864 (Merida, Yucatán: Imprenta Literaria Eligio Ancona, 1865), number 17, pp. 303–304. Luis Gutierrez Muñoz is writing an interesting book on these events.

16. In between Mexico's four clear-cut regions, there are a series of transition states that could fit into either of its neighboring "countries." If Mexico were to break up, who governs and how the debate is framed within these states would determine which faction they join. Geographically, Tamaulipas should be a northern state, but its economy and outlook is quite different from that of Nuevo León and other northern neighbors. Oil and nationalism remain powerful forces within the state. Tamaulipecos see their Nuevo León neighbors as far too friendly with the U.S., and Tamaulipas' odd shape, particularly the long thin branch along the border, effectively cuts off almost all of Monterey's direct access to the U.S. Within Mexico City, Tamaulipas has long been seen as a guarantor of "Mexicanness" in an oft-suspect region. But the rapid growth of maquiladoras within Tamaulipas as well as the decline of the PEMEX oil worker's union has altered the balance of power within the state. Other northern states, like Sinaloa, Zacatecas, San Luis Potosí, and Durango are also, historically, more pro-Mexico. But over the past decades, poverty has led more and more to seek employment within the U.S. Many are staying longer, but keeping ties back home. Los Angeles is now "Mexico's" second largest city. The same is true even farther south, in Guanajuato, Querétaro, and Aguascalientes. A couple of decades ago, if there had been a movement toward northern autonomy, none of these states would have been likely candidates to join a northern regional moment. Things are not so cut and dry today.

TRANSITION STATES

State	Area Square Km	Population 2000	GDP (Billions Dollars) 2001	GDP Per Capita 2001
Aguascalientes	5,589	944,285	$7.06	$7,484
Colima	5,455	542,627	$3.10	$5,706
Durango	119,648	1,448,661	$7.28	$5,025
Guanajuato	30,589	4,663,032	$18.2	$3,895
Michoacán	59,864	3,985,667	$12.7	$3,190

State	Area Square Km	Population 2000	GDP (Billions Dollars) 2001	GDP Per Capita 2001
Nayarit	27,621	920,185	$3.32	$3,609
Querétaro	12,114	1,404,306	$9.09	$6,474
San Luis Potosí	62,848	2,299,360	$9.55	$4,155
Sinaloa	184,934	2,536,844	$10.95	$4,316
Tamaulipas	79,829	2,753,222	$17.67	$6,417
Tlaxcala	3,914	962,646	$3.23	$3,354
Veracruz	72,815	6,908,975	$23.03	$3,333
Zacatecas	75,040	1,353,610	$4.27	$3,156

17. Paper presented by Adolfo Chavez, researcher (Instituto Nacional de la Nutricion, Dia Mundial de la Alimentacion, Facultad de Economia de la UNAM, October 15, 1998) Instituto Nacional de Estadistica Geografia e Informática (INEGI), *Censo de Poblacion y Vivienda 1995* (Mexico: Banamex-Accival, p. 102).

18. INEGI, 2003, pp. 105–106.

19. Instituto Nacional de la Nutricion Salvador Zubiran, *Encuesta Nacional de Alimentacion y Nutricion en el medio Rural, 1996* (Mexico Distrito Federal; 1997). Figures are proportional to population. Source: *Mexico-Social 1996–1998, Estadisticas Seleccionadas* (Mexico Distrito Federal: Banamex-Accival, 1998), p. 451.

20. Defined as percent of people older than five who speak an Indian language. Calculations based on census data and Banamex, p. 644. If one excludes Tabasco, the percent of the Yucatán Peninsula indigenous population shoots up from 17% and exceeds the 21% of southern Mexico. Northern Mexico hosts about 2% indigenous population.

21. Alberto Barrientos, "Aventajan los Norteños," *Reforma,* October 12, 2004, p. A1.

22. INEGI, *Cuaderno de Información Oportuna*, no. 307, October 1998, p. 256; *Cuaderno de Información Oportuna Regional,* no. 55, first trimester 1998, p. 113. Mexico City's gap is likely overstated because company headquarters are there, but not all production.

23. Some would argue that the North has gotten much more because programs like Fobaproa bailed out major northern

industrial groups. This is true but it does not constitute a wide-spread, common use of tax funds. It simply benefits and supports one group. Furthermore, these occasional bailouts quit being attractive and useful when the central state goes broke.

24. Enrique Lomas, "Conciliacion si, Sumision No," *Reforma*, April 26, 1999. Estados, p. 1. The government blocked several credit lines provided by Banobras.

25. "Defienden a Particio," *Reforma*, April 27, 1998, p. 6a.

26. Jose Luis Undiano and Miriam and Clacudia Garcia "Proponen Frente de Gobernadores," *Reforma*, April 28, 1999, p. 1; Claudia Garcia, "Propone el PAN Apoyar a Estados Productivos," *Reforma*, October 18, 1999, p. 1.

27. Ernesto Zedillo, speech in Nayarit, April 26, 2000. Soon thereafter the PRI-dominated Senate vetoed the congressional initiative.

28. David Zuniga, *"Sin Freno la Entrada de Automóviles Illegales a México, Denuncia la AMIA,"* *La Jornada*, October 9, 2004, p. 27.

29. Translated from the highly derogatory Fuerza Bruta Indigena (Brute Indian Force).

30. John Coatsworth, "Free Trade" (presented during the Spring 2004 DRCLAS Corporate Partners Seminar, Harvard Business School, April 2, 2004).

31. Legend has it that those who founded Tenochtitlán, the Aztec capital, wandered until they found this eagle. Today all government paperwork and official seals re-create this eagle, and reinforce the dominance of the Aztec Empire and its legends.

32. IMF, *Government Financial Statistics Yearbook*, 2001. U.S. data is 1999. Mexico data, 1998.

33. *"Tlaxcala Anfitrion Por Tradicion."* Needless to say this led to some snickers and outrage among Mexico's nationalists. Hong Kong then tried to match this gaffe when, in the middle of their SARS scare, they launched: "Hong Kong will take your breath away" and "Hong Kong, a once in a lifetime destination."

34. Central Mexico figures are from *El Pequeño Almanaque Mexicano*, edited by Sergio Aguayo Quezada (Mexico: Hechos Confiables-Grijalbo, 2004).

35. Poland figures are from *New York Times Almanac*, edited by John W. Wright (New York: Penguin Group, 2005).

36. So the average value added, that is, the amount of nonlabor Mexican products used as a maquiladora product is assembled, is still around 3%.

37. Eduardo Zepeda, Center for U.S. Mexican Studies, "Liberalization and Employment in Mexico," *Enfoque*, Fall 1997, p. 5. Large and medium nonmaquila jobs fell from 948,000 (1988) to 747,000 (1995); meanwhile, by 1998, 1,021,724 people were working in maquiladoras (INEGI).

38. Joel Millman, "Data Processing Booms Along Mexican Border," *Wall Street Journal*, December 1, 1998, p. A14. Most of these data-processing jobs are concentrated on the border: Baja, Calif., 1750 jobs; Sonora, 2300; Chihuahua, 7900; Nuevo Leon; 2500; Puebla, 300.

39. Federal Reserve Bank of Dallas/El Paso Branch, "Maquiladora Downturn: Structural Change of Cyclical Factors?" *Business Frontier*, issue 2, 2004, p. 1.

40. INEGI 2003, pp. 31, 374.

41. *Time Almanac 2003*, p. 747.

42. Enrique Alducin, *Los Valores de los Mexicanos. Mexico en los Tiempos de Cambio* (Mexico Distrito Federal: Banamex-Accival, 1993), p. 218.

43. Home ownership and clear land title is a nontrivial matter in Mexico. See, for example, Dennis John Peyton, "Negotiating in a Tricky Real Estate Market," *Business Mexico*, February 1, 2003.

44. I was able to interview a participant in this conversation.

45. John Rawls, *A Theory of Justice* (Cambridge, Mass.: Belknap Press, 1971).

46. "Mirror on the Americas" Poll, *Wall Street Journal*, March 1999.

47. Depending how ambitious he is feeling, President Fox describes himself as either the president of 117 or 123 million Mexicans, 100 million of whom live in Mexico; the rest live in the U.S.

48. Martin Wolf, "Humanity on the Move: The Myths and Realities of International Migration," *Financial Times*, July 30, 2003, p. 11. An estimated six million Mexicans left home. Mexico's competitors for most wanting to leave? Bangladesh (4.1m), Afghanistan (4.1m), Phillipines (2.9m). Globally about one out of every thirty-five people has left home.

49. Calculations based on "*Poblacion Indigena por Entidad Federa-*

tiva," *Mexico-Social 1996–1998, Estadisticas Seleccionadas* (Mexico Distrito Federal: Banamex-Accival, 1998), p. 186.

50. Great book on this subject: John McPhee, *La Place de la Concorde Suisse* (New York: Farrar, Strauss and Giroux, 1984).

51. Paul Sullivan, *Mayas and Foreigners Between Two Wars* (Berkeley: University of California, 1991). One of the great experts on the Maya today is Prof. Kay Warren. See, for example, *Indigenous Movements and Their Critics: Pan-Maya Activism in Guatemala* (Princeton: Princeton University Press, 1998) and *The Violence Within: Cultural and Political Opposition in Divided Nations* (Boulder, Colo., and Oxford, UK: Westview, 1993).

52. In 1993 GDP per person was $6,730 per capita in the Yucatán, $5,570 in the north, $5,090 in central Mexico, and $2,330 in southern states. *Mexico Social, 1996–1998 Estadisticas Seleccionadas*, p. 392. This is distorted due to oil income. . . .

53. INEGI 2003, pp. 31, 374.

54. *Time Almanac 2003*, p. 833.

55. INEGI 2003, p. 598 (2001 data).

56. "Acta de Independencia de Comitan," *Broadside*, August 28, 1821. Mexico City's political squabbles tore apart the new country. Iturbide's government collapsed on March 19, 1823. By the summer of 1823, most of Central America revoked their union agreement with Mexico, which gave birth to the United Provinces of Central America. Then they, too, began to squabble and fragment.

57. The union of Central America and Mexico lasted from October 1848 through March 1849.

58. You can see a map of how Chiapas is divided: http://www.non violentways.org/mapas.html.

59. *Subcomandante Marcos Communiqué*, January 1, 1994.

60. *Plan de Chiapa Libre*, October 26, 1823.

61. The vote took place on September 12, 1824, although some argue Chiapas had already joined Mexico on January 16, 1822.

62. Soconusco became part of Mexico on May 3, 1824, then returned to Guatemala on July 24, 1824. Then it became a no-mans-land through 1842, when it was absorbed by Mexico. Ma Salas, Esther and Diana Guillen, *Chiapas, una Historia Compartida* (Mexico: Instituto de Investigaciones Dr. Jose Maria Luis Mora, 1994).

63. Gov. Patrocinio Gonzalez Garrido (meeting with intellectuals

from Chiapas and Central America, Tuxtla Gutierrez, April 8–12, 1991). This was a particularly politically inept governor who repressed first and then listened. . . .

64. Thomas L. Benjamin, *"El Camino a Leviatan, Chiapas y el Estado Mexicano, 1891–1947"* (Mexico: Conaculta, 1990), p. 41.

65. *"Nota del 24 de Marzo de 1825"* in Luis Chavez Orozco, comp., *Historia de Mexico 1808–1836* (Mexico: Instituto Nacional de Estudios Historicos de la Revolucion Mexicana, Editorial Patria, 1947–1985), p. 529. The plenipotentiary minister of Central America, Juan de Dios Mayorga, answered using the same logic to contest Mexico's takeover of the Soconusco. "If it is true that a fraction of the people that used to be united cannot separate from the will of the majority, the Chiapas, who have indisputably always been part of Guatemala, and have decided to separate from their old association, why not Soconusco? So united have the Chiapas been of Guatemala, as Soconusco from Chiapas." *"Nota del 26 de Marzo de 1825"* in Luis Chavez Orozco, comp *Historia de Mexico 1808–1836;* p. 529.

66. Argument put forward by the Diputacion Provincial for the Pbro. Pedro Jose Solorzano to use it in his task of incorporating Chiapas to Mexico. *"Sobre que la provincia de Chiapas quede separada del Gobierno de Guatemala y admitirla como independiente, entre las que componen el Imperio Mexicano,"* in *Documentos Historicos de Chiapas* (Archivo General de la Nacion, Tuxtla Gutierrez, 1983, Boletin 12), p. 43.

67. Although, there are certainly pockets of extreme poverty among indigenous communities in places like Otomi in Hidalgo and the Tarahumara in Northern Mexico.

68. In the 1970s and 1980s some of the poorest peasants from the rest of Mexico migrated to the Chiapas jungles in search of land. Just as Guatemalans, Nicaraguans, and Salvadorians, fleeing brutal civil wars, also came in droves. All newcomers were caught in century's-long conflicts between various ethnic groups, which were later accentuated by religious differences. Chiapas was already the state with the greatest number of non-Catholics in Mexico. Mexico City has not dealt effectively with very complex, overlapping agendas revolving around drugs, land tenure, political, ethnic, and religious conflicts. Violence

is a constant, and globalization has, so far, accentuated conflict. Many people, be they guerrillas, paramilitary, military, or police of various ilk, are still running around with guns. See, for example, Juan Enriquez and Ray Goldberg; *Chiapas: Reconciling Agriculture and Ecology* (Harvard Business School Case Study, 1988).

69. AP, "Bolivia's Coca Boss Sets an Ultimatum," October 21, 2003. Peter Beaumont, "Coca Farmer's Hero Holds Sway in Bolivia," *Observer*, October 26, 2003.

70. *Global Competitiveness Report 1997* (World Economic Forum, Geneva), p. 22. The Anglo-Saxon countries are United Kingdom, Canada, Ireland, New Zealand, Australia, and the United States.

71. *Congo* is shorthand for the ironically named Democratic Republic of the Congo (formerly Zaire).

72. William J. Bernstein, *The Birth of Plenty* (New York: McGraw Hill, 2004), p. 376.

73. European Union Commission, *Financing the European Union*, a report 1998.

74. Luis Serven, "The Lessons of NAFTA After Ten Years: What Comes Next" (presented during the Spring 2004 DRCLAS Corporate Partners Seminar, Harvard Business School, April 2, 2004).

75. Mary Jordan, "Malnutrition Blights Mexico's Young," *Washington Post*, June 9, 2003, p. 1. Jordan and her husband, Kevin Sullivan, have done an outstanding job of covering Mexico, particularly the disastrous justice system. They won a Pulitzer in 2003.

CHAPTER 7: EUROPE AND ITS DISCONTENTS

1. Europe 1898, history.sandiego.edu/_gen/maps/list europe.html.

2. Angus Maddison, *The World Economy: Historical Statistics* (OECD, Paris 2003).

3. In a strict sense, the supranational level refers only to those institutions in which the leaders do not officially represent specific countries. The decisions these institutions make are then

implemented by a group of countries, for example the European Commission. But multilateral organizations such as the UN, IMF, or WB increasingly behave like supranational organizations, to the chagrin of neocons.

4. Austin covers 252 square miles. Want to know which are the world's smallest countries? See http://geography.about.com/cs/countries/a/smallcountries.htm.

5. Although, some might argue convincingly that Italy was a single country through the fifth century under the Romans. But this is clearly before the era of the modern nation-state. It was only after the annexation of Venetia in 1866 and of Papal Rome in 1870 that one can call Italy one country.

6. In Italian: *In quest 'aula/ que mando 'gli ultimi aneliti / la liberta fiorentina / dopo tre secondi di silezio / I reppresentanti della toscana / affermarono nel MDCCCLIX / l'unita e la liberta d' italia.* . . .

7. Carlo Ruzza and Oliver Schmidtke, "The Northern League: Changing Friends and Foes, and Its Political Opportunity Structure" in D. Cesarini and M. Fulbrook (eds.), *Citizenship, Nationality, and Migration in Europe* (London: Routledge, 1996). Also "The Making of the Lombard League," *Telos*, no. 90 (Spring 1992). They cite a study of 43 posters used by the League by F. Todesco; 16 posters railed against political parties, 15 vs. mafia, 12 vs. thieves, 9 vs. Rome, 9 vs. state, 6 vs. South. . . .

8. You can see what the party is up to this week at http://www.leganord.org/.

9. Pascal Boniface, "The Proliferation of States," *Washington Quarterly* 21, no. 3 (Summer 1998): 113.

10. Ronald Ingelhart, "Postmaterialist Values and the Erosion of Institutional Authority" in Joseph S. Nye Jr., Phillip D. Zelikow, and David C. King, *Why People Don't Trust Government* (Cambridge, Mass.: Harvard University Press, 1997). See also Lester Thurow, *The Future of Capitalism* (New York: Penguin, 1996). Basque autonomy is now guaranteed by the Spanish constitution. Basque is, together with Spanish, the official language of the region, and they have a separate parliament. Recent regional elections pushed autonomy even further.

11. Yaroslav Trofimov, "SMOM Is a Mouse that Roars for Respect as a Bona Fide Nation," *Wall Street Journal*, June 28, 2001, p. A1.

12. Jessica T. Matthews wrote an interesting piece on these trends, "Power Shift," *Foreign Affairs*, January/February 1997, pp. 50–66. Part of it is based on the Council on Foreign Affairs study group on "Sovereignty, Nonstate Actors, and New World Politics."

13. Arnold Wolfers, *Discord and Collaboration: Essays on International Politics* (Baltimore: Johns Hopkins University Press, 1962), p. 19.

14. YPO Closing Ceremony, Florence University (Sala Cinquecento, Palazzo Vecchio, October 25, 2003).

15. Nancy Cochrane, "A Historic Enlargement. Ten European Countries Prepare to Join the European Union," *Amber Waves* 2, issue 2 (April 2004): 38–45.

16. John Newhouse, "Europe's Rising Regionalism," *Foreign Affairs* 76, no. 1 (January/February 1997): 70.

17. See the work done on "consociation" by Arend Lijphart ("Consociational Democracy," *World Politics*, vol. 21, no. 2 [Jan. 1969]: pp. 207–25) at the University of California, San Diego, and see Karl E. Meyer's "Some Divided Nations Do Find a Way to Stand," *New York Times*, May 23, 1998, pp. A17, A19.

18. David J. Elkins, *Beyond Sovereignty: Territory and Political Economy in the Twentieth Century* (Toronto: University of Toronto Press, 1995), p. 220.

19. Table is based on and adapted from Carlo Ruzza and Oliver Schmidtke, "The Northern League: Changing Friends and Foes, and Its Political Opportunity Structure" in *Citizenship, Nationality, and Migration in Europe*, Table I: Crucial Elements in Defining Boundaries in Primordially and Culturally Integrated Forms of Cultural Identity, p. 20.

20. Adrian Humphreys, "U.S. Thinks Little of Canada: Poll," *National Post*, May 7, 2002. Most folks mistakenly think Japan and China are bigger partners, despite "the $1.5 billion traded a day, the largest amount of commerce between any two nations in the world."

21. Edouard Cloutier, Jean Guay, and Daniel Latouche, *Le Virage* (Montreal: Quebec-Amerique, 1992).

22. According to Daniele Bedard, of the Assemble Nationale, the Quebec flag has occupied the top of the main tower of the parliament since January 21, 1948. The Canadian flag is raised on the corner tower when a representative of the Canadian government visits Quebec. No flag was displayed inside the national Assembly chamber until December 15, 1976, when the Quebec flag was placed next to the speaker's chair. Also see Anthony DePalma, "To Some Canadians, the Maple Leaf Is a Red Flag," *New York Times*, November 26, 1998, p. A4.

23. Lord Durham, 1839, quoted in Jonathan Lemco, *Turmoil in the Peaceable Kingdom: The Quebec Sovereignty Movement and Its Implications for the Canada and the United States* (Toronto: University of Toronto, 1994), p. 3. Significant parts of the Quebec issue discussed in this book come from his overview of the issues involved.

24. Official Languages Act (1969).

25. These conditions include a clear majority vote on a clear question and a negotiated agreement on separation by the main actors.

26. Anthony DePalma, "Canadians Riled at Plan to Cut Ties to the Queen," *New York Times*, December 27, 1998, p. A4.

27. Nadeem Esmail and Michael Walker, "How Good Is Canadian Health Care: An International Comparison of Health Care Systems" (a Fraser Institute policy briefing, Vancouver, August 2002).

28. Gallup Canada poll published in the *Toronto Star*, January 7, 1992, p. A15. The exact result was 37% per an EKOS Research Associates June 3, 2001, poll reported by Jamie Glazov, *FrontPage Magazine*, June 7, 2001. Adrian Humphreys, "U.S. Thinks Little of Canada: Poll," *National Post*, May 7, 2002.

29. Charles F. Doran wrote an excellent overview of these issues in "Will Canada Unravel?" *Foreign Affairs*, September/October 1996, pp. 97–109.

30. Environics Corp. poll. Question is "Support for distinct society if it would keep Quebec in Canada?" Those who would support: Canada 34%, Atlantic 33%, Ontario 36%, Western Canada 33%, Manitoba 24%. Quebec not polled. Reported by Michael Jenkinson, "English Canada Has Turned Against Quebec Appeasement," *Alberta Report*, 1996.

31. Unity Diversity Respect, "Regionalism and the Senate," *White Paper*, 2002, http://www.uni.ca/whitepaper005.html.

32. Study by André Raynauld. See Peggy Curran, "Sovereignty Carries a Heavy Price Tag," *Montreal Gazette*, December 11, 1990, p. A4.

33. By the 1990s, more than one million people lived under the poverty line in Quebec; this is 14.5% of families versus what has been traditionally the poorest province, Newfoundland with 14.3%. Jonathan Lemco, *Turmoil in the Peaceable Kingdom: The Quebec Sovereignty Movement and Its Implications for the Canada and the United States* (Toronto: University of Toronto, 1994), pp. 86–88.

34. David J. Elkins, *Beyond Sovereignty*, p. 196. But of course French-Canadian nationalists have tried to push changes in Canada's constitution several times, most notably in 1763, 1774, 1791, 1840, and 1867.

35. These results come from a CBC poll reported in "Poll Suggests Commitment to Canada," *Globe and Mail* April 29, 1991, p. A4.

36. Colin Powell speech to the American Chamber of Commerce (São Paulo, Brazil, October 5, 2004).

37. Canadians know a lot about the U.S. The reverse is rarely true. If you would like to begin educating yourself on this complex society, you might start by visiting the links page that Prof. Erick Duchesne put together for his Canadian Politics course at State University of New York at Buffalo. It is quite extensive: http://pluto.fss. buffalo.edu/classes/psc/duchesne/psc345/canlinks.html.

38. There are, and have been, various fringe associations agitating for eliminating the U.S.-Canadian border. Here are a bunch of links: http://www.unitednorthamerica.org/links.htm. One Ontario group's rationale ranges from better roads to more competitive sports teams, http://www.ontariousa.org/.

39. "The Americanization of Canada: Waves of Immigration to Canada," *The National/ CBC*, http://www.tv.cbc.ca/national/ pgminfo/border/waves.html (2004).

40. Richard J. Sweeney, McDonough School of Business, Georgetown University, "Secession and Expulsion: Lessons for the EU from United States History 1789–1861" (LEFIC working paper, August 20, 2003: pp. 2003–2012).

41. Bradley Miller, "An Apostle of Confederation," *National Post,* March 31, 2005, p. A17.

42. Meanwhile, the hard right continues to eat freedom fries while arguing "if it wasn't for us, the French would be speaking German." OK, fair enough, but if it wasn't for the French, those in the U.S. might still be speaking British or Canadian.

43. Talk on Madame Justice Claire L'Hereux-Dube, Canadian Supreme Court justice, Harvard Law School, December 15, 1998. Ironically, it was exiles from the U.S. revolution that took over the territory to the east of Quebec. As supporters of the monarchy left the U.S., they immigrated to Lower Canada in such numbers as to create the new province, New Brunswick. What would become the Maritimes were flooded with Protestants who had also been exposed to debates on democracy.

44. Robert D. Kaplan, *An Empire Wilderness* (New York: Random House, 1998), p. 13.

CHAPTER 8: LIKE YOUR FLAG? WANT TO KEEP IT?

1. Jim Foley has created a wonderful Web site on human evolution: http://www.talkorigins.org/faqs/homs/index.html.

2. Richard Dawkins, an Oxford don, has written a series of great books. I urge you to read them; they will change your view of the world. This quote comes from *The Selfish Gene* (UK: Oxford University Press, 1989), p. 192.

3. Boutros Boutros-Ghali, "An Agenda for Peace" (United Nations, 1992). He goes on to argue: "If every ethnic, religious, or linguistic group claimed statehood, there would be no limit to the fragmentation, and peace, security and economic well-being for all would be ever more difficult to achieve."

4. There is a wonderful map done by the French Encyclopedists that shows who occupied what piece of land and for how long, from 2000 BC through 1700. Bottom line . . . only the Romans, Turks, and Chinese really mattered.

5. Frances FitzGerald, *Fire in the Lake: The Vietnamese and the Americans in Vietnam* (New York: Back Bay Books, 2002), p. 8.

6. Claude Levi-Strauss, *Structural Anthropology* (New York: Basic Books, 1974), p. 229.

7. *Atlas de las Lenguas Perdidas en el Mundo*, UNESCO 2002. According to Carlos Montemayor, *Los Pueblos Indígenas de México*, in Mexico in the 16th century there were about 170 distinct languages and thousands of dialects. At the beginning of the 20th century, about 100. By 2005, only 62 survived. Of these 62 languages, only 23 people still spoke aguaceto, 52 kiliwa, 82 cochimi, and 90 ixil. Arturo Jiménez, "El Aguaceto, Lengua Originaria en Mayor Peligro de Extinción," *La Jornada*, February 18, 2005, p. 4A.

8. Caroline Kovac, General Manager Health Care and Life Sciences, IBM. FasterCures Summit (Getty Museum April 17, 2005). Panel: Patients Helping Doctors: Saving lives One "Bit" at a Time.

9. The *New York Times* did a great series, "Class Matters": www.ny times.com/class. This data comes from David Leonhardt, "The College Boom Dropout," May 24, 2005, pp. 1 and A18–19.

10. Angus Maddison, *Monitoring the World Economy: 1820–1992* (Washington, D.C.: Organization for Economic Development, 1995), p. 23. GDP capita 1990 dollars.

11. International Monetary Fund, *World Economic Outlook Database*, September 2004. www.imf.org/external/pubs/ft/weo/2004/ 02/data/index.htm.

12. Jonathan Weisman. "Aging Population Poses Global Challenges," *Washington Post*, February 2, 2005, p. 1.

13. U.S. Bureau of Labor Statistics. Court Smith, Oregon State University, using BLS numbers: http://oregonstate.edu/ instruct/anth484/minwage.html.

14. Mark Nord, *Household Food Security in the United States, 2002/FANRR-35* (Economic Research Service/USDA, October 2003). These are households "uncertain of having, or unable to acquire enough food."

15. Victor Oliveira, *The Food Assistance Landscape/FANRR-28-4* (Economic Research Service/USDA, March 2003). In one of the richest places on the planet . . . one in five Americans were receiving some form of food assistance in 2003.

16. Average weekly earnings are in constant 1982 dollars. U.S. Bureau of Labor Statistics, *Employment and Earnings Monthly*. Federal Minimum Wage is in 1996 constant dollars.

17. Data from Economy.com and Northeast Apartment Avisors. Reported by Motoko Rich, "Living in a Retirement Village with Mom and Dad," *New York Times*, May 22, 2005, pp. 1 and 25.

18. Abraham Lincoln Republican Senatorial Nomination acceptance speech, June 1858 (known as the "A House Divided Against Itself Cannot Stand" speech).

19. www.multimedialibrary.com/_FramesML/IM1Page5.html.

20. This story was told by General Rokke at a joint seminar between the National Security Program of the JFK School at Harvard and the Council on Foreign Relations, May 28, 1998.

21. Valery A. Tishkov wrote a good overview of the complex trade-offs involved: "Nationalities and Conflicting Ethnicity in Post-Communist Russia" Working Paper Series, (Conflict Management Group, 1993).

22. These failures have been documented for centuries by scholars. One current explanation includes geography/climate (Columbia's Jeff Sachs). Jared Diamond, in *Germs, Guns, and Steel*, emphasizes the ability to produce excess calories, and in *Collapse* focuses on environmental degradation. Alexander Gerschenkron, *Economic Backwardness in a Historical Perspective*, focuses on the divide between leaders and their followers. Francis Fukuyama focuses on the triumph of liberal democracy and capitalism in *The End of History and the Last Man*.

23. When faced with the full weight of the Inquisition and facing torture, Galileo recanted, but in a low voice he whispered, "You may force me to say what you wish; you may revile me for saying what I do. But it moves."

24. Marc Bloom, "At 73, Marathoner Runs As if He's Stopped the Clock," *New York Times*, February 12, 2005, p. B16.

25. David Wilkinson, *Deadly Quarrels: Lewis Richardson and the Statistical Study of War* (Berkeley: University of California Press, 1980), pp. 41–48, 62. See also Taras Kuzio, "Borders, Symbolism and Nation-State Building: Ukraine and Russia," *Geopolitics and International Boundaries* 2, no. 2 (autumn 1997). And Michael Mann, "Nation States in Europe and Other Continents: Diversifying, Developing, Not Dying," *Daedalus* 122, no. 3 (summer 1993).

26. Robert D. Kaplan, *The Ends of the Earth: From Togo to Turk-*

menistan, *From Iran to Cambodia, A Journey to the Frontiers of Anarchy* (New York: Vintage, 1996), p. 8. See also Georgie Anne Geyer, "Our Disintegrating World: The Menace of Global Anarchy," *Encyclopedia Britannica Book of the Year*, 1985.

27. Paul Collier, a World Bank economist, has written extensively on the economics of civil wars. See, for example, "Economic Agendas of Civil Wars" and "Economic Causes of Civil Conflict and Their Implications for Policy," World Bank 2000, http://www.worldbank.org/research/conflict/papers/civilconflict.pdf.

28. Robert Kaplan covers part of this phenomenon in a wonderful article: "Was Democracy Just a Moment?" *Atlantic Monthly* 280, no. 6 (December 1997): pp. 55–80.

29. Talk with Kenichi Omahe at Legal Sea Foods, MIT, 1997. He argues these trends could someday split the Japanese state.

30. The Pew Charitable Trust has done a series of surveys on these issues. See www.people-press.org/trustrpt.htm.

31. As Gallup and other polls reflected these trends, various academics tried to explain them. See, for example, Joe Nye, Phillip D. Zelikow, and David C. King, *Why People Don't Trust Government* (Cambridge, Mass.: Harvard University Press, 1997); Robert D. Putnam, "What Is Troubling Trilateral Democracies" (prepared for the Bertelsmann Foundation Project "Can Democracies Survive," January 1996); and Robert D. Putnam, "Bowling Alone Revisited," *The Responsive Community*, Spring 1995, pp. 18–33. The 2003 numbers are from Princeton Survey Associates, October 9–10, 2003. "Generally speaking, how often do you think you can trust the government to do what's right?" Most of the time, 27%; some of the time, 52%; hardly ever, 13%; never, 6%; unsure, 2%.

32. Edward Bellamy, *Looking Backward: 2000–1888* (New York: Signet, 2002 reissue of 1888), p. 36. Analyzed as a myth in James Robertson, *American Myth, American Reality* (New York: Hill and Wang, 1980), pp. 170–71.

33. Joseph S. Nye, Jr., Phillip D. Zelikow, and David C. King, *Why People Don't Trust Government* (Cambridge: Harvard University Press, 1997), p. 1. The poll answer refers to "They do the right thing most of the time."

34. Karl Popper, *The Open Society and Its Enemies* (London: G. Routledge and Sons, 1945).

35. David D. Kirkpatrick, "Frist Set to Use Religious Stage on Judges Issue," *New York Times*, April 15, 2005, p. 1.

36. The Pew Research Center for People and the Press does interesting research. For instance: http://peoplepress.org/reports/display.php3?PageID=813.

37. Examples provided by Greg Simon, CEO, FasterCures Summit (Getty Museum, April 17, 2005).

38. M. Waters, *Globalization*, 2nd ed. (London: Routledge, 2001).

39. These examples are compiled from diverse sources including Unrepresented Peoples Organization (UNPO) at http://www.unpo.org, James Minahan, *Nations Without States: Contemporary National Movements* (Westport, Conn.: Greenwood Press, 1996). Author's analysis.

40. Mike & the Mechanics, "Can You Hear Me Running?"

41. http://www.unpo.org.

42. Here is a quote from the senator's speech in the senate on January 9, 1900: "It is elemental. It is racial. God has not been preparing the English-speaking and Teutonic peoples for a thousand years for nothing but vain and idle self-contemplation and self-admiration. No! He has made us the master organizers of the world to establish system where chaos reigns. He has given us the spirit of progress to overwhelm the forces of reaction throughout the earth. He has made us adept in government that we may administer government among savage and senile peoples. Were it not for such a force as this the world would relapse into barbarism and night. And of all our race He has marked the American people as his chosen nation to finally lead in the regeneration of the world. This is the divine mission of America, and it holds for us all the profit, all the glory, all the happiness possible to man. We are trustees of the world's progress, guardians of its righteous peace." (Sen. A. J. Beveridge, in *Congressional Record*, January 9, 1900.) You can see just how angry this discourse makes some people today: Bill Templer's "America Imperialism and Anti-Imperialism a Century Ago," http://webdoc.sub.gwdg.de/edoc/ia/eese/artic24/templar/2_2004.html.

43. Richard J. Ellis, *To the Flag* (Kansas: University Press of Kansas, 2005), reviewed in "Ideas," *Boston Globe*, May 29, 2005, p. D3.

44. Sam Dillon, "School Law Spurs Efforts to End Minority Gap," *New York Times*, May 27, 2005, p. 1.

45. Fernando Henrique Cardoso. Talk at David Rockefeller Center for Latin America Studies, Cambridge, Mass., American Academy of Arts and Sciences, December 4, 2004.

46. E. L. Jones, *Growth Recurring* (Ann Arbor: University of Michigan Press, 1988), pp. 73–86.

47. Louise Levathes. *When China Ruled the Seas: The Treasure Fleet of the Dragon Throne, 1405–1433* (U.K.: Oxford University Press, 1997). Gavin Menzies wrote a fun, somewhat speculative book on these trends: *1421, the Year China Discovered the World* (London: Bantam Press, 2002).

48. Angus Maddison, *Monitoring the World Economy, 1820–1992* (Washington, D.C.: Organization for Economic Cooperation and Development, 1995), p. 30 (recalculated using 2003 incomes from the World Bank's *World Development Report 2005*). Some estimate that the dominance of these two countries was even greater, e.g., Jeffrey Sachs et al., *Emerging Asia: Changes and Challenges* (Manila: Asian Development Bank, 1997), estimates that India and China were 58% of world output.

49. Robert D. Kaplan, *An Empire Wilderness* (New York: Random House, 1998), p. xv.

50. As told by Cong. Bernie Tauzin, PhRMA Meeting, Washington, D.C., March 17, 2005.

CONCLUSION: WHAT IS YET TO BE DONE?

1. David Cay Johnson, "The Richest Are Leaving Even the Rich Farther Behind," *New York Times*, June 6, 2005, p. 1.

2. This is the type of common sense retaught to adults by middle schoolers in places like Buckingham Browne and Nichols. It contrasts with the rants of several pundits who base most of their thoughts and data on the work of Dr. Batson D. Seling.

3. Department of Defense Poll, November 2004, cited in Damien Cave, "Growing Problem for Military Recruiters: Parents," *New York Times*, June 3, 2005.

5   *Newt Gingrich* • Reuters/CORBIS

5   *Alan Greenspan* • Reuters/CORBIS

12   *Cartoon* • TOLES © 2004 The Washington Post. Reprinted with permission of UNIVERSAL PRESS SYNDICATE. All rights reserved.

13   *U.S. bankruptcy filings* • Based on data from the U.S. Courts/American Bankruptcy Institute

14   *Paris Hilton* • WENN/Landov

22   *British Empire map* • Victoria and Albert Museum, London/Art Resource, NY

25   *Flag montage* • Robesus, Inc.

26   *Stars in the U.S. flag* • Juan Enriquez

34   *Utility patents map* • U.S. Patent and Trademark Office

35   *States won graph* • Based on data from the U.S. Patent and Trademark Office, U.S. Census, and 2004 election results

38   The Da Vinci Code *book cover* • Jacket cover from *The Da Vinci Code*, by Dan Brown. Used by permission of Doubleday, a division of Random House, Inc.

38   Left Behind *book cover* • Jacket cover from *Left Behind*, by Tim LaHaye and Jerry Jenkins. Used by permission of Tyndale House Publishers, Inc.

40   *Krebs diagram* • Courtesy of Valdis Krebs

43   *Promises/reality gap* • Juan Enriquez

43   *East Germany flag* • Wolfgang Kaehler/CORBIS

44   *Berlin Wall* • David Turnley/CORBIS

45   *Confederate flag photo* • Ron Kuntz/CORBIS SYGMA

47   *Texas flag* • Robesus, Inc.

48   *Alaska map* • Alaska State Library, Alaska/Arctic Photograph Collection, PCA 62-135

52   *Eisenhower and flag* • Bettmann/CORBIS

53   *Philippines flags* • Robesus, Inc.

62   *Soccer* • Reuters/CORBIS

62   *Korea, Samsung* • Samsung Electronics/Handout/Reuters/CORBIS

65   *Juan de Oñate* • Bettmann/CORBIS

65   *Pilgrims* • Bettmann/CORBIS

67   *Deng Xiaoping and Mao* • Bettmann/CORBIS

70   *Darwin cartoon* • Bettmann/CORBIS

72   *Torture scene* • Bettmann/CORBIS

73   *Alhambra Decree* • Reproduction courtesy of Beth Hatefutsoth, the Nahum Goldmann Museum of the Jewish Diaspora, Tel Aviv. Original document in the collection of the municipal archives, Avila, Spain.

77   *Greek god* · Nimatallah/Art Resource, NY

79   *Emerging Biotechonomy* · Juan Enriquez, Rodrigo Martinez, Nigel Holmes

88   *Navajo jewelry* · Danny Lehman/CORBIS

89   *Maori man* · Paul A. Souders/CORBIS

92   *Foxwoods Resort and Casino* · David G. Houser/CORBIS

94   *Indian census map* · U.S. Census Bureau

96   *Fort Laramie Treaty* · Bettmann/CORBIS

99   The Wizard of Oz *still* · John Springer Collection/CORBIS

101 *Native American Rushmore* · Original illustration by Matt Davis

114 *War paint* · Warren Morgan/CORBIS

126 *Nunavut inauguration* · Tom Hanson/AFP/Getty Images

129 *El Paso horse* · Susana Gonzalez/Getty Images

131 A Day Without a Mexican *poster* · Mark Mainz/Getty Images

132 *Mexico map, 1826* · Michael Maslan Historic Photographs/CORBIS

133 *Hispanic census map* · U.S. Census Bureau

136 *Foreign born graph* · Juan Enriquez, based on U.S. Census Bureau data

139 *Caution sign* · Royalty-Free/CORBIS

141 *Schwarzenegger* · Getty Images

145 *Afghanistan poppy field* · Shaul Schwarz/CORBIS

146 *U.S.-Mexico border* · Lynsey Addario/CORBIS

151 *Protestors* · Reuters/CORBIS

158 *U.S. senators* · Original illustrations by Matt Davis

159 *Barack Obama* · Kevin Lamarque/Reuters/CORBIS

170 *Vincente Fox* · Reuters/CORBIS

173 *Map of the four Mexicos* · Juan Enriquez

181 *EZLN* · Reuters/CORBIS

193 *Yucatán flag* · Original illustration by Matt Davis, based on data from
     http://www.yucatan.com.mx/especiales/banderadeyucatan/14090001.asp

210 *Europe, start of 20th century* · Library of Congress
     (created by Rand McNally)

210 *Europe, 1994* · Library of Congress (created by CIA)

214 *European Union flag* · Robesus, Inc.

214 *Sophia Loren* · AFP/Getty Images

214 *Ferrari* · Don Heiny/CORBIS

222 *Tartans* · Jack Hollingsworth/Photodisc/Getty Images

245 *African mother panning for gold* · Caroline Penn/CORBIS

246 *Minimum wage vs. poverty level* · Courtesy of csmith@oregonstate.edu

247 *Heraldic shields* · Dover Publications, Inc.

250 *General Ervin J. Rokke* · Defense Visual Information Center

250 *Soviet symbols of power* · Jerry Cooke/CORBIS

260 *Flag montage* · Robesus, Inc.

Aberdeen Saturday Pioneer, 99
aboriginal people. *See* Native
 Americans; native people
Abourezk, James, 97
Aceh, 20
affirmative action, 157, 162, 297n.47
Afghanistan, 285n.67, 328n.48
 poppy cultivation in, 145,
 315–16n.43
 war in, 6, 8
African-Americans, 87, 135, 155–64
 discrimination against, 156–57
 education of, 152–53
 electoral politics and, 155–56,
 157–61, 162, 321n.88
 jailing of, 161–62
 reparations issue and, 162–63
agriculture, 131, 211, 212
 federal subsidies and, 32
 NAFTA and, 205
airline industry, 252
Akaka, Daniel K., 122, 309n.96
Alabama, 32, 156, 159, 160
Alabama League of the South, 156
Alaman, Lucas, 198
Alaska, 32, 48–52, 98
 land ownership issues in, 49–51,
 290n.41
 native people of, 49–51, 87, 94,
 290nn. 37, 39, 41
 statehood of, 51
Alaskan Independence Party (AIP), 52
Albright, Madeleine, 224
Alhambra Decree (1492), 73
American Dream, 246
American Samoa, 55
Apalachee, 113
apocalyptic rapture, 38–39
Arab-speaking states, 71–72
Arapaho, 101
Argentina, 17, 65
Arizona, 87, 98, 117, 138, 146, 168
 English-only initiative in, 141–42
Arkansas, 98
Armenia, 261
Asakawa, Masatsugu, 7
Asian banks, U.S. deficits and, 8–9,
 280n.19
Asians, 87, 133, 319n.78
Assembly of First Nations, 123

Australia, aboriginal people of, 88–89,
 91, 298–99n.7
Austria, 213, 216
auto industry, 252, 258
Aztecs, 171, 185, 192, 326n.31

Babbitt, Bruce, 111
Baja California, 17, 189–91
Baker, Richard, 10
bankruptcy, 13–14, 31
Baptists, 78
Basques, 21, 115, 216, 223, 332n.10
Baum, L. Frank, 99
Baylies, Francis, 101
Belgium, 213, 216
 secessionism in, 21, 153
Bell, Daniel, 259
Bellamy, Edward, 256
Bellamy, Francis, 262
Belthem, Tony, 101
Berlin Wall, 44
Bernstein, William J., 71
Beveridge, Albert J., 261, 339–40n.42
Biafra, 20
bilingual education, 142–43
biology databases, 79
Bolivia, 200–201
book reading, by right vs. left, 37–38,
 40
Boorstin, Daniel, 29
Boston, law on Indians in, 87
Boutros-Ghali, Boutros, 240,
 335–36n.3
branding, 288n.16
 of countries, 42–43, 46
 of U.S. regions, 46–52
Brazil, 61–62, 63, 64, 65, 69, 203, 254
British Empire, 9, 21–23, 46
Bryan, Frank, 19
Buchanan, Pat, 237
budget, federal, 6
 cuts in, 18
 spending on future vs. past in, 245
 see also deficits
Buffett, Warren, 15
Bulgaria, 44
Bureau of Indian Affairs (BIA),
 116–17, 306n.76
Burke, Edmund, 42, 287–88n.15
Bush, George, I, 82

Bush, George, II, 5, 268
  approval ratings of, 46
  Hispanic vote and, 138, 140,
    314n.28
  in presidential elections, 15, 32–37,
    78, 138, 140, 314n.28
  Schiavo case and, 75
Butler, Samuel, 247

California, 11, 32, 80, 156, 168, 190,
    236
  electoral politics in, 138–41, 319n.78
  Hispanics in, 130, 131, 134, 137,
    138–41, 147, 149, 154
  Native Americans in, 114
Canada, 35–36, 64, 115, 135, 204, 206,
    221, 224–35, 248, 252, 253, 271
  forces contributing to untying of,
    225–31
  lessons to be learned from, 231–32,
    238
  national identity of, 228–29
  native people in, 90–91, 123–27,
    298n.7, 299n.13, 310n.102,
    311n.108
  potential changes in U.S. border
    with, 228, 229, 233–37, 261–62
  secessionism in, 115, 123, 126, 142,
    216, 225–26, 227, 228, 230,
    232–33, 255, 333n.22
  transfer payments among provinces
    of, 229–30, 231, 233
  see also Quebec
Carrillo, Felipe, 193
Carter, Jimmy, 37, 53
casinos, Native American, 92–93, 103,
    107
Castañeda, Emilia, 134
Catalans, 21, 115, 216
Catholic Church, 72–74
Cayuga, 107
Census Bureau, U.S., 107–9
Central America, 168, 183, 195–96,
    197–98, 328nn. 56, 57
  see also specific countries
Central Valley, CA, 114
change, 66, 240–49
  adaptability and, 253, 258–59,
    264–65
  avalanche metaphor for, 248–49
  in dominant code or language,
    241–43
  evolution and, 240
  income declines and, 245–47
  investing in future vs. past and, 245,
    263
  national myths and, 241, 247–48,
    262
  in standards of individual power
    and success, 282n.41

technology and, 252, 258
  trust issues and, 258
Cheeshahteaumuck, Caleb, 127
Cherokee, 96, 288n.21
Cheyenne, 101
Chiapas, 20, 179–80, 195, 196, 197–200,
    202, 205, 329nn. 61, 65, 330n.68
Chihuahua, 177
children:
  proxy votes for, 272
  U.S. spending on, 245
  see also education
Chiles, Lawton, 147
China, 8, 9, 46, 56, 81, 167, 187, 241,
    254, 280n.19, 322n.7
  economic growth in, 66–69
  education in, 63, 82
  failure of, to adapt and grow, 264–65
Chinese Exclusion Act (1882), 81
Chivington, John, 101
Citibank, 16
citizenship:
  dual, 80
  exceptional, of Native Americans, 93
  of Hispanics, 136–37
  in U.S. territories, 53, 54, 56, 293n.66
civil wars, 254, 285n.67
Cleveland, Grover, 119
Clinton, Bill, 6, 121, 128, 308n.90
Club for Growth, 257
Coatsworth, John, 180
coca production, 200
college education, 243
Colombia, 53, 64, 285n.67
colonies, as burden, 212
Colorado, 32, 48, 138, 168
computers, 69, 258
Confederacy, 45, 46, 156, 288n.21
Congo, 20, 203
Congress, U.S., 13, 27, 49, 50, 53, 54,
    148, 255, 265
  Alaskan Indian lands and, 49, 50
  gerrymandering and, 36–37
  Hawaiian annexation and, 121,
    307n.83
  representation of African-
    Americans in, 158–61
  Schiavo case and, 75
  treaties with Indian nations and,
    103, 300nn. 20, 21
Connecticut, 32, 91–93, 98
  Native Americans in, 92–93
constitutions, Anglo vs. Latin, 65
corporations:
  coziness between government and,
    255–56
  debts of, 10
  keeping intact vs. splitting, 209
Costa Rica, 168, 183
Coulter, Ann, 102

countries:
    branding of, 42–43, 46
    hallmarks of, 217–18
    myths of, 21, 27, 44, 100, 241,
        247–48, 262, 284n.58
    use of term, 285n.66
Cox, Cathy, 78
creationism, 78
credit card debt, 11, 13
Cuba, 64, 307n.82
cultural identities, 223
currency valuations, 15
    federal budget deficits and, 8–9
    government power over, 16–17
    speculators and, 15–16, 17
Czechoslovakia, 19–20, 191, 213

Danforth, John, 76
Dark Ages, 72
Darwin, Charles, 70, 239
databases, scientific, 66, 79
Da Vinci Code, The (Brown), 38, 287n.8
Davis, Gray, 141, 149, 272
Davis, Paul, 160
death penalty, 75
debt, 245
    bankruptcy and, 13–14, 31
    corporate, 10
    of individuals, 11–14, 247
    national. *See* deficits
deficits, 4–9, 275, 279n.6
    accounting problems and, 6–7
    Asian banks and, 8–9, 280n.19
    currency valuations and, 8–9
    interest payments on, 5, 8
    tax cuts and, 6, 8, 273, 275
    trade, 7
deities, 76–78
Delaware Indians, 95
DeLay, Tom, 75, 255, 257
Delgamuukw, 90, 125
Democratic National Convention
    (2004), 87
Democratic party, 34, 257
    in California, 138, 140–41
Deng Xiaoping, 66, 67
Denmark, 213, 216, 244
derivatives, 17
Descartes, Rene, 63
digital era, 242
Dobbs, Lou, 131
Dobyns, Henry, 102
Doctrine of Discovery, 91
dollar, U.S., 8, 9, 15, 17, 53
Dornan, Robert, 139–40
drug trafficking, 110, 144–46, 161–62,
    285n.67, 315nn. 42, 43
    in Afghanistan, 145, 315–16n.43
    in Mexico, 170, 189, 200
Dunn, Joe, 134

East Germany, 43–44, 285n.67
Ecuador, 17
education, 60–63, 243, 275
    belief systems and, 78
    bilingual, 142–43
    college, 243
    ethnic disparities in, 82–83,
        152–53, 262–63, 297n.47
    in foreign languages, 147–48
    of Hispanics, 136, 142–43, 152–53,
        319n.72
    in math, science, and engineering,
        62–63, 68–69, 81–82, 83, 273
    of native people, 115, 127, 152–53
    No Child Left Behind and, 262–63
    post-9/11 reduction in foreign
        students and, 81, 263
Eisenhower, Dwight, 51
elderly:
    spending on, 7, 8, 245
    voting power of, 272
electoral politics, 32–37
    African-Americans and, 155–56,
        157–61, 162, 321n.88
    differences in world view and, 41
    federal subsidies and, 32
    gerrymandering and, 36–37, 161
    Hispanics and, 138–41, 158, 314n.28
    increased polarization in, 256–57
    knowledge gap and, 33–35
    "none of the above" option and, 272
    proxy votes for children and, 272
    urban vs. suburban-rural
        environments and, 35
    voting rights and, 157, 162, 319n.78,
        321n.88
El Salvador, 168, 183, 196, 322–23n.7
engineering, education in, 63, 68, 82
English common law, 298–99n.7
Environmental Protection Agency
    (EPA), 105
Eritrea, 20
Estonia, 213, 261
Ethiopia, 20
ethnicity:
    coping with, 221–24
    educational disparities and, 82–83,
        262–63, 297n.47
    see also African-Americans;
        Hispanics; Native Americans;
        specific ethnicities
Europe, 209–24, 238
    changing economic realities in,
        211–13
    devolution of sovereignty and
        control in, 212–13, 216–21
    historic nations contained within
        countries of, 214–15
    overlapping of multiple
        sovereignties in, 221–23

Europe (*cont.*):
    proliferation of states in, 210–11,
        213, 214, 216–17, 223–24
    secessionism in, 19–20, 21, 153,
        154, 155, 215–17
    see also specific countries
European Economic Community
    (EEC), 213
European Hymn, 219–20
European Union (EU), 20, 21, 146,
    203, 204–5, 219, 253
    cost of independence reduced by,
        216, 217
    history of, 213
    sovereignty ceded to, 220–21
    stars in flag of, 213–14, 223–24
euros, 8, 9, 15, 17, 216
evolution, 70, 78, 240, 274, 296n.32
expansionism, 293n.65

Fannie Mae, 10
Feather, William, 240
Ferdinand, king of Spain, 73
Finland, 213, 221
Fisher, Russ, 252
FitzGerald, Frances, 241
flags:
    Confederate, 45, 288n.21
    Iraqi, 28, 285n.65
    Texas, 47
    U.S., desecration of, 27
    U.S., stars in, 24–27, 45, 261–62
Fleming, John, 87
Florida, Hispanics in, 138, 147
Folta, George, 87
food assistance, 246, 337n.15
Ford, Gerald, 37
Fort Laramie Treaty (1868), 97, 301n.24
Fox, Vicente, 170, 196, 328n.47
France, 89, 95, 213, 216, 234, 253,
    307n.81
Freddie Mac, 10
Free Trade Area of the Americas
    (FTAA), 204
Frist, Bill, 75
fundamentalism, 71–76
    in Arab-speaking states, 71–72
    polarization and, 75–76, 256–57
    Schiavo case and, 75
    in Spain, 72–74
future, investing in, 245, 263

Galileo, 253, 337n.23
Galloway, Scott, 42
Garreau, Joel, 235
GE, 209
genomics, 79
George III, king of England, 95
Georgia (country), 261
Georgia (state), 78, 158–59, 160

Germany, 46, 213, 216, 234, 253, 307n.81
    reunification of East Germany and,
        43–44
gerrymandering, 36–37, 161
Gingrich, Newt, 5, 117
Giovanni, Nikki, 271
globalization, 82, 180–81, 253, 259,
    281n.20, 282n.37, 330n.68
GM, 252
gold standard, 9, 15
Google, 82
Gorbachev, Mikhail, 249, 250
Gore, Al, 35, 37
Goshute, 105
Gover, Kevin, 116
Grant, Ulysses S., 97
Great Britain, 14, 64, 115, 144, 228
    in colonial era, 89, 91, 94–95
    Scottish autonomy and, 21, 115, 155
Great Sioux Reservation, 97, 301n.24
Greece, 205, 213
Greenspan, Alan, 5–6, 10
Guam, 55
Guatemala, 168, 183, 196, 197–98,
    199, 202, 329n.65
Guerrero, 195, 199, 201

Haiti, 285n.67, 293n.63
Harvard University, 16, 64, 82, 127,
    153
Havel, Václav, 20
Hawaii, 32, 51, 98, 132
    native people of, 118–22,
        307–8n.83, 308–9n.90
    sovereignty issue in, 120, 121,
        308n.90, 309nn. 91, 92, 96
    U.S. annexation of, 119, 121, 307nn.
        82, 83, 308n.90
H bombs, 63
health care, 8, 13, 229, 242, 252
    Medicare and Medicaid and, 6, 7,
        279n.6, 280n.15
hedge funds, 10
Held, David, 219
heroin, 145
high school dropouts, 63, 152–53
Hispanics, 83, 87, 129–55, 237
    census map showing distribution
        of, 133
    citizenship of, 136–37
    deportations of, 134
    education of, 136, 142–43, 152–53,
        319n.72
    electoral politics and, 138–41, 158,
        314n.28
    immigration of, 131–37, 143–44,
        146–47, 149–50, 152, 166–67,
        191, 205, 313–14n.25, 317n.60,
        322–23n.7, 328n.48
    language issues and, 141–43

population statistics on, 130, 131,
   133, 134, 135, 148
potential autonomy-secession
   demands and, 153–55
in work force, 131, 134
home ownership, 11–12
Honcharenko, Agapius, 49
Honduras, 168
Hong Kong, 8, 81, 203
housing costs, 247
Human Rights Watch, 161
Huntington, Sam, 131, 132

Illinois, 32, 98, 236
immigration:
   border security and, 143–47
   in Europe, 144
   of Hispanics, 131–37, 143–44,
      146–47, 149–50, 152, 166–67,
      191, 205, 313–14n.25, 317n.60,
      322–23n.7, 328n.48
   historic perspective on, 151–52
   laws and quotas on, 133, 134, 136,
      137, 313n.21
   melting pot myth and, 135, 312n.14
Immigration and Naturalization
   Service (INS), 24, 143, 146,
   315n.38
income:
   declines in, 245–47
   per capita, top five countries for,
      244
income gaps, 67, 80, 152
   between Anglo America and Latin
      America, 66, 147, 313n.25, 316n.49
   before industrial revolution, 211
   in northern vs. southern Mexico, 175
India, 46, 187, 254, 285n.67, 322–23n.7
   failure of, to adapt and grow, 264–65
Indian Imprisonment Act (Boston,
   1675), 87
indigenous people. See Native
   Americans; native people
Indonesia, 20
industrial revolution, 66, 211–12, 265
inequalities, 18, 31–35
   knowledge gap and, 33–35
   in tax payments and subsidies, 31–32
   see also income gaps
innovation, 61
Inouye, Daniel K., 122
Inquisition, 72, 74, 337n.23
interest rates, 5, 8, 16
Inuit, 126, 290n.41
Iraq, 285n.67
   new flag of, 28, 285n.65
   war in, 6, 8, 45
Ireland, 46, 205, 213, 244, 289–90n.22
Isabella, queen of Spain, 73
Italy, 21, 213, 214–17, 219–20

Jackson, Andrew, 52, 96
Jackson, Janet, 78
Jackson, Jesse, 75
jails, African-Americans in, 161–62
Japan, 8, 79, 81, 271, 280n.19
   education in, 69
   potential secessionism in, 254
Jews, banished from Spain, 73
John XXII, Pope, 72
Jones-Shafroth Act (1917), 54
Jordan, David Starr, 23
Justice Department, U.S., 107

Kaho'olawe, 120
Kamehameha School, 121, 309n.94
Kansas, 48, 78, 98
Kaplan, Robert D., 265
Katanga, 20
Kentucky, 32, 98
Kerry, John, 32, 33, 36, 37
Kickapoo, 110
Killington, VT, 19
King, Mackenzie, 234
knowledge, 66
   belief systems and, 70–72
   change and, 241–43
   education and, 60–63, 68–69, 243,
      273
   patents and, 34–35, 61, 66
   regional inequalities in, 33–35, 80, 82
   scientific databases and, 66, 79
knowledge economy, 66, 69, 80, 82,
   212, 241–43, 245, 273
Krebs, Valdis, 40
Krugman, Paul, 257
Kuna Indians, 221

Lakota, 99
Lamberth, Royce C., 111, 112
languages:
   banned by conquering nations, 155
   dominant, changes in, 241–42
   extinction of, 242, 336n.7
   official, populations speaking other
      languages and, 141–43, 225, 226,
      230, 233
   trends in studies of, 147–48
Latin America, 69, 203, 253, 263
   colonial legacy in, 64–66
   constitutions in, 65
   see also specific countries
Latvia, 213, 261
Laurier, Wilfried, 234
League of Nations, 221
Left Behind series (LaHaye and
   Jenkins), 38, 287n.9
legitimacy gap, 43
Levesque, Rene, 232
Lewis, Joseph C., 15
Lili'uokalani, queen of Hawaii, 119, 121

Lincoln, Abraham, 30, 101, 248, 302n.33
Little Bighorn, Battle of, 97
Looking Horse, Arvol, 115
LTCM, 10
Luxembourg, 203, 213, 244

Maine, 105, 161, 236
Makah, 104
Mankiw, Gregory, 4
Maori, 89–90
Mao Tse-tung, 66
maquiladoras, 186–87, 189, 194,
    324n.16, 327nn. 36, 37
Marcos, Subcomandante, 180, 200
Margold, Nathan, 50
Marshall, John, 96
Marshall Islands, 56
Martha's Vineyard, MA, 105–6
Martinez, Mel, 148
Maryland, 160
Massachusetts, 32, 98, 105–6, 119,
    235, 236
math, education in, 62, 68, 81, 273
Maya, 172–73, 192, 197
McArthur, John, 261
McClaughry, John, 19
McEwan, Bonnie, 113
media, 37–40
    book reading and, 37–38, 40
    rapture news and, 39
Medicaid, 7, 280n.15
Medicare, 6, 7, 279n.6
melting pot, myth of, 135, 312n.14
Mercosur, 204
methamphetamines, 105, 304n.47
Mexico, 20, 46, 64, 65, 66, 74, 110, 154,
    166–206, 248, 252, 253, 254, 271
    advantages of small states and, 203
    Car Wars in, 176–78
    Central, 171–72, 173–74, 184–86
    Central America's split from, 168,
        183, 195–96, 328nn. 56, 57
    in colonial era, 182, 185, 193
    control over U.S. border with, 110,
        143–44, 146–47, 304n.54,
        317n.60
    currency problems in, 15, 17
    economic outlook for, 168
    history of, 168–69
    immigration from, 131–37, 143–44,
        146–47, 149–50, 166–67, 191,
        205, 313–14n.25, 317n.60,
        322–23n.7, 328n.48
    income gap between U.S. and, 66,
        147, 313n.25, 316n.49
    Indians in, 175, 179–82, 192,
        304n.54, 325n.20
    indigenous region of, 172, 173–74,
        195–201
    languages in, 336n.7

NAFTA and, 171, 180, 203–5
New Maya region of, 172–74, 191–94
    northern vs. southern, 174–83
    North of ("NAFTA" country), 171,
        173–74, 186–91
    potential expansion of U.S. into,
        261–62
    pre-1845 border of, 132–33
    questions to ask about untying of,
        201–2
    regional rivalries and divisions in,
        169–202, 323n.11
    transition states in, 174,
        324–25n.16
    U.S. annexation of portions of, 130,
        132, 148–49, 166–67, 168
    Zapatista guerrilla movement in,
        179–82, 197–200
Mexico City, 49, 171, 174, 176, 182,
    184–85, 186, 187, 193, 194, 195,
    197
Michigan, 98
Micronesia, 56
military service, 45, 273
minimum wage, 7, 246
Minnesota, 32, 98
Minook, 50
miscegenation, bans on, 119, 156
Mississippi, 7, 32, 36, 98, 156, 159,
    160, 280n.15
Missouri, 78, 98
Miss Universe, 55
Miss USA, 55
moderates, targeted by own parties, 257
Mohawks, 107
Monet, Jean, 213
monetary problems, 15–18
Montana, 32, 158–59
Moore, Roy S., 156
Moors, 73
Morales, Evo, 200–201
mortgages, 10, 12, 13, 247
Morton, Bob, 19
Muckleshoot, 103–4
Musgrove, Ronnie, 156
Muslim immigrants, 144
Myanmar, 145, 285n.67
myths:
    adapting of, 241
    of countries, 21, 27, 44, 100, 241,
        247–48, 262, 284n.58
    not shared by Native Americans,
        100–101

nation, use of term, 285n.66
National Football League (NFL), 55
National Guard, 45
nationalism, 75, 219
National Museum of the American
    Indian, 112

National Origins Act (1924), 133
Nation of Hawaii, 121, 309n.91
Native American Rights Fund (NARF), 111
Native Americans, 52, 86–87, 91–118
  American symbols, myths, and heroes rejected by, 100–101
  Bureau of Indian Affairs and, 116–17, 306n.76
  casinos of, 92–93, 103, 107
  citizens self-identifying as, 113
  in colonial era, 64, 94–95, 102, 113
  communities of (list), 107–9
  discrimination against, 87–88
  disease spread among, 102, 116
  education of, 152–53
  international law and, 115–16
  land ownership issues and, 93, 94–98, 103–4, 105–7, 112, 114, 301n.24
  massacres of, 99, 101, 302n.33
  racial hatred toward, 117–18
  resurfacing of extinct tribes and, 113
  sovereignty issues and, 93–100, 103–7, 110, 112, 117, 300n.20, 303n.39
  state names originating from languages of, 98
  trust assets of, 110–12
  U.S. treaties with, 95–98, 103, 112, 300nn. 20, 21
  U.S.-Mexico border and, 110, 304n.54
native peoples:
  of Alaska, 49–51, 87, 94, 290nn. 37, 39, 41
  of Australia, 88–89, 91, 298–99n.7
  of Canada, 90–91, 123–27, 298n.7, 299n.13, 310n.102, 311n.108
  of Hawaii, 118–22, 307–8n.83, 308–9n.90
  land ownership issues and, 49–51, 88–91, 93, 94–98, 103, 112, 114, 123, 124, 125, 290n.41
  in Mexico, 175, 179–82, 192
  of New Zealand, 89–90, 91, 105–7
  in Spanish empire, 102, 299n.9
  United Nations and, 115–16, 120
  see also Native Americans
natural resources, 203
Navajo, 105, 117
Navassa, 293n.63
NBA dream team, 55
Nebraska, 98
Neruda, Pablo, 76
Netherlands, 144, 213, 216
Nevada, 32, 156, 168
New England, 228
  secessionism in, 19, 52, 236

Newfoundland, 228
New Hampshire, 19, 32
New Mexico, 32, 48, 138, 158, 168
  Native Americans in, 87, 88
Newton, Isaac, 104
New York City, 153
New York State, 32, 138
  Oneidas in, 106–7
New Zealand, aboriginal people of, 89–90, 91
Nicaragua, 168, 183, 196
Nigeria, 20
"Night Before Christmas, The," Tex-Mex version of, 150
Nixon, Richard, 15, 139
No Child Left Behind Law, 262–63
North American Free Trade Agreement (NAFTA), 171, 180, 203–5
North Dakota, 32, 97, 98, 158–59
Northern Mariana Islands, 56
Norton, Eleanor Holmes, 159
Norton, Gale, 111
Norway, 244
Nunavut, 126

Oaxaca, 176, 195, 198, 199, 201
Office of Hawaiian Affairs (OHA), 121
oil:
  in Alaska, 51
  in Mexico, 172, 173, 194, 324n.16
Oklahoma, 48, 104
Olympics, 55, 248, 282n.41
Oñate, Juan de, 129
Oneidas, 106–7
O'Neill, Tip, 265
Onondaga Nation, 107
O'odham, 110, 304n.54
Oregon, 236, 319n.78
Organic Act (1884), 49

Pacific islands:
  annexations of, 119, 307n.81
  U.S. territories, 55–56
  see also Hawaii
Palau, 56, 261
Panama, 17, 221, 254
  canal zone and, 53, 291n.48
Passamaquoddies, 105
Pataki, George, 107
patents, 34–35, 61, 66, 186
Paul, Saint, 77, 296n.31
Páz, Octavio, 166
Penobscot, 105
Pension Benefits Guaranty Corp. (PBGC), 10
Pequot, 92–93
Perry, Rick, 47
Peru, 64, 271
peso, Mexican, 15, 17
Peterson, Pete, 4

PhDs, 69
Philippines, 53, 132, 322–23n.7,
    328n.48
pilgrims, 64
Pledge of Allegiance, 262
Plymouth colony, 100
political discourse, 255, 256–57,
    265–66, 274–75
poppy cultivation, 145, 315–16n.43
Portugal, 64, 205, 213, 216
pound, British, 15
Powell, Colin, 234
Powell, Enoch, 244
primordial identities, 223
Producers Rice Mill, Inc., 32
promises, broken, 42–45
Puerto Rico, 53, 54–55, 120, 132,
    291nn. 49, 51, 292n.54, 307n.82
    Vieques bombings and, 120,
        308n.88

Quebec, 216, 237
    as beneficiary of transfers and
        subsidies, 229, 230, 231, 233
    Inuit claims in, 126
    secessionism in, 115, 123, 142, 216,
        225–26, 227, 228, 230, 232–33,
        333n.22
Quiñones, Denise, 55

race, 155–64
    see also African-Americans
rapture media, 38–39
Reagan, Ronald, 190
real estate, 11–12, 80, 247, 269–70, 271
    in Baja California, 189–90
Regan, Don, 190
Reich, Robert, 6
religion, 70–78
    bestselling books and, 37–38
    deities and, 76–78
    fundamentalism and, 71–76,
        256–57
    and gaps between reality and
        dogma, 70–72, 77
    mixing governance with, 72–76
    positive aspects of, 71, 75
    science and, 70–71, 75, 274
    separation of church and state and,
        220
rental discrimination, 87
renting vs. owning home, 11
rents, increases in, 247
reparations, 162–63
Republican party, 33–34, 51, 76
    in California, 138–41
Riceland Foods, Inc., 32
Robertson, Julian, 16
Rokke, Ervin J., 249–51
Romney, Mitt, 119

Roosevelt, Teddy, 100
Rove, Karl, 279n.6, 308n.88
Rubin, Robert E., 4, 111
Rumsfeld, Donald, 120, 265
rural vs. urban regions, 35
Russia, 46, 83, 203, 251, 254
    Alaska and, 48–49

same-sex marriage, 36, 119
Samsung, 62
Sanchez, Loretta, 139–40
Sand Creek Massacre (1864), 101
Sarbanes-Oxley, 6
savings, 11, 13
Savonarola, Girolamo, 72
Schiavo, Terry, 75
Schroeder, Gerhard, 253
science, 66, 69
    belief systems and, 70–71, 75, 78,
        274
    databases and, 66, 79
    education in, 62, 68, 83, 273
Scotland, 21, 115, 155
secessionism, 19–21, 161, 254–55
    avalanche metaphor for, 248–49
    in Canada, 115, 123, 126, 142, 216,
        225–26, 227, 228, 230, 232–33,
        255, 333n.22
    economic disparities and, 19–21
    in Europe, 19–20, 21, 153, 154, 155,
        215–17, 332n.10
    as global phenomenon, 259
    governmental failures leading to,
        251–52, 337n.22
    Hispanic population and, 153–55
    internal vs. external threats and, 254
    in Mexico, 193, 195–201
    in New England, 19, 52, 236
Senecas, 107
September 11 attacks, 144
Seward, William, 49
Sharpton, Al, 120
Sheridan, Phil, 47
Singapore, 8, 9, 81, 203
Sioux, 97, 101, 301n.24
slaves, 52, 113, 180, 212
    reparations issue and, 162–63
Slovenia, 20, 213
smallpox, 102
small states, advantages of, 203
Smithsonian Institution, 112
soccer, 61–62, 135
social mobility, 83
Social Security, 5, 6, 7, 152, 279n.6
Soconusco, 198, 329nn. 62, 65
Soros, George, 15
South, 113, 236
    race and electoral politics in, 156,
        160–61
    secessionism in, 52

South Carolina, 156, 159, 160
South Dakota, 97, 101, 158–59
South Korea, 8, 9, 69, 81, 280n.19
  education in, 62, 63
  sovereignty, 240, 284n.57
  devolution of, in Europe, 212–13,
    216–21
  overlapping of, in Europe, 221–23
  secessionism and, 19–21
  "tartan rules" of, 222–23
Soviet Union. *See* Russia; USSR
Spain, 21, 46, 115, 182, 213, 271
  in colonial era, 64–66, 74, 102, 130,
    182, 185, 193, 299n.9
  religious fanaticism in, 73–74
  secessionism in, 21, 115, 216, 254,
    332n.10
Spanish speakers, 141–43, 147–48
  see also Hispanics
Specter, Arlen, 257
Starr, Ken, 10
state, notion of, 285n.66
  Burke on, 287–88n.15
stem cell research, 76
Stockbridge-Munsee, 107
Stoeckel, Baron Eduard de, 49
suburban regions, 18, 19, 35
Sung Dynasty, 264
supranational organizations, 212,
  220–21, 223, 260, 331n.3
Supreme Court, U.S., 54, 75, 121, 156,
  290n.41, 291n.49
  Indian law cases and, 106, 303n.39
Swineford, Alfred P., 49
Switzerland, 203, 221, 244

Taiwan, 8, 9, 69, 81, 280n.19
Taliban, 315–16n.43
Tall Oak, 100
Tamaulipas, 188–89, 324n.16
taxes, 6, 7, 221
  cuts in, 6, 8, 268, 273, 275, 279n.6
  in Mexico, 176–78, 184
  Native Americans and, 93, 100
  states paying more than they receive
    from, 31–32
technology, 15, 63, 66, 69, 252, 258,
  273, 274
  foreign talent and, 81
  regional disparities in, 80–81
television, 40, 69
terra nullius concept, 88–89, 91
territories, U.S., 53–56, 132, 291n.49,
  292nn.57, 63, 293n.66
Texas, 46–48, 100, 168, 185, 289n.26
  autonomy sentiments in, 47–48
  flags flown over, 46
  Hispanics in, 131, 138, 140, 142,
    148–49, 154
  victory over Mexico of, 148–49

Thanksgiving, 100
Tibet, 81
Tiger Management, 16
Tohono O'odham, 110, 304n.54
trade:
  NAFTA and, 171, 180, 203–5
  U.S. deficits in, 7
Trade and Intercourse Act (1790), 106
Treasury bonds, U.S., 6, 8
Treaty of Six Nations (1784), 106
trust:
  in fellow Americans, 257–58
  in U.S. institutions, 255–56
Tully, Shawn, 11
Tuscarora, 106

Uighur, 81
United Airlines, 10
United Kingdom (UK), 46, 155, 213,
  216, 307n.81
United Nations, 28, 219, 260
  native people and, 115–16, 120,
    310n.102
Unrepresented People's Organization
  (UNPO), 261
urban vs. suburban-rural regions, 35
US Air, 10
USA Patriot Act (2001), 144
USSR (Soviet Union), 262
  collapse of, 24, 249–51, 285n.67
  see also Russia
Utah, 98, 105

Vargas Llosa, Mario, 168
Venezuela, 203
Vermont, 19, 235, 236
Vieques, 120, 308n.88
Vietnam War, 235
Virgin Islands, U.S., 56
Vogler, Joe, 52
voting rights, 157, 319n.78
  felony convictions and, 162,
    321n.88

Waitangi, Treaty of (1840), 89–90
Wales, 155
Wampanoag, 105–6, 127
wars, change in nature of, 254
Washington, D.C., 159
Washington, George, 100, 106
Washington State, 236
  Native Americans in, 87, 103–4
welfare, 153
West, Jonathan, 68
whaling, 104
Whitlock, Ed, 253
Wickersham, James, 50
Wilson, Pete, 138–39, 141
Winnemem Wintu, 114
Wisconsin, 236

women, marginalization of, 61, 76
Woolhandler, Steffie, 13
World War I, 23, 54, 219
World War II, 134, 219, 228
Wounded Knee, massacre at (1890), 99
Wyoming, 158–59

xenophobia, 81

Yaqui, 110, 185
Yucatán, 172–73, 176, 191–94, 195, 197, 206, 324n.15, 325n.20
Yugoslavia, 20, 29, 191, 285n.67

Zanguill, Israel, 135
Zapatistas, 179–82, 197–200
Zedillo, Ernesto, 149, 178, 180

JUAN ENRIQUEZ has a career that spans business, domestic and international politics, and science. He was the founding director of the Life Sciences Project at Harvard Business School, a fellow at Harvard's Center for International Affairs, and a peace negotiator during Mexico's Zapatista rebellion. He has appeared on *60 Minutes*, is the author of *As the Future Catches You*, and has published his work in *Harvard Business Review*, *Foreign Policy*, *Science*, the *New York Times*, *Los Angeles Times*, *Philadelphia Inquirer*, and *Boston Globe*. Mr. Enriquez is the CEO of Biotechonomy, a life-sciences research and venture capital firm.